Careers in Healthcare

Careers in Healthcare

Editor
Michael Shally-Jensen, Ph.D

SALEM PRESS
A Division of EBSCO Information Services, Inc.
Ipswich, Massachusetts

GREY HOUSE PUBLISHING

Library of Congress Cataloging-in-Publication Data

Careers in healthcare / editors: Marylane Wade Koch, Michael Shally-Jensen. --
[1st ed.].
p. : ill. ; cm. -- (Careers in--)
Includes bibliographical references and index.
ISBN: 978-1-61925-232-5
1. Medical personnel--Vocational guidance. 2. Allied health personnel--Vocational guidance. I. Koch, Marylane Wade. II. Shally-Jensen, Michael.

R690 .C66 2014
610.69

First Printing

PRINTED IN THE UNITED STATES OF AMERICA

CONTENTS

PUBLISHER'S NOTE

Careers in Healthcare contains twenty-six alphabetically arranged chapters describing specific fields of interest in healthcare. These chapters provide a current overview and a future outlook of specific occupations in the healthcare industry. Merging scholarship with occupational development, this single comprehensive guidebook provides healthcare students and researchers alike with the necessary insight into potential careers, and provides instruction on what job seekers can expect in terms of training, advancement, earnings, job prospects, working conditions, and more. *Careers in Healthcare* is specifically designed for a high school and undergraduate audience and is edited to align with secondary or high school curriculum standards.

Scope of Coverage

Understanding the interconnected nature of the different and varied branches of healthcare is important for anyone preparing for a career in this field. *Careers in Healthcare* comprises twenty-six lengthy chapters on a broad range of branches and divisions within the industry, including traditional and long-established fields such as Dentist and Registered Nurse, as well as in-demand allied health fields such as Medical Assistant, Cardiovascular Technician, Physical Therapist, and Home Health Aide. This excellent reference also presents possible career paths and occupations within high-growth and emerging fields in these industries.

Careers in Healthcare is enhanced with numerous charts and tables, including projections from the US Bureau of Labor Statistics, and median annual salaries for those occupations profiled. Each chapter also notes those skills that can be applied across broad occupation categories. Interesting enhancements, like **Fun Facts**, **Famous Firsts**, and dozens of photos, add depth to the discussion. A highlight of each chapter is **Conversation With** – a two-page interview with a professional working in a related job. The respondents share their personal career paths, detail potential for career advancement, offer advice for students, and include a "try this" for those interested in embarking on a career in their profession.

Essay Length and Format

Each chapter ranges in length from 3,500 to 4,500 words and begins with a Snapshot of the occupation that includes career clusters, interests, earnings and employment outlook. This is followed by these major categories:
- **Overview** includes detailed discussions on: Sphere of Work; Work Environment; Occupation Interest; A Day in the Life. Also included here is a Profile that outlines working conditions, educational needs, and physical abilities. You will also find the occupation's Holland Interest Score, which matches up character and personality traits with specific jobs.

- **Occupational Specialties** like Basic EMTs, Intermediate EMTs and Paramedics, with detailed comparisons. This section also includes a list of Duties and Responsibilities.
- **Work Environment** details the physical, human, and technological environment of the occupation profiled.
- **Education, Training, and Advancement** outlines how to prepare for this occupation while in high school, and what college courses to take, including licenses and certifications needed. A section is devoted to the Adult Job Seeker, and there is a list of skills and abilities needed to succeed in the job profiled.
- **Earnings and Advancements** offers specific salary ranges, and includes a chart of metropolitan areas that have the highest concentration of the profession.
- **Employment and Outlook** discusses employment trends, and projects growth to 2020. This section also lists related occupations.
- **Selected Schools** list those prominent learning institutions that offer specific courses in the profiles occupations.
- **More Information** includes associations that the reader can contact for more information.

Special Features

Several features continue to distinguish this reference series from other career-oriented reference works. The back matter includes:
- Appendix A: Guide to Holland Code. This discusses John Holland's theory that people and work environments can be classified into six different groups: Realistic; Investigative; Artistic; Social; Enterprising; and Conventional. See if the job you want is right for you!
- Appendix B: General Bibliography. This is a collated collection of annotated suggested readings.
- Subject Index: Includes people, concepts, technologies, terms, principles, and all specific occupations discussed in the occupational profile chapters.

Acknowledgments

Special mention is made of editor Michael Shally-Jensen, who played a principal role in shaping this work with current, comprehensive, and valuable material. Thanks are due to the many academicians and professionals who worked to communicate their expert understanding of the healthcare industry to the general reader. Finally, thanks are also due to the professionals who communicated their work experience through our interview questionnaires. Their frank and honest responses provide immeasurable value to *Careers in Healthcare*. The contributions of all are gratefully acknowledged.

EDITOR'S INTRODUCTION

An Industry Overview

The healthcare industry is dedicated to the prevention, diagnosis, treatment, and management of disease and the preservation of health through services provided by trained medical and allied healthcare professionals. These professionals usually have specific educational degrees, as well as certifications and licensure, qualifying them to provide care. Healthcare providers include medical doctors (MDs), dentists, nurses, dietitians, physical therapists, chiropractors, emergency medical technicians, home health aides, pharmacists, and many more. These and other such occupations make up the subject of the present book. One must realize, however, that the industry is very broad and not every occupation could be included here.

Industry Makeup

In the twenty-first century, many new advances have been made in diagnosis, treatment of illness, and disease management. The healthcare industry continues to offer a wide range of services and products to prevent, treat, and manage disease, as well as to promote wellness. Emphasis on healthy lifestyle choices has heightened, as have early diagnosis and treatment of preventable diseases. Americans have been encouraged to take an active part in their health, and portions of the industry are transitioning from thinking of themselves as providing illness care to instead providing health and wellness. Living healthful lifestyles remains the most cost-effective solution to the many complications and adverse outcomes of sickness and disease; more than half of all U.S. healthcare dollars are spent to treat and manage illnesses that can be prevented or reduced through lifestyle change.

Another major advance in understanding has come about through the Genome Project, a project devoted to the discovery and identification of the more than 20,000 human genes. The program (completed in 2003) studied the sequence of some three thousand unites of deoxyribonucleic acid (DNA). Knowledge of DNA sequencing can enable scientists to crack the code of human genetics and treat and prevent devastating infectious and inherited diseases. These discoveries are especially important to understand the human immune system and to predict how each person will intake and utilize medications; this level of genetic analysis is expected to produce a future field of personalized medicine, in which care will be tailored meticulously to the genetically determined needs of each individual body. One day, these discoveries may also assist people to stay well by uncovering the secrets in the human genes that enhance health.

Medical and healthcare services today are provided by a diverse group of providers in various settings. In the past, the majority of services were delivered within healthcare institutions such as hospitals. Today, many procedures and treatments once limited to inpatient settings have moved to outpatient settings and to patients' homes.

Ambulatory healthcare services help patients remain in their residences within their communities, decreasing costs and improving patient satisfaction. Many medical procedures can safely be performed in physician or dentist offices. Physical therapists and others offer their services in outpatient centers, rehabilitation centers, and patients' homes. Innovative medical equipment allows patients to remain outside the walls of institutional care facilities such as hospitals.

Ambulatory outpatient settings include mental health and substance abuse centers, family planning centers, kidney dialysis centers, and surgical centers. Medical and diagnostic laboratories play an important role in patient care, as do diagnostic imaging centers. Although many hospitals offer these services through dedicated department staff and high-technology equipment, laboratories and diagnostic imaging establishments are becoming more available in the ambulatory healthcare setting. The improved technology of these services allows more options for diagnosis and treatment than ever before in healthcare history.

Traditional medicine still remains primary in patient care management; physicians and nurses provide the majority of care. However, many people have also adopted alternative practices to enhance wellness and treat illness. Specialists such as chiropractors, homeopaths, acupuncturists, and naturopaths offer Americans additional choices for medical and healthcare services. Consultants in nutrition and fitness provide services to support lifestyle changes for disease prevention and wellness. Healthcare professionals work as educators as well as care providers to improve patients' quality of life.

History

The American Colonies had few educated physicians and many healthcare needs. Poor sanitation practices, such as pouring waste into local streams, bred infectious diseases. Doctors had little formal training, often limited to knowledge of stabilizing broken bones and administering herbs and liquors. In 1765, the College of Pennsylvania founded the first medical school in the United States, modeled after the school at the University of Edinburgh. Courses included basic anatomy, and students received experience in bedside care at the Pennsylvania Hospital.

Historically, care of the sick was delegated to women with little training. Generations passed down various folk remedies. In the late 1800s, nurses, sponsored by charitable organizations and churches, delivered care in the homes of new mothers and people with infectious diseases. Following the standards of Great Britain's pioneering Florence Nightingale, American nurses established a professional training process through schools of nursing. By the early 1900s, nurses were licensed and credentialed by the states. The need for nurses expanded during World War I and II, so the federal government funded nursing education and provided stipends.

Traditionally, physicians were viewed as selfless professionals putting the welfare of their patients before any other concerns. However, over time physicians became central figures in the business of health care in order to be paid for their services. In 1929 Baylor Hospital in Dallas, Texas, began a prepaid healthcare plan called Blue

Cross to provide hospital services for teachers. Physicians joined this plan as Blue Shield to cover the cost of their services, forming Blue Cross-Blue Shield. Eventually similar insurance and managed care organizations arose to cover the healthcare needs of individuals and families and to secure payment for medicine and healthcare services.

With advanced technology and disease management, the life expectancy of Americans increased, resulting in more seniors needing health care. In 1965, the federal government enacted landmark legislation, establishing Medicare and Medicaid. Medicare was a federal government-funded program designed to pay for basic medical care for Americans over 65 years old. Medicaid, funded with federal dollars but managed by the states, paid for basic healthcare services for indigent citizens and children.

Today, Americans enjoy many options for high-technology, sophisticated drug therapies and advanced medical and healthcare services. In March 2010, the federal government passed the Patient Protection and Affordable Care Act (PPACA), which was designed to greatly expand the availability of affordable medicine and healthcare services. Although there have been delays in rolling out the new law's provisions (the bulk of which were to take effect in 2014), the healthcare industry as a whole is expected to grow as a result.

Future Outlook

The outlook for this industry shows it to be on the rise. Healthcare spending in the United States accounts for a larger share (about 18 percent) of Gross Domestic Product (GDP) than in any other country in the world. According to the BLS, some 16 million Americans are currently employed in the industry, and that number is expected to grow steadily over the next decade. On the bureau's list of the twenty fastest-growing occupations, half were in the medicine and healthcare industry. The BLS has projected that 5.7 million new jobs will be created in the industry between 2010 and 2020, more than in any other industry. Another positive statistic is that the BLS projects that healthcare wages and salaries will rise 27 percent through 2014 and should continue to increase thereafter (albeit not at the same rate).

The healthcare industry has a long history of employment growth, offering good to excellent wages and benefits. Work environments are generally positive. Most healthcare employees receive access to health insurance and other benefits such as retirement plans. Some claim that this industry is recession proof, as, even in economic decline, people need and seek healthcare services. Some sectors, such as nursing, are usually in a state of shortage to meet the country's needs. The choice of vocations available is diverse, with new roles evolving yearly to meet developing needs. Economic challenges encourage creative thinking and allow variations on traditional approaches to care. Workers can choose among various settings, from institutional to community-based businesses. Skills are sometimes transferable to other settings or industries and allow for advancement. For example, businesses may hire occupational healthcare nurses. Although professional healthcare providers usually require four-year college degrees or higher education and training, most roles in the health care field require either two-year associate's degrees, vocational training, or on-the-job training, minimizing the educational investment costs to support staff and other nonphysician workers.

Services and Occupations

The U.S. healthcare industry includes nearly 600,000 establishments, varying in size, services, and location. Ambulatory (outpatient) healthcare services are provided either directly or indirectly. These services constitute more than 85 percent of all healthcare establishments. Ambulatory care includes outpatient care centers, home healthcare services, medical and diagnostic laboratories, radiology services, and offices of physicians and other healthcare professionals. The U.S. Bureau of Labor Statistics (BLS) notes that hospitals account for only 1 percent of these establishments, but they account for 35 percent of jobs in the industry. Whatever the type of establishment or the form of service, the work performed is done by professional staff, support and allied staff, along with administrative and other personnel.

Professional Staff

The healthcare industry is a service business that relies heavily on the professional staff who provide skilled medical and patient care services. Many jobs are available for those seeking a career in this industry. Most professional staff roles require a college education with a minimum of a baccalaureate degree. Some, such as physicians and nurse practitioners, require graduate and postgraduate education and internships. Additional certifications are available for health care professionals desiring specialization or economic enhancement. Many professional roles require licensure by state boards. If providers move to a different state, they may need to apply for new licenses to continue practicing.

Just as education varies from job to job, wages and salary vary as well. General practice physicians in rural areas may earn incomes of $100,000, while urban neurosurgeons may earn $500,000. Pay, practice parameters, and patient base depend on the selected area of practice, size of the business, and geographic location. Physicians are regulated by the states where they are licensed and work, and they may be required to complete continuing education to keep current on their chosen specialty areas.

Registered nurses (RNs) make up the largest segment of healthcare professionals, with around 6.2 million positions in the United States. Their basic educational path may be through two-year associate's degrees, three-year diploma degrees, or four-year baccalaureate degrees. Additional education to the master's or doctoral level offer more career opportunities. RNs can work in diverse settings, as almost all medicine and healthcare establishments utilize these healthcare professionals. They offer assessment, treatments, health teaching, resource referral, and support for patients and families.

Nurses are licensed under the regulations of the states where they live and work, and they may be required to complete continuing education to keep current on their chosen areas of practice. Their work environment depends on the setting where they work. Annual salaries for staff RNs range from around $57,000 to $68,000. Salaries may also vary based on the shifts nurses work, as evening and night shifts usually pay a differential. Advanced degree nurses, such as nurse practitioners, earn $80,000 to $85,000 or more depending on the place of employment.

Continued rehabilitation therapy is needed by many Americans in the course of their illness, injury, or after surgery to restore function and return to the activities of daily living. Healthcare professionals who provide these therapies are physical or rehabilitative therapists (sometimes also considered allied health professionals). The work options for such therapists are diverse, with good opportunities for employment. Education necessary for these roles includes a minimum baccalaureate degree and a further degree from an accredited program in a specialty area. Annual salaries range from $72,800 to $78,000 for lead physical therapists, and slightly less for related occupations.

As healthcare delivery changes under new reimbursement guidelines and more Americans gain insurance, new jobs may emerge, while traditional ones may evolve into new roles. Job seekers would be wise to research thoroughly roles of interest and contact someone in the field for further discussion before committing the time and financial investment necessary to achieve these occupations.

Support and Allied Staff

Allied healthcare providers are important to the delivery of services in the medicine and healthcare industry. Their specialized skills support patients in many settings. A growing group of healthcare providers with increasing job opportunities consists of healthcare technologists and technicians. Education requirements for these positions usually include baccalaureate degrees with one to two years of additional training and licensure or certification. Examples of jobs in these areas include clinical laboratory technologists and technicians, radiologic technicians, medical records and health record technicians, dental hygienists, and ultrasound technicians (diagnostic medical sonographers). Salaries depend on the setting and specialty area of practice. Medical or health record technicians can expect to earn between $26,000 and $47,000, dental hygienists between $55,000 and $79,000, and radiologic technicians between $42,000 and $63,000.

Many healthcare industry support jobs require high school diplomas, associate's degrees, specialized vocational training, or on-the-job training. The BLS has stated that most healthcare jobs require less than a four-year college degree. For example, licensed practical nurses (LPNs) or vocational nurses require one year of dedicated training and earn $35,000 to $45,000. Other allied health jobs include emergency medical technician ($30,000 to $40,000), medical assistant ($25,000 to $30,000), and home health aide ($17,000 to $28,000).

—Marylane Wade Koch and Michael Shally-Jensen

Sources

Bureau of Labor Statistics. 2013. Occupational Outlook Handbook.
http://www.bls.gov/ooh/

KPMG. 2013. "Media and Telecom Execs Optimistic on Revenue Growth." http://www.kpmg.com/US/en/
IssuesAndInsights/ArticlesPublications/Press-Releases/Pages/Media-And-Telecom-Execs-Optimistic-On-
Revenue-Growth-Worry-About-Keeping-Pace.aspx

Cardiologist

Snapshot

Career Cluster: Health Science, Medicine

Interests: Medicine, Science, Anatomy & Physiology

Earnings (Yearly Average): $488,799

Employment & Outlook: Faster Than Average Growth Expected

OVERVIEW

Sphere of Work

Cardiologists are medical doctors who specialize in the diagnosis, treatment, and prevention of diseases of the heart and cardiovascular system. There are several areas of specialization, but most cardiologists fall into the following classifications: non-surgical, invasive, and interventional. Further specialization in pediatric cardiology, nuclear cardiology, or electrophysiology and other fields is also possible. Other cardiologists focus on conducting research and teaching cardiology at medical schools.

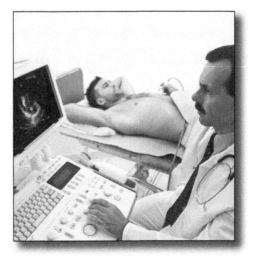

Non-surgical cardiologists provide medical advice on how patients

can maintain heart health, and they perform non-invasive tests to determine whether patients have a heart condition. These tests include electrocardiograms and stress tests, and are performed in a medical office.

Invasive cardiologists do much of the same work as non-surgical cardiologists, but they have the added ability and training to perform catheterizations, a procedure that helps the physician understand blood flow to the heart and determine the heart's ability to pump.

An interventional cardiologist has the skill and training to perform more invasive procedures, such as angioplasty, a form of surgery used to open blocked arteries and insert stents, in a clinical setting. These clinical procedures involve more risk and are most often performed at a hospital.

Profile

Working Conditions: Work Indoors
Physical Strength: Light Work
Education Needs: Medical Degree
Licensure/Certification: Required
Physical Abilities Not Required: No Heavy Work
Opportunities For Experience: Prior Military Service, Volunteer Work
Holland Interest Score*: ISR

* See Appendix A

Work Environment

Cardiologists generally work in medical environments, such as hospitals and medical offices. These environments can be very busy. Hospitals, in particular, are extremely active, with frequent, daily interaction between the cardiologist and nurses, other doctors, medical technicians, and patients. Medical facilities and hospitals are sterile environments, and physicians and staff follow daily procedures to ensure that each patient is protected from germs and other health hazards.

To conduct patient consultations for on-going treatment and non-invasive work, cardiologists use medical offices with examination rooms where they can meet privately with patients. Medical offices keep a limited supply of related medical technology on the premises, which is used for non-invasive or non-surgical patient testing. When the cardiologist must use more invasive techniques to treat a patient, he or she might consult with a fellow cardiologist (trained to perform a specific procedure) or other medical personnel, such as nurses and medical technicians, to treat the patient in a clinical setting.

Cardiologists often work erratic, long hours. Their work day is further extended when the doctor is assigned to provide "on-call" services, which include answering patient calls after hours and, when necessary, going to the hospital to treat patients who need urgent care.

Occupation Interest

Because heart disease is one of the most common public health issues, cardiologists work in a busy environment where their services are in high demand. Cardiology is also a growing field, where new discoveries and research lead to frequent changes in best practices. Cardiologists enjoy the benefits of working with state-of-the-art technology, which is constantly being refined and upgraded. Cardiologists earn significant salaries, but are also subject to significant malpractice insurance costs.

A Day in the Life—Duties and Responsibilities

The daily responsibilities of a cardiologist vary based on his or her specialty. For example, a non-invasive cardiologist works primarily in the office of his or her medical practice, seeing as many as 30 patients a day. He or she will conduct tests, recommend medication, and/or dietary changes and exercise. When more invasive procedures are warranted, the non-surgical cardiologist may refer patients to other cardiologists. Invasive, non-interventional cardiologists perform these tasks as well, but they perform catheterizations in a special laboratory ("cath lab") that also contains medical imaging equipment used during the procedure.

Interventional cardiologists perform the above duties and are further qualified to perform angioplasty (a procedure in which a balloon is used to enlarge arteries and clear arterial blockages as well as insert stents) and other procedures. Interventional cardiologists tend to work longer hours in the hospital than non-interventional specialists.

Other cardiologists choose to obtain additional training to work specifically with certain types of patients, for example, children. Many also receive training in the field of electrophysiology (the bioelectrical impulses that make the heart beat); this training qualifies them to implant pacemakers and to perform other procedures to correct irregular heartbeats.

Some cardiologists perform research in addition to practicing cardiology and teaching medical students. These doctors usually work in research laboratories, medical libraries, and universities, studying samples and conducting studies to learn more about cardiac and cardiovascular problems and treatments. They write frequent medical articles and share the results of their studies with peers at conferences and meetings.

Duties and Responsibilities

- Examining heart patients or those with cardiovascular conditions
- Ordering or performing various tests and procedures
- Prescribing and administering medications and treatments
- Diagnosing diseases and conditions of the heart and circulatory system
- Teaching patients about preventative medicine
- Working with other medical professionals

WORK ENVIRONMENT

Physical Environment

Cardiologists spend a great deal of time working in medical offices. Non-invasive procedures and patient follow-ups take place in medical offices. The hospital environment is more complex and frenetic, with a great deal of social interaction and a higher caseload assigned to each doctor.

Human Environment

Cardiologists are in constant contact with patients during the course of their work, providing consultations, performing procedures, and studying patients for the purpose of medical research. Cardiologists also work closely with colleagues, nurses, physician assistants, medical technologists, hospital administrators, and other medical professionals. Empathy, patience, and effective communication skills enhance patient interaction and treatment.

Relevant Skills and Abilities

Analytical Skills
- Analyzing and understanding data

Communication Skills
- Speaking and writing effectively
- Listening attentively
- Expressing thoughts and ideas clearly

Interpersonal/Social Skills
- Being able to remain calm under pressure
- Being able to work independently and as part of a team
- Cooperating with others
- Providing support to others
- Having good judgment
- Being objective

Organization & Management Skills
- Paying attention to and handling details
- Performing duties that change frequently
- Managing time
- Demonstrating leadership

Planning & Research Skills
- Developing evaluation strategies
- Using logical reasoning
- Identifying and solving problems
- Identifying resources

Technical Skills
- Performing scientific, mathematical and technical work
- Understanding and using technology

Technological Environment

Cardiologists must understand the application of a wide range of medical equipment, including electrocardiograms, diagnostic equipment, and surgical supplies. They rely on smart phones, computer systems, and related databases, all of which enable them to efficiently communicate with peers, conduct research, order medications, and organize patient records. The field of cardiology is dynamic, and technologies are constantly being improved and developed to enable doctors to perform with more precision. reduced customer spending can lead to layoffs. This tends to create an atmosphere of intense competition.

EDUCATION, TRAINING, AND ADVANCEMENT

High School/Secondary

High school students interested in cardiology should take a wide range of mathematics and science courses, such as algebra, biology, chemistry, trigonometry, physiology, geometry, and psychology. Because doctors must be effective communicators, students can benefit from English and other humanities courses.

Suggested High School Subjects
- Algebra
- Biology
- Chemistry
- College Preparatory
- English
- Geometry
- Health Science Technology
- Humanities
- Mathematics
- Physics
- Physiology
- Psychology
- Science
- Sociology
- Statistics
- Trigonometry

Famous First

The first heart surgery in which stitches were applied to the heart to heal a wound took place in Montgomery, Ala., in 1902. The patient was a 13-year-old boy who had been stabbed in the heart. The operation was performed on a kitchen table under dim light provided by kerosene lamps.

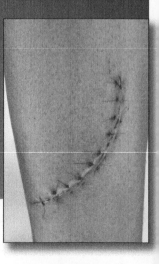

College/Postsecondary

Future cardiologists should earn a bachelor's degree in science with a focus on pre-medical studies. They must attend medical school for another four years to receive a medical degree, followed by several more years of internships and residency. Upon completion of the residency, they are expected to obtain a cardiology fellowship, which lasts an additional two to five years.

Related College Majors
- Anatomy
- Human & Animal Physiology
- Medicine (M.D.)
- Osteopathic Medicine
- Pre-Medicine Studies

Adult Job Seekers

Adults seeking a career in cardiology must follow the same academic and clinical training path as any other, beginning with a bachelor's degree, medical school, internship, and residency.

Professional Certification and Licensure

Like other medical doctors, cardiologists are required to have a medical degree from an accredited medical school. They are also expected to obtain a professional medical license from the state in which they seek to practice, and to pass the United States Medical Licensing Examination upon graduation from medical school.

Additional Requirements

Cardiologists should have a strong interest in helping others, promoting good health practices, and restoring the health of patients. Strong communication skills and proven research capabilities are a necessity. Because cardiologists often treat patients with life-threatening illnesses, they should take particular care to develop communication skills that enable them to interact with patients in a sensitive yet concise manner. They should enjoy learning, because it is vital for them to keep up with current procedures and studies. Last but not least, they must be highly motivated individuals in order to successfully complete the years of specialized training that their field requires.

EARNINGS AND ADVANCEMENT

Cardiologists have among the highest earnings of any occupation. Earnings depend on geographic location, whether the cardiologist is salaried or in private practice, number of years in practice, skill, personality and professional reputation. According to Allied Physicians, Inc., median annual earnings of each type of cardiologist in 2012 were: non-invasive cardiologists, $457,524; invasive cardiologists, $466,791; and interventional cardiologists, $542,080.

Cardiologists may receive paid vacations, holidays, and sick days; life and health insurance; and retirement benefits. Self-employed cardiologists must arrange for their own health insurance and retirement programs. Some employers provide for paid educational leave.

Metropolitan Areas with the Highest Employment Level in this Occupation (Physicians and Surgeons)

Metropolitan area	Employment	Employment per thousand jobs	Hourly mean wage
New York-White Plains-Wayne, NY-NJ	26,080	5.06	$73.84
Chicago-Joliet-Naperville, IL	12,140	3.33	$72.56
Los Angeles-Long Beach-Glendale, CA	7,740	2.00	$94.73
Atlanta-Sandy Springs-Marietta, GA	6,210	2.75	$97.02
Nassau-Suffolk, NY	6,110	5.00	$97.38
Bethesda-Rockville-Frederick, MD	5,910	10.56	$78.24
Boston-Cambridge-Quincy, MA	5,750	3.36	$62.33
Washington-Arlington-Alexandria, DC-VA-MD-WV	5,170	2.21	$81.05

Source: Bureau of Labor Statistics

EMPLOYMENT AND OUTLOOK

Cardiologists held about 25,000 jobs nationally in 2012. Employment of cardiologists is expected to grow faster than the average for all occupations through the year 2020, which means employment is projected to increase about 24 percent. This is due to the continued growth of the healthcare industry. Demand for all physicians will continue to increase as consumers are looking for high levels of care using the latest technologies, tests and therapies.

Employment Trend, Projected 2010–20

Health Diagnosing and Treating Practitioners: 26%

Physicians and Surgeons: 24%

Total, All Occupations: 14%

Note: "All Occupations" includes all occupations in the U.S. Economy. Source: U.S. Bureau of Labor Statistics, Employment Projections Program

Related Occupations
- Neurologist
- Pediatrician
- Physician
- Radiologist
- Surgeon

Related Military Occupations
- Physician & Surgeon

Conversation With . . .
EDWARD KOSINKSI

Cardiolgist, 35 years

1. What was your individual career path in terms of education, entry-level job, or other significant opportunity?

My career path was pretty traditional. I went to college and directly from there, to medical school. I did a medical residency and followed that up with a cardiology fellowship. It was 13 years of schooling before I started practicing. That was the norm then, but now it's even longer.

2. Are there many job opportunities in your profession? In what specific areas?

There are a lot of opportunities. There's going to be an ever-increasing need for cardiologists because of the aging population in our country.

3. What do you wish you had known going into this profession?

I don't think I appreciated how varied the occupation is. That's the beauty of cardiology. There are so many different avenues to pursue. You can be involved in doing procedures, you can focus on congestive heart failure, heart rhythm management issues, structural heart disease. You can also do research. I specialize in interventional cardiology, which typically is using stents to open up arteries.

4. How do you see your profession changing in the next five years?

We're going to become more dependent on "position extenders," meaning nurse practitioners and physician assistants, to manage the increasing number of patients who are going to need our services. There will also continue to be a movement away from the small private practice of cardiology to much larger groups, which are typically either parts of large medical entities or incorporated into hospitals.

5. What role will technology play in those changes, and what skills will be required?

There is, in general, going to be a de-emphasis on buying new technology to diagnose and treat patients just for the sake of having it. I think the cost is going to be the issue. We're going to start looking at technology as either a friend or enemy and we'll be moving away from making decisions about whether to buy technology based on the "pizzazz" marketing of it.

To justify the use of the technology, we're going to have to improve its cost, efficiency, or effectiveness. If it can't make it on one of those grounds it won't be utilized. It will be up to companies and physicians to prove that the technology is worth using. I think hospitals are going to employ individuals to make that determination for them. People are recognizing that unless a certain new technology will offer improved safety, efficiency, or a reduction in cost, they shouldn't buy it.

6. Do you have any general advice or additional professional insights to share with someone interested in your profession?

I think there's nothing more rewarding than being a doctor. It makes your life meaningful because you're able to help people. You're placed in a unique role. It's probably the only profession where you're trusted immediately, and that is a privilege and an honor. It takes dedication and a huge time commitment. You give things up, you may delay having a family, you may delay your life, there are a lot of hours, you work hard, but you get enormous personal satisfaction. There's no better feeling. I think it's a really unique group of people who become physicians. If you want to make that type of commitment, you are amply rewarded.

7. Can you suggest a valuable "try this" for students considering a career in your profession?

I don't believe that internships or walking around in a hospital give you any sense of what it's like to be a cardiologist. I recommend exposing yourself to as many different circumstances as you can during your high school and college years. That's the best preparation. I recommend that you get to know lots of different types of people. Understand what they're going through. Understand what their problems are. A marvelous preparation is to expose yourself as best as you can to people who are different than you and you'll be amazed at what you find. That will give you the greatest skill set and prepare you to work with the wide range of people you will see as a cardiologist.

SELECTED SCHOOLS

Columbia University
535 W. 116th Street
New York, NY 10027
212.854.1754
www.columbia.edu

Duke University
450 Research Drive
Durham, NC 27705
919.684.811
www.duke.edu

Harvard University
1350 Massachusetts Avenue
Cambridge, MA 02138
617.495.1000
www.harvard.edu

Johns Hopkins University
3400 N. Charles Street
Baltimore, MD 21218
410.516.2300
www.jhu.edu

Stanford University
450 Serra Mall
Stanford, CA 94305
650.723.2300
www.stanford.edu

University of California, San Francisco
745 Parnassus Avenue
San Francisco, CA 94143
415.476.9000
www.ucsf.edu

University of Michigan, Ann Arbor
1032 Greene Street
Ann Arbor, MI 48109
734.764.1817
www.umich.edu

University of Pennsylvania
3451 Walnut Street
Philadelphia, PA 19104
215.898.5000
www.upenn.edu

University of Washington
1410 NE Campus Parkway
Seattle, WA 98195
206.543.9686
www.washington.edu

Washington University, St. Louis
1 Brookings Drive
St. Louis, MO 63130
314.935.5000
wustl.edu

MORE INFORMATION

American College of Cardiology
2400 N Street, NW
Washington, DC 20037
202.375.6000
www.acc.org

American College of Physicians
190 North Independence Mall W.
Philadelphia, PA 19106-1572
800.523.1546
www.acponline.org

American Heart Association
7272 Greenville Avenue
Dallas, TX 75231
800.242.8721
www.heart.org

American Medical Association
515 N. State Street
Chicago, IL 60654
800.621.8335
www.ama-assn.org

Centers for Disease Control and Prevention (CDC)
1600 Clifton Rd
Atlanta, GA 30333
www.cdc.gov

Michael Auerbach/Editor

Cardiovascular Technician

OVERVIEW

Sphere of Work

Cardiovascular technicians, also referred to as EKG/ECG technicians, use highly advanced imaging technologies to evaluate a patient's heart health and to identify any abnormalities as directed by a cardiologist. In particular, cardiovascular technicians perform electrocardiograms (EKGs or ECGs) to assist in the assessment and diagnosis of cardiovascular or heart health, function, or pathology. Electrocardiograph machines record and measure heart activity, heartbeats, and electrical activity. Physicians use these electrocardiograms to make diagnoses, rule out illness, assess change over time, and develop appropriate treatment plans.

Work Environment

Cardiovascular technicians spend their workdays in hospitals, doctors' offices, catheterization laboratories, and medical imaging centers. They may perform electrocardiogram tests in medical imaging suites, operating rooms, emergency rooms, or patient rooms. Cardiovascular technicians generally work forty-hour weeks, but it is not unusual for them to work longer hours. Typical shifts may include days, evenings, weekends, and on-call hours to meet the medical community's need for electrocardiograms.

Profile

Working Conditions: Office Environment
Physical Strength: Light Work
Education Needs: Bachelor's Degree
Licensure/Certification: Usually Not Required
Physical Abilities Not Required: No Heavy Physical Work
Opportunities For Experience: Prior Employment As Advertising & Marketing Manager
Holland Interest Score*: ESA

* See Appendix A

Occupation Interest

Individuals drawn to the profession of cardiovascular technician tend to be intelligent, analytical, and detail oriented. Those most successful as cardiovascular technicians display traits such as good eyesight, physical strength, stamina, hand-eye coordination, focus, problem-solving skills, calm demeanor, and tact. Cardiovascular technicians should enjoy working in a medical environment and have training in ultrasound technology.

A Day in the Life—Duties and Responsibilities

Cardiovascular technicians' daily occupational duties and responsibilities are determined by their area of job specialization and work environment. Cardiovascular technicians can specialize in electrocardiograms, invasive cardiology, echocardiography (heart sonography or ultrasound), vascular technology, and stress testing.

Cardiovascular technicians may begin their day by preparing and sterilizing the electrocardiogram equipment and coordinating with office or hospital staff to schedule and plan appointments. When they receive information about patient appointments, they review paperwork from the cardiologist or other referring doctor to determine the type and extent of testing required. This helps them plan their day and work as efficiently as possible.

When a patient arrives for testing, the cardiovascular technician typically greets the patient and explains the role of the electrocardiogram test. The cardiovascular technician then helps the patient position his or her body correctly for the test. Testing may involve attaching electrodes to the patient's body to monitor his or her heart rate, performing a basic electrocardiogram as part of routine examinations or pre-surgery clearance procedures, or performing so-called Holter monitoring procedures to track a cardiac patient's heart activity over a twenty-four hour period. The cardiovascular technician may examine the heart's chambers, valves, and vessels using ultrasound imaging. Patients with pacemakers may visit the cardiovascular technician periodically so that their pacemakers' level of function can be monitored. Cardiovascular technicians may also be called to perform emergency or bedside electrocardiograms. Throughout each exam, the cardiovascular technician works to maintain the comfort and safety of the patient.

All exams done by a cardiovascular technician have the potential to reveal life-threatening results, so he or she must use tact when interacting with patients. In most cases, the cardiovascular technician

Duties and Responsibilities

- Obtaining patient information
- Escorting patients to treatment room or wheeling equipment to patient's bedside
- Explaining test procedures and instructing patients
- Attaching electrodes to specified body areas
- Operating the selector switch to record pulse from electrodes by moving the electrode across specific chest areas
- Entering information into a computer to analyze EKG reading
- Recognizing technical errors that prevent a correct reading
- Putting patient through exercises on treadmill stress tester
- Operating machine to produce tracing paper indicating electrode positions
- Recognizing emergencies and assisting physicians
- Sending tracing to physician for interpretation
- Scheduling appointments and maintaining files

is instructed not to share test results with patients, and that duty is usually deferred to the patient's physician.

After completing the ordered exams, the cardiovascular technician must note all normal and abnormal heart activity for the physician's evaluation. Printouts of each exam's results are usually collected and passed on to the patient's doctor as well. If the test was difficult to conduct accurately or effectively, the results were inconclusive or hard to decipher, or the results showed evidence of abnormal cardiac activity, the cardiovascular technician will notify the referring physician that additional examinations are necessary.

In addition to the range of responsibilities described above, all cardiovascular technicians are responsible for educating themselves about the administrative, physical, and technical patient privacy safeguards included in the Health Insurance Portability and Accountability Act.

OCCUPATION SPECIALTIES

Cardiac Sonographers

Cardiac Sonographers use ultrasound to examine the heart's chambers, valves, and vessels. They use ultrasound instruments to create images called echocardiograms. The echocardiogram may be done while the patient is either resting or physically active.

Vascular Technologists

Vascular Technologists help physicians diagnose disorders affecting blood flow. Vascular technologists listen to the blood flow in the arteries and veins to check for abnormalities. They do noninvasive procedures using ultrasound instruments to record information, such as blood flow in veins, blood pressure, and oxygen saturation. Many of these tests are done during or immediately after surgery.

WORK ENVIRONMENT

Physical Environment

Cardiovascular technicians generally perform electrocardiograms in hospitals, doctors' offices, catheterization laboratories, and medical imaging centers. Such medical settings are usually clean and brightly lit. Cardiovascular technicians must take care to prevent work-related injuries and exposure to radiation.

Human Environment

Cardiovascular technicians should be comfortable interacting with patients, physicians, laboratory technicians, nurses, scientists, and office staff. Owing to the sensitive nature of medical diagnosis, cardiovascular technicians must use empathy, tact, and confidentiality when interacting with patients.

Relevant Skills and Abilities

Communication Skills
- Speaking clearly

Interpersonal/Social Skills
- Cooperating with others
- Working as a member of a team

Organization & Management Skills
- Following instructions
- Paying attention to and handling details

Technical Skills
- Working with data or numbers
- Working with machines, tools or other objects

Technological Environment

To complete their work, cardiovascular technicians use electrocardiograph machines, electrodes, vascular catheters, calipers, cardiac ultrasound equipment, defibrillators, pacemakers, and sterilizing equipment.

EDUCATION, TRAINING, AND ADVANCEMENT

High School/Secondary

High school students interested in pursuing a career as a cardiovascular technician should prepare themselves by developing good study habits. High school classes in anatomy, physiology, physics, and mathematics will provide a strong foundation for college-level work in the field. High school students interested in this career path should seek internships or part-time work opportunities that expose the students to medical settings.

Suggested High School Subjects
- Biology
- Chemistry
- English
- Health Science Technology
- Mathematics
- Physiology

Famous First

The first pacemaker used to aid a patient (by regularizing his heart beat) was a large machine invented in 1952 by Dr. Paul Zoll of Boston. Wires were attached to the patient's heart, and the machine generated an electric pulse at the desired rate. Within six years pacemakers were being made small enough to fit inside a breast pocket and run on transistor batteries.

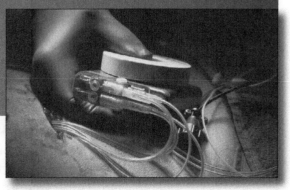

College/Postsecondary

Postsecondary students interested in becoming cardiovascular technicians should work towards an associate's degree or a bachelor's degree in cardiovascular technology, medical sonography, ultrasound technology, or a related field. The Commission on

Accreditation of Allied Health Professionals (CAAHEP) has accredited approximately 200 training programs in cardiovascular technology and diagnostic medical sonography. Coursework in anatomy, physiology, instrumentation, physics, and ethics may also prove useful in students' future work. Postsecondary students can gain work experience and potential advantage in their future job searches by securing internships or part-time employment in medical settings.

Related College Majors

- Anatomy & Physiology
- Electrocardiograph Technology
- Medical Sonography

Adult Job Seekers

Adults seeking employment as cardiovascular technicians should have, at a minimum, an associate's degree in cardiovascular technology from a program accredited by the Commission on Accreditation of Allied Health Professionals. Adult job seekers should educate themselves about the educational and professional license requirements of their home states and the organizations where they seek employment. They may benefit from joining professional associations to help with networking and job searching. Professional medical imaging associations, such as the American Registry of Radiologic Technologists and the Society of Diagnostic Medical Sonography, generally offer job-finding workshops and maintain lists and forums of available jobs.

Professional Certification and Licensure

Since cardiovascular technicians receive extensive on-the-job training from a supervisor or cardiologist, certification and licensure is not legally required for cardiovascular technicians; however, it may be required as a condition of employment or promotion. Options for voluntary cardiovascular technician certification include the American Registry for Diagnostic Medical Sonography's Registered Diagnostic Cardiac Sonographer (RDCS) designation and the Cardiovascular Credentialing International's Certified Cardiographic Technician (CCT) designation. These voluntary certifications are earned by completing a training program and passing a national examination.

Additional Requirements

Individuals who find satisfaction, success, and job security as cardiovascular technicians will be knowledgeable about the profession's requirements, responsibilities, and opportunities. Cardiovascular technicians have access to confidential medical information and may be present when patients receive life-changing diagnoses, so they must adhere to strict standards of professional ethics and confidentiality. Membership in professional medical imaging associations is encouraged among all cardiovascular technicians as a means of building professional community and networking.

EARNINGS AND ADVANCEMENT

Earnings of cardiovascular technicians depend on the employee's training, experience and specific responsibilities, as well as the size and geographic location of the hospital. Median annual earnings of cardiovascular technicians were $52,375 in 2012. The lowest ten percent earned less than $28,207, and the highest ten percent earned more than $81,641.

Cardiovascular technicians may receive paid vacations, holidays, and sick days; life and health insurance; and retirement benefits. These are usually paid by the employer.

Metropolitan Areas with the Highest
Employment Level in this Occupation

Metropolitan area	Employment	Employment per thousand jobs	Hourly mean wage
New York-White Plains-Wayne, NY-NJ	1,290	0.25	$26.85
Los Angeles-Long Beach-Glendale, CA	1,120	0.29	$27.64
Chicago-Joliet-Naperville, IL	1,050	0.29	$24.30
Tampa-St. Petersburg-Clearwater, FL	830	0.74	$22.64
Philadelphia, PA	820	0.45	$27.00
Miami-Miami Beach-Kendall, FL	810	0.82	$20.95
Dallas-Plano-Irving, TX	790	0.38	$24.22
Boston-Cambridge-Quincy, MA	730	0.43	$32.91

Source: Bureau of Labor Statistics

EMPLOYMENT AND OUTLOOK

Cardiovascular technicians held about 51,000 jobs in 2012. Employment of cardiovascular technicians is expected to grow much faster than the average for all occupations through the year 2020, which means employment is projected to increase 29 percent or more. Job growth will occur as the population ages and people stay more active later in life.

Employment Trend, Projected 2010–20

Cardiovascular Technicians/Technologists: 29%

Health Technologists and Technicians: 26%

Total, All Occupations: 14%

Note: "All Occupations" includes all occupations in the U.S. Economy. Source: U.S. Bureau of Labor Statistics, Employment Projections Program

Related Occupations
- Medical Laboratory Technician
- Radiologic Technologist
- Ultrasound Technician

Conversation With . . .
JOYCE UKLEJA
Cardiovascular technician/manager
35 years

1. **What was your individual career path in terms of education, entry-level job, or other significant opportunity**

   Back in 1977 I went to the Medical Careers Institute, I started out an as electrocardiogram technologist and was trained to do stress tests, attaching Holter monitors, etc. After eight years of that I moved on to become a supervisor. I went back to school for my Master's degree in management. Ever since, I've been a supervisor or office manager for a cardiologist in addition to working with patients.

2. **Are there many job opportunities in your profession? In what specific areas?**

   There are not many job opportunities for cardiovascular technicians. Many hospitals and cardiology practices have people in other positions handle those tasks. Exercise physiologists will do stress tests, for example. Also, more hospitals are outsourcing Holter monitor readings. A Holter monitor is a small device that the patient wears for 24 to 48 hours, and which records the heart's rhythms. The readings are downloaded into a report and the results read by the cardiologist. A cardiovascular technician is trained to attach the monitor and create the report. Cardiologists used to have their cardiovascular technicians do that, but now many outsource the work to outside companies.

3. **What do you wish you had known going into this profession?**

   I wish I could have foreseen how the area of echocardiogram technology would grow. When I first went into the profession, that wasn't a very big thing so I didn't go into that program. Then it became a very big thing.

4. **How do you see your profession changing in the next five years?**

   That's hard to say. It seems like there's less and less that cardiology practices are expecting their cardiovascular technicians to do. A lot of times the jobs that we used to do are being handled by other people. Respiratory therapists, medical technicians who work on the floor, nurses, exercise physiologists, they all handle the tasks that we do.

5. What role will technology play in those changes, and what skills will be required?

You need to have really good computer skills to keep up with the changes in this profession. Hospitals are going paperless now and medical records are computerized. You have to be able to learn how to use different software programs.

6. Do you have any general advice or additional professional insights to share with someone interested in your profession?

My advice to anyone starting out in this profession is to treat all of your patients as if they were family members.

If you're interested in this profession, volunteer in the cardiology department of a hospital to see if you like it. You really should have that experience before you pursue this as a career because without it, it's difficult to know if you'll enjoy the profession.

Find a hospital where you can shadow someone. Some programs require their students to do internships. You have to intern for a certain number of hours in order to fulfill your requirements. Often, those internships lead to jobs at those hospitals. If you're not in a program that has that requirement, find a volunteer opportunity on your own. If you're shadowing someone, make sure that person is doing the type of work that you're thinking of doing. If you want to go into cardiology, it wouldn't make any sense to volunteer or shadow someone in a unit other than cardiology.

Some of the cardiovascular technicians that I work with got their start that way – by volunteering.

7. Can you suggest a valuable "try this" for students considering a career in your profession?

It's important that you find out beforehand whether you have the stomach for it. Some people are squeamish about hospitals. You can't be afraid. You're going to see all kinds of things when you go to the floors and do EKGs.

When I first started, I had to go to the intensive care units and the burn unit. I thought, 'What was I thinking, going into this field?' On the other hand, when I worked as an office manager in a cardiology department, I found I didn't like that. I didn't like sitting behind the desk all day. I enjoy the patient care aspect of the job. Now I do both.

SELECTED SCHOOLS

Many technical and community colleges offer programs leading to either
certification (one year) or an associate's degree (two years) in cardiovascular
technology. Interested students are advised to consult with a school guidance
counselor or research area postsecondary schools. The website of the Commission
on the Accreditation of Allied Health Education Programs (see below) allows
users to search for accredited cardiovascular technology programs in their state.

MORE INFORMATION

**Alliance of Cardiovascular
Professionals**
P.O. Box 2007
Midlothian, VA 23112
804.632.0078
www.acp-online.org

**American Registry of Diagnostic
Medical Sonographers**
1401 Rockville Pike, Suite 600
Rockville, MD 20852-1402
800.541.9754
www.ardms.org

**Cardiovascular Credentialing
International (CCI)**
1500 Sunday Drive, Suite 102
Raleigh, NC 27607
800.326.0268
www.cci-online.org

**Commission on Accreditation
of Allied Health Education
Programs**
1361 Park Street
Clearwater, FL 33756
727.210.2350
www.caahep.org

**Joint Review Committee on
Education in Diagnostic Medical
Sonography**
6021 University Boulevard, Suite 500
Ellicott City, MD 21043
443.973.3251
www.jrcdms.org

**Society of Diagnostic Medical
Sonography**
2745 Dallas Parkway, Suite 350
Plano, TX 75093-8730
800.229.9506
www.sdms.org

Simone Isadora Flynn/Editor

Chiropractor

Snapshot

Career Cluster: Health Science
Interests: Science, Health & Wellness, Physical Education
Earnings (Yearly Average): $71,232
Employment & Outlook: Faster Than Average Growth Expected

OVERVIEW

Sphere of Work

A chiropractor is a health care practitioner who mainly employs alternative, noninvasive methods to treat problems related to the human muscular, nervous, and skeletal systems, as well as to improve the overall health of the patient. Chiropractic medicine is founded on the idea that spinal misalignment and compression adversely affect the nervous system, limiting the immune system's ability to fight off disease and chronic conditions. A chiropractor uses techniques such as manual adjustment of the patient's spine and body parts in order to correct or treat health problems.

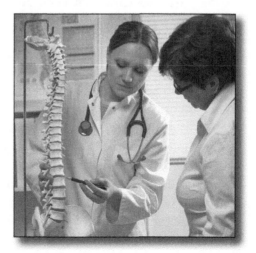

Work Environment

Like a variety of other health care and alternative health professionals, chiropractors often work in private practices, often alone or with a small number of employees. In some cases, several chiropractors join together to establish a group practice affiliated with a larger hospital or clinic. Chiropractors usually work forty hours or more per week. Because most chiropractors are self-employed, they can maintain a flexible schedule, seeing patients during evenings and weekends, being "on-call," or making house calls. They stand for long periods and use their hands and arms extensively.

Profile

Working Conditions: Work Indoors
Physical Strength: Medium Work
Education Needs: Specialized Degree
Licensure/Certification: Required
Physical Abilities Not Required: No Strenuous Labor
Opportunities For Experience: Part-Time Work
Holland Interest Score*: ISR

* See Appendix A

Occupation Interest

Those interested in pursuing a career in chiropractic must have an affinity for effective, holistic treatment of bodily diseases. In essence, a chiropractor must understand and appreciate the merits of traditional Western medicine while also applying the tenets of alternative medicine. The aspiring chiropractor should be physically strong and dexterous, as a chiropractor repeatedly performs bodily adjustments in his or her efforts to produce successful results.

A Day in the Life—Duties and Responsibilities

A chiropractor spends the majority of his or her day meeting, diagnosing, and treating patients. Like other front-line health care professionals, chiropractors evaluate the state of a patient's health through physical examinations and interviews. They regularly order laboratory tests, x-rays, and other imaging procedures to determine whether a patient's problems can be adequately treated through chiropractic methods. They suggest appropriate treatment programs and usually manipulate and adjust a patient's spine using their hands and fingers. Most importantly, chiropractors study a patient's neuromusculoskeletal system using chiropractic diagnoses. Chiropractors also study a patient's medical history and recommend alternative treatments, which may include exercise regimes, a change of diet, herbal or vitamin supplements, massage, electric currents, acupuncture, or therapies involving light, water, or heat. Chiropractors may refer patients to other medical professionals if those patients require medical care beyond what chiropractic treatment can offer. Unlike medical doctors, chiropractors cannot prescribe medication or perform any surgical procedure.

Some chiropractors specialize in a specific area of chiropractic, including orthopedics, pediatrics, internal disorders, or sports injuries. These specialists see patients with problems related to their specific area of expertise.

Self-employed chiropractors must also take on various administrative and management responsibilities, such as scheduling, bookkeeping, purchasing equipment, hiring staff, and communicating with insurance companies and other vendors. All chiropractors must document patient case histories and treatment plans.

Duties and Responsibilities

- Analyzing a patient's condition through questioning, observation, examination, x-ray and laboratory services
- Advising the patient regarding the course of treatment to be followed, including counseling the patient about such matters as nutrition, exercise, and stress management
- Performing a series of spinal adjustments from the base of the skull to the tip of the spine by hand and finger manipulation
- Treating patients using such measures as exercise, water, light, massage, and heat therapy
- Referring patients requiring drugs or surgery to other health care specialists
- Maintaining accurate case history records of all patients

WORK ENVIRONMENT

Physical Environment

The majority of chiropractic care is performed in comfortable, clean, bright private office settings. Chiropractors who work in a hospital or clinic are exposed to a more bustling, noisy environment than those who work in private practices.

Human Environment

Chiropractors see multiple patients on a daily basis, and, like physicians, they must be friendly, accommodating, and reassuring. They normally work with a small administrative staff, other chiropractors, acupuncturists, and/or massage therapists.

Relevant Skills and Abilities

Communication Skills
- Speaking and writing effectively

Interpersonal/Social Skills
- Being sensitive to others
- Cooperating with others
- Working independently and as a member of a team

Organization & Management Skills
- Making decisions
- Paying attention to and handling details
- Managing a schedule

Technical Skills
- Familiarity with massage/body work
- Working with your hands

Technological Environment

Chiropractors use a wide variety of medical equipment to diagnose and treat patients. They commonly work with stethoscopes, x-ray and ultrasound machines, otoscopes (for examining the ear), percussion hammers, traction units, electrocardiograph machines, and nerve interference detection instruments, among other devices. Familiarity with medical, scheduling, accounting, and database software is also important.

EDUCATION, TRAINING, AND ADVANCEMENT

High School/Secondary

High school students who are interested in becoming chiropractors should focus their academic studies in the sciences, anatomy, health, and communications. They should also supplement their foundational coursework with classes in mathematics, physiology, nutrition, and physical education. At home or in the local library, students can research and learn about alternative healing and holistic practices. They can also seek part-time assistant positions at local chiropractor clinics to gain familiarity with the profession.

Suggested High School Subjects
- Algebra
- Applied Math
- Applied Physics
- Biology
- Chemistry
- College Preparatory
- English
- Health Science Technology
- Physical Science
- Physics
- Physiology
- Psychology
- Trigonometry

Famous First

The first chiropractor was Daniel David Palmer (pictured) of Davenport, Iowa. He performed his first treatment in 1895, and five years later opened the Palmer School of Chiropractic in Davenport. The school remains one of the best known institutions in the field today.

College/Postsecondary

In order to receive a doctor of chiropractic (DC) degree, prospective chiropractors must complete a four-year chiropractic program accredited by the Council on Chiropractic Education (CCE). To be admitted to a chiropractic program, candidates must have at least two or three years of undergraduate education. Many applicants have earned a bachelor's of science degree. Most undergraduates looking to enter chiropractic programs study biology, physics, and chemistry. Chiropractic programs offer students classroom, clinical, and laboratory experience in the sciences, spinal adjustment and manipulation, and physical and laboratory diagnosis.

Those interested in specializing in a particular chiropractic area pursue advanced training in their field of interest. Chiropractic specialties include rehabilitation, pediatrics, and neurology, among others. To be granted "diplomate" status in a particular subfield, chiropractors must successfully pass specialty examinations offered by chiropractic specialty boards.

Related College Majors
- Anatomy & Physiology
- Chiropractic (D.C., D.C.M.)
- Pre-Medicine

Adult Job Seekers

Chiropractors typically form strong networking connections with faculty members and colleagues during the course of their formal education. Many chiropractic programs offer work-study opportunities that allow students to gain practical experience in the field. Membership in a professional chiropractic association such as the American Chiropractic Association (ACA) can also provide networking, job-finding, and professional development opportunities.

After they receive their degree, some chiropractors join a multidiscipline practice where they work alongside physical therapists, massage therapists, acupuncturists, medical doctors, or other medical professionals. This kind of arrangement can provide new chiropractors with an existing patient base when they are starting out in the field. Many chiropractors later establish a solo practice.

Professional Certification and Licensure

All chiropractors must acquire a state license in order to perform chiropractic medicine and may only practice within the state in which they are licensed. Chiropractors must meet all requirements mandated by the state licensing board. Every state licensing board requires prospective chiropractors to have completed a minimum of two years of undergraduate coursework and hold a doctor of chiropractic degree in order to qualify for licensure. To be licensed, chiropractors must pass the National Board of Chiropractic Examiners examination, which consists of written and practical sections. Some states may administer additional or supplemental examinations. Licensed chiropractors must participate in continuing education programs each year to maintain their licensure.

Additional Requirements

Chiropractors, like other health care professionals, must possess strong problem-solving skills and desire to help improve the lives of their patients. They must also be empathic, understanding, and supportive of people who are suffering from serious ailments. Unlike other medical treatments, chiropractic treatment coverage varies greatly among health insurance carriers; therefore, chiropractors should be aware of and sensitive to their patients' financial constraints. Since many years of education are required to become a chiropractor, prospective chiropractors should be passionate about learning and committed to their goal.

Fun Fact

The word chiropractic is derived from the Greek and means "to perform with the hands." . . . David Palmer is credited with founding modern chiropractic medicine in the U.S. in 1895.
Source: Wikipedia

EARNINGS AND ADVANCEMENT

Earnings depend on the number of years in practice, individual initiative and professional ability, and the location of the practice or employer. Median annual earnings of chiropractors were $71,232 in 2012. The lowest ten percent earned less than $34,206, and the highest ten percent earned more than $152,290. In chiropractic medicine, as in other types of independent practice, earnings are relatively low in the beginning and increase as the practice grows.

Chiropractors may receive paid vacations, holidays, and sick days; life and health insurance; and retirement benefits. These are usually paid by the employer. Self-employed chiropractors must provide their own benefits.

Metropolitan Areas with the Highest
Concentration of Jobs in this Occupation

Metropolitan area	Employment[1]	Employment per thousand jobs	Hourly mean wage
Chicago-Joliet-Naperville, IL	960	0.26	$49.04
New York-White Plains-Wayne, NY-NJ	720	0.14	$44.45
Los Angeles-Long Beach-Glendale, CA	710	0.18	$45.74
Atlanta-Sandy Springs-Marietta, GA	630	0.28	$24.17
Minneapolis-St. Paul-Bloomington, MN-WI	550	0.32	$41.48
Phoenix-Mesa-Glendale, AZ	540	0.31	$29.90
Portland-Vancouver-Hillsboro, OR-WA	530	0.53	$28.54
Warren-Troy-Farmington Hills, MI	500	0.46	$40.43

[1]Does not include self-employed. Source: Bureau of Labor Statistics, 2012

EMPLOYMENT AND OUTLOOK

There were approximately 28,000 chiropractors employed nationally in 2010;another 25,000 were in solo practice (i.e., self-employed). A small number teach, conduct research at chiropractic institutions, or work in hospitals and clinics. Employment is expected to grow faster than the average for all occupations through the year 2020, which means employment is projected to increase about 28 percent. This is a result of the continued demand by consumers for alternative healthcare. Chiropractors emphasize the importance of healthy lifestyles and do not prescribe drugs or perform surgery. As a result, chiropractic care is appealing to many health-conscious Americans. Chiropractic treatment of the back, neck, extremities and joints has become more accepted as a result of research and changing attitudes about alternative, noninvasive healthcare practices. The rapidly expanding older population will also increase demand for chiropractors. Most job openings arise from retirements. Chiropractors usually remain in the occupation until they retire; few transfer to other occupations.

Employment Trend, Projected 2010–20

Chiropractors: 28%

Health Diagnosing and Treating Practitioners: 26%

Total, All Occupations: 14%

Note: "All Occupations" includes all occupations in the U.S. Economy. Source: U.S. Bureau of Labor Statistics, Employment Projections Program

Related Occupations
- Physical Therapist
- Physician

Conversation With . . .
DR. LAUREN E. HAMM
Chiropractor, 16 years

1. What was your individual career path in terms of education, entry-level job, or other significant opportunity?

I did my undergraduate work at Assumption College in Central Massachusetts. I received my bachelor's in Psychology and also was pre-med. After college, I went to Palmer College of Chiropractic in Davenport, Iowa, where I received my D.C. (Doctor of Chiropractic) degree. This is a five-year program after college. I started my own practice after I graduated from chiropractic school (no entry level job for me). I then went on to get my specialization in pregnancy and pediatrics and this is my focus today.

2. Are there many job opportunities in your profession? In what specific areas?

There are many job opportunities as a chiropractor. Many people choose to become an associate after they graduate and work for another chiropractor. As health care is changing and people are more focused on wellness, they are turning to the chiropractic profession to help keep them well, instead of waiting until they get sick.

As a chiropractor, we can set our own hours and work for ourselves, or we can choose to work in a facility with integrated health care and work with professionals in different fields. We also have the ability to teach. Many chiropractors practice and also teach in colleges. The possibilities are endless.

3. What do you wish you had known going into this profession?

I wish I had visited more offices while I was in school. All chiropractors are not the same and I wish I had the opportunity to visit more while I was in school, because so many chiropractors practice in different ways. I knew I would be setting up my own practice, and I was looking at office layout, how they run their business, how they interact with their patients, and how their offices look.

4. How do you see your profession changing in the next five years?

With the Affordable Care Act, health care is changing rapidly, especially the way it is administered. All health care professionals are already seeing this in the form of more paperwork. There's more paperwork and there are more hoops to jump through. This is making it more difficult and more expensive for us to operate. Although my practice already is predominantly a cash practice, I believe that more and more health care practitioners will be moving to a cash model.

In terms of delivery of care, there are always new techniques you can learn. There are hundreds of techniques out there. But in terms of how I actually deliver care, I hope it doesn't change. I like my model. I hope that what I'm doing today is what I'm doing in 20 years.

5. What role will technology play in those changes, and what skills will be required?

The biggest changes with technology involve record keeping. It is mandated that all health care go to a digital format. Our office has been computerized for more than six years now. Our records and notes are documented in computerized patient files.

Also, all our patient analysis is done with specific computerized instrumentation, things like surface EMG, thermography, and digitized posture analysis. In terms of working on patients, they're coming out with instrumentation technology. I don't like it. I like to use my hands. But there are chiropractors who work solely with instruments

6. Do you have any general advice or additional professional insights to share with someone interested in your profession?

If you're planning to be a chiropractor, I think you have to be an outgoing person, because you're dealing with the public every single day. You need to be a good communicator. You will need to know how to run a business, because so many chiropractors are in business for themselves. You do get some business courses in chiropractic school, but not nearly enough. You'll need to know banking, balancing books, and QuickBooks. You need to be able to ask for money, to be comfortable doing that. And you will need to be a boss and know how to deal with the people who are working for you.

7. Can you suggest a valuable "try this" for students considering a career in your profession?

Go ahead and visit some chiropractors. We are usually more than happy to have someone shadow us for a day. Look at a few chiropractic schools and see what the requirements are to become a chiropractor. I recommend http://www.sherman.edu/ and http://www.life.edu/ as fantastic places to start.

SELECTED SCHOOLS

Below are listed a selection of specialized schools in chiropractic. The website of the Association of Chiropractic Colleges (see "More Information," below) provides a complete list of accredited programs.

Cleveland Chiropractic College
10850 Lowell Avenue
Cleveland, OH
913.234.0600
www.cleveland.edu

D'Youville College
320 Porter Avenue
Buffalo, NY 14201
716.829.7725
www.dyc.edu

Logan College of Chiropractic
P.O. Box 1065
Chesterfield, MO 63006
636.230.1934
www.logan.edu

National University of Health Sciences
200 E. Roosevelt Road
Lombard, IL 60148
630.889.6604
www.nuhs.edu

New York Chiropractic College
P.O. Box 800
Seneca Falls, NY 13148
315.568.3100
www.nycc.edu

Northwestern Health Sciences University
2501 W. 84th Street
Bloomington, IN 55431
952.888.4777
www.nwhealth.edu

Palmer College of Chiropractic
1000 Brady Street
Davenport, IA 52803
563.884.5500
www.palmer.edu
Also has branches in Port Orange, FL, and San Jose, CA.

Sherman College of Chiropractic
P.O. Box 1452
Spartanburg, SC 29304
864.578.8700
www.sherman.edu

Texas Chiropractic College
5912 Spencer Highway
Pasadena, TX 77505
281.487.1170
www.txchiro.edu

University of Western States
2900 NE 132nd Avenue
Portland, OR 97230
503.251.5712
www.uws.edu

MORE INFORMATION

American Chiropractic Association
Member Information Center
1701 Clarendon Boulevard
Arlington, VA 22209
703.276.8800
www.acatoday.com

Association of Chiropractic Colleges
4424 Montgomery Avenue, Suite 202
Bethesda, MD 20814
800.284.1062
www.chirocolleges.org

Congress of Chiropractic State Associations
12531 East Meadow Drive
Wichita, KS 67206
316.613.3386
www.cocsa.org

Council on Chiropractic Education
8049 N. 85th Way
Scottsdale, AZ 85258-4321
480.443.8877
www.cce-usa.org

Council on Chiropractic Guidelines and Practice Parameters
P.O. Box 2542
Lexington, SC 29071
803.356.6809
www.clinicalcompass.org

Federation of Chiropractic Licensing Boards
5401 W. 10th Street, Suite 101
Greeley, CO 80634-4400
970.356.3500
www.fclb.org

International Chiropractors Association
6400 Arlington Boulevard, Suite 800
Falls Church, VA 22042
800.423.4690
www.chiropractic.org

National Board of Chiropractic Examiners
901 54th Avenue
Greeley, CO 80634
800.964.6223
www.nbce.org

World Chiropractic Alliance
2683 Via de La Valle, Suite G 629
Del Mar, CA 92014
800.347.1011
www.worldchiropracticalliance.org

Briana Nadeau/Editor

Dental Assistant

Snapshot

Career Cluster: Health Science

Interests: Science, Health Care, Dentistry, Patient Care Techniques, Film Production

Earnings (Yearly Average): $35,478

Employment & Outlook: Faster Than Average Growth Expected

OVERVIEW

Sphere of Work

Dental assistants are responsible for assisting dentists, oral surgeons, and orthodontists with patient care, equipment and exam room set up and care, and record keeping. During an exam or procedure, a dental assistant may hand tools or materials to the dentist, suction the patient's mouth, tighten or repair braces, operate the x-ray machine, take "before" and "after" dental-work photographs, stay with the patient until the numbing process is complete or the patient wakes from sedation, or make notes in the patient's record. In addition, dental assistants assist dentists, orthodontists, and dental

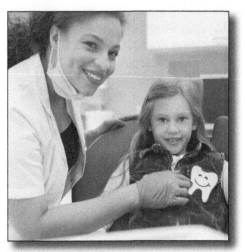

laboratory technicians with the construction of orthodontic appliances, crowns, full dentures, partial dentures, or veneers. Dental assistants may specialize in general, pediatric, or trauma dentistry, as well as orthodontics, oral surgery, or dental laboratory work.

Work Environment

Dental assistants spend their workdays sitting and standing in dental offices, orthodontic offices, oral surgery offices, and dental laboratories. Dental offices and laboratories tend to be clean, well-lit, well-ventilated, and temperature-controlled environments. Dental assistants generally work forty-hour weeks but may be required to work more during periods of increased business or emergencies. Both full-time and part-time employment opportunities are available in this occupation.

Occupation Interest

Individuals drawn to the dental assistant field tend to be intelligent and detail oriented. Successful dental assistants display traits such as strong interpersonal and effective time management skills. Dental assistants should enjoy working closely with others, be interested in health or science, and have a strong background in patient care and dental record keeping.

A Day in the Life—Duties and Responsibilities

A dental assistant spends most of his or her day providing patient care alongside a dentist, orthodontist, or oral surgeon. Prior to a patient appointment, the dental assistant sterilizes the exam or procedure room and dental equipment, and prepares the dental instrument tray. He or she greets each patient in the waiting room, brings the patient to the exam or procedure room, and obtains the patient's dental history and vital signs. Where permitted, a dental assistant may take and process x-rays of the patient's teeth, mouth, or surrounding jaw

Profile

Working Conditions: Work Indoors
Physical Strength: Light Work
Education Needs: On-The-Job Training, High School Diploma With Technical Education, Technical/Community College, Apprenticeship
Licensure/Certification: Required
Physical Abilities Not Required: No Heavy Labor
Opportunities Or Experience: Internship, Apprenticeship, Military Service, Part-Time Work
Holland Interest Score*: SAI

* See Appendix A

structure. During the exam or procedure, the dental assistant may assist the dentist, orthodontist, or oral surgeon by applying numbing cream to the patient's gum and tooth area as directed, handing over tools and materials, and vacuuming saliva or blood to keep the patient's mouth dry. A dental assistant may also make dental molds or impressions, mix cements and putties used for fillings, or assist in the construction of orthodontic appliances, crowns, bridges, ceramics, partial dentures, or full dentures. After an exam or procedure, the dental assistant instructs the patient on proper post-exam or post-procedure dental care and about proper brushing and flossing techniques to prevent plaque buildup and gum disease.

Dental assistants perform some administrative duties as well. They record current and future treatment in patient charts, take "before" and "after" photographs for patient files, and help with patient scheduling, billing, and general clerical work as required. They may also be responsible for maintaining supply inventory and placing orders. In addition, all dental assistants are responsible for educating themselves about and complying with the administrative, physical, and technical patient privacy safeguards included in the federal Health Insurance Portability and Accountability Act (HIPAA).

Duties and Responsibilities

- Obtaining and recording patients' medical histories
- Preparing patients for dental treatment
- Keeping patients' mouths free of saliva buildup by use of a suction pump
- Arranging dental instruments, materials and medications on chairside tray
- Mixing and preparing materials such as fillings and cements
- Making impressions of patients' teeth to make study casts
- Handing instruments to the dentist
- Assisting during oral surgery
- Sterilizing instruments

WORK ENVIRONMENT

Physical Environment

The immediate physical environment of dental assistants varies based on their employer and specialization. Dental assistants spend their workdays in dental offices, orthodontic offices, oral surgery offices, and dental laboratories. To minimize potential exposure to infectious diseases, radiation, and mercury, dental assistants wear safety glasses, surgical masks, and gloves.

Human Environment

Dental assistants interact with patients, dental laboratory technicians, dental hygienists, and office staff. They work under the direction of a supervising dentist, orthodontist, or oral surgeon. Dental assistants must be comfortable working in very close physical proximity to patients and dentists during exams and procedures.

Relevant Skills and Abilities

Communication Skills
- Speaking effectively
- Recording information

Interpersonal/Social Skills
- Being able to remain calm
- Being sensitive to others
- Providing support to others

Organization & Management Skills
- Adhering to a schedule
- Following instructions
- Handling challenging situations
- Organizing information or materials

Technical Skills
- Performing technical work
- Working with machines, tools or other objects
- Working with your hands

Technological Environment

A dental assistant's tools may include sterilizers or autoclaves, amalgamators, aspirators, dental or orthodontic pliers, tongue forceps, molar clamps, rubber dams, x-ray machines, cameras, water sprays, and cheek and tongue retractors. Materials used in laboratory work include powdered plaster and cements, mercury, disinfectants, and waxes. In addition, dental assistants use computers, Internet communication tools, phones, billing and scheduling software, spreadsheets, photocopiers, and fax machines to fulfill administrative duties.

EDUCATION, TRAINING, AND ADVANCEMENT

High School/Secondary

High school students interested in pursuing a career as a dental assistant should prepare themselves by developing good study habits. High school–level study of biology, chemistry, anatomy, health, computer science, communications, and mathematics will provide a strong foundation for work as a dental assistant or college-level work in the field. Due to the diversity of dental assistant responsibilities, high school students interested in this occupation may benefit from seeking internships or part-time jobs that expose the students to dental or medical settings and procedures.

Suggested High School Subjects
- Applied Biology/Chemistry
- Biology
- Bookkeeping
- Business
- Business & Computer Technology
- Business English
- Chemistry
- Dental Assisting
- Health Science Technology
- Keyboarding
- Mathematics
- Science

Famous First

The first gauge to measure tooth-wear effectively was developed in 1990. Whereas earlier tools might help to detect major wear over long periods of time, the new gauge could measure weekly or even daily rates of wear by means of a scanning electron microscope.

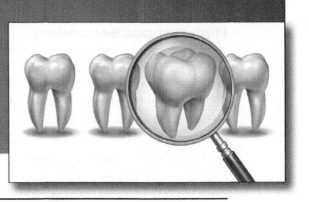

Postsecondary

Postsecondary students interested in becoming dental assistants should work toward a certificate or an associate's degree in that field, dental technology, clinical sciences, or a related field. The Commission on Dental Accreditation (CODA) has approved nearly 300 dental-assisting training programs that can be completed in one year. These training programs instruct students in subject areas such as dental materials, tools and techniques, pharmacology, dental anatomy, and radiology. Postsecondary students can gain work experience and potential advantage in their future job searches by securing co-ops or part-time employment in dental or medical settings.

Related College Majors
- Dental Assistant Training
- Health Science

Adult Job Seekers

Adults seeking employment as dental assistants should have, at a minimum, a certificate or an associate's degree from an accredited CODA training program. Adult job seekers should educate themselves about the educational and professional licensure requirements of their home states and the organizations where they seek employment. Joining professional dental associations may help qualified job seekers with networking and job searching. Professional dental associations, such as the American Dental Assistants Association (ADAA) and the National Dental Association (NDA), generally maintain lists of available jobs.

Professional Certification and Licensure

Registration or licensure is required of dental assistants as a condition of professional practice in most states. Most states recognize and accept the Certified Dental Assistant (CDA) designation offered by the Dental Assisting National Board (DANB) and the Registered Dental Assistant (RDA) designation offered by the American Medical Technologists (AMT). The CDA and the RDA certifications have education, training, CPR certification, testing, and continuing education requirements. Licensing requirements for dental assistants vary significantly by state and dental assistant specialty. Dental assistants should consult with the department of health in their home state for specific licensing requirements.

Additional Requirements

Individuals who find satisfaction, success, and job security as dental assistants will be knowledgeable about the profession's requirements, responsibilities, and opportunities. As they have access to patients' private medical information, dental assistants must demonstrate integrity and professional ethics. Membership in professional dental associations is encouraged among all dental assistants as a means of building professional community and networking.

Fun Fact

One of the fastest growing occupations in the United States, the demand for dental assistants is expected to grow 31 percent between 2010 and 2020.
Source: Dental Assisting National Board, Inc.

EARNINGS AND ADVANCEMENT

Earnings depend on the individual's training and practical experience, the duties of the job and the geographic location of the employer. Median annual earnings of dental assistants were $35,478 in 2012. The lowest ten percent earned less than $24,041, and the highest ten percent earned more than $49,915.

Dental assistants may receive paid vacations, holidays, and sick days; life and health insurance; and retirement benefits. These are usually paid by the employer. Some employers also provide an allowance for the purchase of uniforms, time off to attend professional meetings, and free dental care.

Metropolitan Areas with the Highest Employment Level in this Occupation

Metropolitan area	Employment	Employment per thousand jobs	Hourly mean wage
Los Angeles-Long Beach-Glendale, CA	10,340	2.67	$16.85
New York-White Plains-Wayne, NY-NJ	9,350	1.81	$17.63
Chicago-Joliet-Naperville, IL	9,180	2.52	$15.94
Houston-Sugar Land-Baytown, TX	6,020	2.28	$16.04
Atlanta-Sandy Springs-Marietta, GA	5,120	2.26	$17.84
Santa Ana-Anaheim-Irvine, CA	5,000	3.55	$17.59
Washington-Arlington-Alexandria, DC-VA-MD-WV	4,750	2.03	$19.40
Riverside-San Bernardino-Ontario, CA	4,560	3.93	$15.80

Source: Bureau of Labor Statistics

EMPLOYMENT AND OUTLOOK

Dental assistants held about 300,000 jobs in 2012. About one-third of dental assistants worked part time, sometimes in more than one dentist's office. Almost all dental assistants work in private dental offices, although some work in dental schools, private and government hospitals, and state and local public health departments or clinics.

Employment is expected to grow much faster than the average for all occupations through the year 2020, which means employment is projected to increase 30 percent or more. This increase is due to greater demand for dental care and dentists' desire to increase productivity by using dental assistants for routine tasks. Population growth, greater retention of natural teeth by middle-aged and elderly people, and a focus on preventative care for younger patients are also adding to this increasing demand. In addition, some job openings will arise from the need to replace dental assistants who leave the occupation or retire.

Employment Trend, Projected 2010–20

Healthcare Support Occupations: 34%

Dental Assistants: 31%

Total, All Occupations: 14%

Note: "All Occupations" includes all occupations in the U.S. Economy. Source: U.S. Bureau of Labor Statistics, Employment Projections Program

Related Occupations
- Dental Hygienist
- Medical Assistant

Related Military Occupations
- Dental & Optical Laboratory Technician
- Dental Specialist

Conversation With . . .
COLLEEN GILBOW
Dental Assistant, 3 years

1. What was your individual career path in terms of education, entry-level job, or other significant opportunity?

My career path began with a 14-month course for Expanded Function Dental Assisting at All-State Career School. It was a lot fun! You learn everything there is to know about the in's and out's of assisting and the basic anatomy of the head and neck, along with learning about and how to take X-rays. The 14 months included one month at the University of Maryland Dental School. There I completed what they call "clinicals," which is when you're put into rotation to work with all the students practicing in each different field of dentistry. I then had to complete a one month externship in an actual office. After that I was able to start working as a dental assistant. I'm happy with the path I have chosen. I originally wanted to be a dentist but financially that wasn't an option for me. All-State offered the next best thing, so I jumped on the opportunity.

2. Are there many job opportunities in your profession? In what specific areas?

As far as job opportunities, they are plenty! There are dental offices everywhere and many different types to choose from, including endodontists, orthodontists, periodontists, oral surgery offices, and general practices.

3.   What do you wish you had known going into this profession?

My biggest mistake was not taking the Expanded Function Exam (a state exam) immediately after my schooling. So, if there's one thing I wish I had known, it would have been how important it is to have this certification in advance.

4. How do you see your profession changing in the next five years?

I don't see my profession changing that much in the next five years. However, technology is getting more advanced each year making things in the office faster and easier.

5. What role will technology play in those changes, and what skills will be required?

Technology has made taking X-rays much faster. By using digital X-rays we no longer have to develop film, which saves a lot of the assistant's time. But that is just the beginning. A lot of the hands-on procedures that we do in the office are becoming digital, like taking impressions, which will not only be easier on the assistant, but for the patient as well.

6. Do you have any general advice or additional professional insights to share with someone interested in your profession?

Take the radiology and expanded function exam right away after school. The radiology license is a requirement for the position. The expanded function is not a requirement in all offices, but will allow you to do more, like take impressions, fabricate and cement temporary crowns, and remove sutures. All will save the doctor time in the chair, making you more valuable, which results in higher pay. It's also important because all the information will be fresh in your brain. It's a lot to remember and the longer you wait, the less you will remember. Second, really think about the type of office you'd like to work in. Whether it be working with children in a pediatric office, doing oral surgery, or just working in a general office, it will make going to work much more enjoyable if you're in the right place.

7. Can you suggest a valuable "try this" for students considering a career in your profession?

My "try this" would be to reach out to your personal dentist first. Ask to shadow someone in the office, or possibly volunteer for a few days to get an idea of what it would be like. If the opportunity is there to make sure that's the direction you want to go in, take it.

SELECTED SCHOOLS

Hundreds of technical and community colleges across the United States offer programs leading to either certification (one year) or an associate's degree (two years) as a dental assistant. Interested students are advised to consult with a school guidance counselor or research area postsecondary schools. The website of the Commission on Dental Accreditation (see below) allows users to search for allied dental education programs (dental assisting, hygiene, and lab technology) in their state.

MORE INFORMATION

American Association of Public Health Dentistry
3085 Stevenson Drive, Suite 200
Springfield, IL 62703
217.529.6941
www.aaphd.org

American Dental Assistants Association
35 East Wacker Drive, Suite 1730
Chicago, IL 60601-2211
312.541.1550
www.dentalassistant.org

American Dental Association
211 East Chicago Avenue
Chicago, IL 60611-2678
312.440.2500
www.ada.org

American Medical Technologists
10700 West Higgins, Suite 150
Rosemont, IL 60018
800.275.1268
www.amt1.com

Commission on Dental Accreditation
American Dental Association
211 East Chicago Avenue
Chicago, IL 60611-2678
312.440.2500
www.ada.org/117.aspx

Dental Assisting National Board
444 N. Michigan Avenue, Suite 900
Chicago, IL 60611
312.642.3368
www.danb.org

National Dental Assistants Association
3517 16th Street, NW
Washington, DC 20010
202.588.1697
www.ndaonline.org

National Dental Association
3517 16th Street, NW
Washington, DC 20010
202.588.1697
admin@ndaonline.org
www.ndaonline.org

Simone Isadora Flynn/Editor

Dental Hygienist

Snapshot

Career Cluster: Health Science

Interests: Science, Health Care, Dentistry, Patient Care

Earnings (Yearly Average): $72,345

Employment & Outlook: Faster Than Average Growth Expected

OVERVIEW

Sphere of Work

Dental hygienists assist dentists with patient preventive dental care and treatment. In particular, they take diagnostic images, perform examinations and cleanings, and provide patient instruction in order to prevent tooth decay, oral disease, and other dental problems. Dental hygienists partner with supervising dentists to support and promote oral health for their patients. In addition to patient care and treatment, dental hygienists update patient records with details of dental services provided and notes for future care.

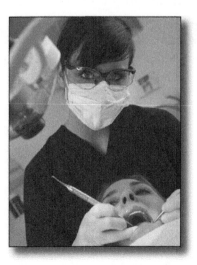

Work Environment

Dental hygienists spend their workdays in private dental offices, hospitals, long-term care facilities, government agencies, schools, prisons, and health care centers. These medical settings tend to be clean, well-lit, well-ventilated, and temperature-controlled environments. Dental hygienists generally work thirty-five to forty hours per week in a private dental office. Both full-time and part-time work opportunities are available in this occupation.

Occupation Interest

Individuals drawn to the profession of dental hygienist tend to be detail oriented and caring. Those who succeed as dental hygienists exhibit traits such as good hand-eye coordination, physical stamina, thoroughness, and effective time management. Dental hygienists should enjoy working with people, be interested in oral health, and have a strong background in patient care and dental recordkeeping.

A Day in the Life—Duties and Responsibilities

A dental hygienist typically spends his or her workdays in a general or pediatric dentistry practice. At the beginning of a patient appointment, the hygienist greets the patient in the waiting room and brings the patient to the exam or procedure room, where he or she interviews the patient about dental and physical health histories. The hygienist then examines the patient's teeth, mouth, gums, lymph nodes, and neck for evidence of tooth decay, oral disease, or other abnormalities. He or she may also take film or digital x-rays of the teeth, mouth, or surrounding jaw structure for diagnostic purposes. During the cleaning, the dental hygienist uses various hand instruments and tools to remove tartar, calcifications, deposits, and plaque from teeth and may polish teeth to remove stains or improve appearance or health. The hygienist may also perform root planing (scraping bacteria from a decaying part of a tooth) and

Profile

Working Conditions: Work Indoors
Physical Strength: Light Work
Education Needs: Technical/ Community College
Licensure/Certification: Required
Physical Abilities Not Required: No Heavy Labor
Opportunities Or Experience: Internship, Apprenticeship, Military Service,
Holland Interest Score*: SAI

* See Appendix A

deep gum cleaning, treat teeth with fluoride, and apply sealants to help prevent tooth decay (especially for children). For some patients, a hygienist may need to insert or detach restorative devices or remove oral stitches. Throughout the exam and cleaning, the dental hygienist records the exam findings as well as the current and future treatment plan in the patient's chart. During or after the visit, the hygienist teaches the patient about proper brushing and flossing techniques to prevent future plaque buildup and gum disease.

To ensure health and safety, dental hygienists must use clean, sterile equipment and they are responsible for sterilizing exam or procedure rooms and dental equipment between patient appointments. In addition, all dental hygienists are responsible for educating themselves about and complying with the administrative, physical, and technical patient privacy safeguards included in the federal Health Insurance Portability and Accountability Act (HIPAA).

Duties and Responsibilities

- Removing deposits and stains from patients' teeth
- Polishing teeth
- Applying topical medications to teeth and between teeth to help prevent decay
- Taking and processing x-rays
- Examining and recording the condition of the mouth and teeth on charts
- Cleaning, sharpening and sterilizing equipment
- Instructing patients in home oral health care procedures such as brushing and flossing

WORK ENVIRONMENT

Physical Environment

The immediate physical environment in which dental hygienists work varies based on their employer and specialization. Most dental hygienists spend their workdays in either general family dentist offices or pediatric dentist offices. To minimize potential exposure to infectious diseases, dental hygienists wear safety glasses, surgical masks, and gloves. They also follow strict protocols regarding radiology.

Relevant Skills and Abilities

Communication Skills
- Speaking effectively
- Recording information

Interpersonal/Social Skills
- Being patient
- Cooperating with others
- Working as a member of a team

Organization & Management Skills
- Adhering to a schedule
- Paying attention to and handling details

Technical Skills
- Performing technical work

Human Environment

Dental hygienists interact with patients, supervising dentists, dental assistants, and office staff. Dental hygienists must be comfortable working in very close physical proximity to patients and dentists during exams and procedures.

Technological Environment

Dental hygienists use a wide variety of technology, materials, and equipment. Their tools and materials may include mouth mirrors, sterilizers or autoclaves, sealant lights and sealants, tongue forceps, hand instruments, polishers, toothbrushes, dental floss, fluorides, x-ray machines, powdered plaster and cement, curettes, cameras, water sprays, disinfectants, and topical anesthetics. In addition, dental hygienists may also use Internet communication tools, phones, spreadsheets, copiers, fax machines, and software programs for dental imaging, patient records, invoices, and scheduling.

EDUCATION, TRAINING, AND ADVANCEMENT

High School/Secondary

High school students interested in pursuing a career as a dental hygienist should prepare themselves by developing good study habits. High school–level study of biology, chemistry, health, communications, computer science, and mathematics will provide a strong foundation for college-level work in the field. Students interested in this career path may benefit from seeking internships or part-time work opportunities that expose the students to dental or medical settings and procedures.

Suggested High School Subjects
- Algebra
- Applied Biology/Chemistry
- Applied Math
- Biology
- College Preparatory
- Dental Assisting
- English
- Health Science Technology
- Mathematic

Famous First

The first efficient toothpick machine and the first dental floss dispenser arrived in the same year, 1872, and were produced in the same state, Massachusetts. The toothpick machine was made by Silas Noble and James Cooley of Granville, Mass. The dental floss dispenser was made by Asahel Shurtleff of Randolph, Mass.

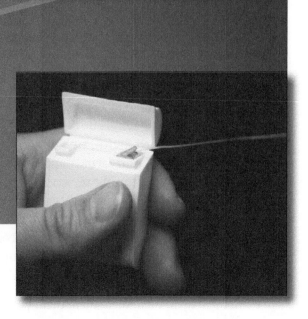

College/Postsecondary

IPostsecondary students interested in becoming dental hygienists should work toward a certificate or an associate's degree in dental hygiene from a training program accredited by the Commission on Dental Accreditation (CODA). These programs commonly provide courses in anatomy and physiology, chemistry, microbiology, nutrition, radiography, pharmacology, and pathology. Program trainees also receive hands-on clinical instruction. Postsecondary students can gain work experience and potential advantage in their future job searches by securing internships or part-time employment in dental or medical settings.

Related College Majors
- Dental Hygienist Training
- Health Science

Adult Job Seekers

Adults seeking employment as dental hygienists should have, at a minimum, a certificate or an associate's degree in dental hygiene from a CODA-accredited program. Many dental assistants choose to pursue additional education to become dental hygienists. Adult job seekers should educate themselves about the educational and professional licensure requirements of their home states and the organizations where they seek employment. Joining professional dental associations, such as the American Dental Hygienists Association (ADHA), may help job seekers with networking and job searching.

Professional Certification and Licensure

Licensure is required for dental hygienists as a condition of professional practice. Requirements for becoming a licensed dental hygienist (LDH) or registered dental hygienist (RDH) include education, a background check, valid CPR certification, a written national board dental hygiene examination, a state or regional clinical examination, and formal application to a state licensing board. Individuals planning to work as registered dental hygienists must complete a CODA-accredited dental hygienist training program to earn a certificate, associate's degree, or bachelor's degree. License renewal is usually contingent on continuing education. Due to differences in individual state dental practice requirements, dental hygienists should consult with the department of health in their home state for licensing specifics.

Additional Requirements

Individuals who find satisfaction, success, and job security as dental hygienists will be knowledgeable about the profession's requirements, responsibilities, and opportunities. As professionals in this role have access to private medical information, dental hygienists must be honest and ethical. Membership in professional dental associations is encouraged among all dental hygienists as a means of building professional community and networking.

EARNINGS AND ADVANCEMENT

Earnings of dental hygienists are affected by the type and geographic location of the employer, and the education and experience of the individual. Median annual earnings of dental hygienists were $72,345 in 2012. The lowest ten percent earned less than $47,700, and the highest ten percent earned more than $99,449.

Dental hygienists may receive paid vacations, holidays, and sick days; life and health insurance; and retirement benefits. These are usually paid by the employer.

Metropolitan Areas with the Highest
Employment Level in this Occupation

Metropolitan area	Employment	Employment per thousand jobs	Hourly mean wage
Chicago-Joliet-Naperville, IL	5,060	1.39	$31.49
Los Angeles-Long Beach-Glendale, CA	4,780	1.24	$47.48
New York-White Plains-Wayne, NY-NJ	3,870	0.75	$38.86
Dallas-Plano-Irving, TX	3,170	1.51	$37.18
Warren-Troy-Farmington Hills, MI	3,120	2.91	$29.22
Atlanta-Sandy Springs-Marietta, GA	3,100	1.37	$34.97
Minneapolis-St. Paul-Bloomington, MN-WI	3,090	1.77	$34.07
Seattle-Bellevue-Everett, WA	2,720	1.93	$44.91

.Source: Bureau of Labor Statistics, 2012

EMPLOYMENT AND OUTLOOK

Dental hygienists held about 190,000 jobs in 2012. About one-third of dental hygienists worked full-time; most worked part-time. Employment is expected to grow much faster than the average for all occupations through the year 2020, which means employment is projected to increase up to 38 percent. This is due to population growth, greater retention of natural teeth by older people, increased substitution of dental hygienists for services previously performed by dentists, and the growing awareness of the importance of preventative dental care.

Employment Trend, Projected 2010–20

Dental Hygienists: 38%

Health Technologists and Technicians: 26%

Total, All Occupations: 14%

Note: "All Occupations" includes all occupations in the U.S. Economy. Source: U.S. Bureau of Labor Statistics, Employment Projections Program

Related Occupations
- Dental Assistant

Conversation With . . .
LAUREN HERON
Dental Hygienist, 9 years

1. What was your individual career path in terms of education, entry-level job, or other significant opportunity?

I began my career at an "entry level" in terms of education. As a dental hygienist, you are able to work under the supervision of a dentist with just as Associate's degree. Including prerequisite classes and the full Associate's Degree program, you could be working in as little as three years. I earned an Associate's in Dental Hygiene at a community college, which can make it financially easier to get into the field. Then I went on and, in two semesters, earned a Bachelor's of General Studies with a focus in Allied Health from The University of Connecticut. That was when I began clinical teaching with a hygiene program. After a year, I enrolled in the Master's program at Albertus Magnus College in New Haven, CT and received a Master's in Management. I chose management because a dental office is a business. This broadened my scope, so that I can be an office manager or a hygiene coordinator in a large practice. The management degree also could open the door to product representation, since selling dental products is another side of the dental world.

2. Are there many job opportunities in your profession? In what specific areas?

Every state has different guidelines for dental hygienists; some states even allow hygienists to have their own practice. So, other states may have more opportunities given the different scope of practice, but I can only speak for Connecticut, where we have some limitations. Here, at this time, the job market is flooded, but there are a few opportunities in private practice, teaching, and product representation. Given the different scope of practice allowed in each state, it's advisable to do your research on job opportunities.

3. What do you wish you had known going into this profession?

I wish I had known how much I was going to love dentistry! If I knew then what I know now, I would have become a dentist. Don't get me wrong, dental hygiene is a great career, but by the time I realized I wanted more I was at a time in life when going back to school was not an option.

4. How do you see your profession changing in the next five years?

Advancements in research and technology are big in dentistry. I see the daily appointment having more chair-side diagnostic technology, such as saliva testing for mouth bacteria levels that influence gum disease and cavities, or high tech oral cancer screenings. These are adjunct services that are offered now. In the last 25 years, dentistry has changed dramatically. We have come so far with infection control, computers, digital radiology/imaging, lasers, and dental materials.

5. What role will technology play in those changes, and what skills will be required?

The skill level for further technology will most likely only be in-office training from the product representative. Some things may require more in-depth education, like a day seminar, but in my experience I have never had more than a weekend course.

6. Do you have any general advice or additional professional insights to share with someone interested in your profession?

Never get hung up on gear or equipment. What you need are customers.

It is truly a fun profession. Yes, there are days when the schedule is busy, but the patients make those days wonderful. I have been fortunate to find a great dentist to work with. I look forward to seeing my patients every visit.

7. Can you suggest a valuable "try this" for students considering a career in your profession?

It may be helpful for someone with no dental background to shadow a dental hygienist. It is a simple way to see how a "day in the life" can go. Many hygienists get their feet wet in dentistry as dental assistants. But oral health is not for everyone. It is not all bright, white perfect smiles. It can be difficult dealing with gum disease, bloody gums, broken teeth, and bad breath. It's not always pretty and you are literally hands-deep in it.

SELECTED SCHOOLS

Hundreds of technical and community colleges across the United States offer programs leading to either certification (one year) or an associate's degree (two years) as a dental hygienist. Interested students are advised to consult with a school guidance counselor or research area postsecondary schools. The website of the Commission on Dental Accreditation (see below) allows users to search for allied dental education programs (dental assisting, hygiene, and lab technology) in their state.

MORE INFORMATION

American Association of Public Health Dentistry
3085 Stevenson Drive, Suite 200
Springfield, IL 62703
217.529.6941
www.aaphd.org

American Dental Association
211 East Chicago Avenue
Chicago, IL 60611-2678
312.440.2500
www.ada.org

American Dental Hygienists Association
Division of Professional Development
444 North Michigan Avenue, Suite 3400
Chicago, IL 60611
312.440.8900
www.adha.org

Commission on Dental Accreditation
American Dental Association
211 East Chicago Avenue
Chicago, IL 60611-2678
312.440.2500
www.ada.org/117.aspx

National Dental Association
3517 16th Street, NW
Washington, DC 20010
202.588.1697
www.ndaonline.org

National Dental Hygienists Association
3517 16th Street, NW
Washington, DC 20010
202.588.1822
www.ndhaonline.org

Simone Isadora Flynn/Editor

Dentist

Snapshot

Career Cluster: Health Science, Medicine
Interests: Science, Health Care, Dentistry
Earnings (Yearly Average): $155,735
Employment & Outlook: Faster Than Average Growth Expected

OVERVIEW

Sphere of Work

Dentists assess, diagnose, and treat health issues concerning a patient's teeth and oral tissue. Using magnifiers, dental tools, and X-rays, they perform thorough examinations, searching for cavities, plaque, gum disease, exposed nerves, and other conditions. Dentists use handheld tools, drills, and other equipment to fix cavities and broken teeth, reset teeth, clear away plaque, and remove teeth as needed. They also provide guidance on measures patients can take to ensure good oral hygiene. Many dentists are general practitioners. A large number of dentists become specialists in one of the following eight subfields: orthodontics, endodontics, oral pathology, pediatric dentistry,

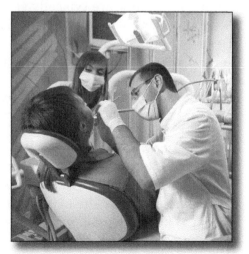

periodontics, public health dentistry, oral maxillofacial surgery, or prosthodontics. (See "Occupation Specialties," below.)

Work Environment

Dentists generally work in medical office environments. These settings are clean, well lit, and well ventilated. Dentist offices feature a main reception and waiting area, records rooms, and individual rooms equipped with patient chairs, dentist equipment, and X-ray machines. Dentists usually work as solo practitioners or with one or two partners. Some are employed in large medical facilities, research departments of pharmaceutical companies, or government agencies. These professionals generally work thirty-five to forty hours per week with a normal schedule. They may work longer hours when an emergency arises.

Profile

Working Conditions: Work Indoors
Physical Strength: Light Work
Education Needs: Medical Degree
Licensure/Certification: Required
Physical Abilities Not Required: No Heavy Labor
Opportunities Or Experience: Military Service
Holland Interest Score*: ISR

* See Appendix A

Occupation Interest

Dentists are respected as experts in oral health, care, and hygiene. They use their interest in science and concern for others to help people repair and maintain their teeth and gums for the long term. Physical stamina, a calm demeanor, and a high tolerance for stress are necessary to endure long hours of standing and handling patients who may be agitated. Dentists are typically very well compensated for their work. More experienced dentists often work reduced and more flexible hours. Demand for dentists is expected to continue to increase over the next several years, so many employment opportunities are available.

A Day in the Life—Duties and Responsibilities

Dentists usually see several patients each day, performing examinations, diagnosing problems, and implementing treatment plans. A dentist examines patients' teeth using small, sterilized metal tools, power tools such as suction devices and air-water syringes, and hand mirrors. He or she may use local anesthetics or gas to minimize pain and keep the patient calm during the procedure. During an exam, a dentist may clear additional plaque and debris, fill cavities, or straighten and file errant teeth. After this examination, the dentist or an assistant takes X-rays of the patient. If an issue is detected that warrants another appointment, the dentist assesses the issue and discusses treatment options with the patient. Antibiotics or other medications may be prescribed, decayed teeth may be extracted, protective sealants may be applied to growing teeth, and devices may be created to address gaps. The dentist may also provide a referral for the patient to visit a specialist for further care and treatment. If the appointment yields no issues, the dentist provides information about oral care so that the patient will continue to follow good oral hygiene practices.

In addition to the general practice procedures above, dental specialists may provide focused care for a particular condition, oral structure, or patient population. Depending on their specialty, they may perform surgeries and root canals, affix braces, take tissue samples, implant artificial replacement teeth, or otherwise diagnose and treat conditions in the gums, interior tooth pulp, bones, or head and neck areas of patients. Some dentists, such as dental public health specialists, work in the community to promote good oral health and hygiene.

Those in solo practices are additionally responsible for the daily operations of their business. This may entail hiring and managing staff, maintaining records and inventory, and handling finances.

Duties and Responsibilities

- **Diagnosing oral conditions and determining treatment**
- **Administering anesthetics**
- **Locating and filling cavities**
- **Treating diseased gums**
- **Extracting teeth**
- **Replacing missing teeth**
- **Fitting and providing artificial dentures**
- **Cleaning teeth**
- **Teaching preventive care**

OCCUPATION SPECIALTIES

Orthodontists

Orthodontists diagnose and correct or prevent irregularities and deviations in the position of teeth and the development of the jaws, primarily (though not exclusively) in adolescents. They design and fabricate appliances such as braces and mouthguards.

Oral and Maxillofacial Surgeons

Oral and Maxillofacial Surgeons perform surgical operations on the mouth and jaws to remove teeth, tumors and other abnormal growths or to correct abnormalities in the jaw or palate.

Periodontists

Periodontists treat diseased gum and bone tissue by performing surgical procedures, eliminating the irritating margins of fillings, removing plaque, and other methods. They also provide dental implants (artificial teeth attached to the bone).

Prosthodontists

Prosthodontists specialize in making artificial teeth or dentures to correct deformations of the mouth and jaws.

Endodontists

Endodontists specialize in the internal structures of teeth and perform root canals, or the removal of the nerves and blood supply of an injured or infected tooth.

Pediatric Dentists

Pediatric Dentists, or Pedodontists, are dentists for infants, children and adolescents. They treat primary and secondary teeth and construct suitable appliances for growing mouths

Public Health Dentists

Public Health Dentists concern themselves with community dental health. They plan, organize and maintain dental health programs of public health agencies and analyze the dental needs of a community to determine necessary changes that need to be made.

WORK ENVIRONMENT

Relevant Skills and Abilities

Analytical Skills
- Analyzing and understanding information

Communication Skills
- Speaking and writing effectively
- Describing complex phenomena to others

Interpersonal/Social Skills
- Cooperating with others
- Working as a member of a team
- Making others feel reassured

Organization & Management Skills
- Coordinating tasks
- Managing people/groups
- Paying attention to and handling details
- Performing duties that change frequently

Planning & Research Skills
- Developing evaluation strategies
- Researching information

Technical Skills
- Performing scientific, mathematical and technical work

Physical Environment

Dentists work in medical offices, which are usually private practices. These locations have individual rooms with patient chairs, mobile lights, X-ray machines, hand tools, water-draining systems, and power tools. Dentist offices must be very clean and well organized, with patient records easily accessible and enough waiting space for multiple patients. Although dentists wear protective masks, gloves, and safety glasses and follow safety protocols, they may be exposed to patients' saliva and blood, infectious diseases, or radiation, and risk injury from equipment.

Human Environment

In addition to patients, dentists interact with dental hygienists, dental assistants, laboratory technicians, and dental students. As business owners, solo practitioners must also work with building managers, medical equipment and pharmaceutical salespeople, office suppliers, and receptionists.

Technological Environment

Dentists must use an array of technologies and equipment, although the specifics depend on their area of specialty. Their tools include mouth mirrors, handheld probing and cleaning tools, drills, powered water syringes, X-ray and digital imaging equipment, and surgical devices. They must also use patient databases, office management systems, Internet communication tools, and medical and accounting software.

EDUCATION, TRAINING, AND ADVANCEMENT

High School/Secondary

High school students interested in dentistry should study biology, chemistry, anatomy, physics, physiology, and other natural sciences. Mathematics, health, psychology, and nutrition courses are also very important. High school students should also hone their writing and public speaking skills through English and communications classes.

Suggested High School Subjects
- Algebra
- Applied Math
- Biology
- Chemistry
- Child Growth & Development
- College Preparatory
- English
- Foods & Nutrition
- Geometry
- Physics
- Physiology
- Science
- Speech

Famous First

The first dental drill appeared in 1790. Modeled on a spinning wheel, it was powered by means of a foot pedal. Another modern tool of dentistry, the dental chair (adjustable, with headrest, etc.), didn't appear until nearly 60 years later, in 1848.

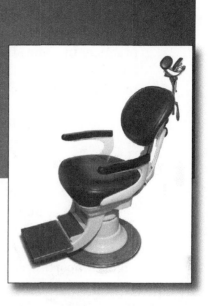

College/Postsecondary

Prospective dentists should receive a bachelor's degree with a major or concentration in biology, chemistry, or a related discipline. Upon completion of their undergraduate training, aspiring dentists must take and pass the Dental Admissions Test and attend a four-year dental college, where they will pursue either a doctor of dental surgery (DDS) or a doctor of dental medicine (DMD) degree. Dentists who wish to become specialists must complete an additional two to four years of training after receiving their DDS or DMD degree. Those who intend to establish their own practices may also benefit from some formal instruction in economics, accounting, and business management.

Related College Majors
- Biology
- Chemistry
- Dentistry (D.D.S., D.M.D.)
- Pre-Dentistry Studies
- Pre-Medicine

Adult Job Seekers

Most dentists are independent business owners in private practices. In order to start a dental office, new dentists may begin their careers by working with established dentists, which enables them to gain return patients over time.

Professional Certification and Licensure

Dentists must complete dental college and pass written and practical exams to obtain licensure in the state or states in which they seek to practice. In some states, the National Board Dental Examinations can be taken in lieu of the written portion of the state exam. Specialists may also be required to pass special state licensing exams.

Additional Requirements

Dentists must demonstrate exceptional dexterity and manual skills. They must also possess a strong attention to detail and the ability to quickly identify and diagnose oral health issues. A calm and agreeable bedside manner can keep a patient still and composed during examinations. Strong managerial and organizational skills are also highly important, as most dentists are independent business owners.

Fun Fact

There are 65 accredited dental schools in the United States from which 5,000 dentists graduated in 2010.
Source: American Dental Association

EARNINGS AND ADVANCEMENT

Earnings depend on the type and geographical location of the practice and the number of years in practice. Self-employed dentists in private practice tend to earn more than salaried dentists. Dentists earned median annual salaries of $155,735 in 2012. The lowest ten percent earned less than $75,483, and the highest ten percent earned more than $176,384.

Dentists may receive paid vacations, holidays, and sick days; life and health insurance; and retirement benefits. These are usually paid by the employer.

Metropolitan Areas with the Highest
Employment Level in this Occupation

Metropolitan area	Employment(1)	Employment per thousand jobs	Hourly mean wage
New York-White Plains-Wayne, NY-NJ	5,260	1.02	$67.95
Los Angeles-Long Beach-Glendale, CA	3,420	0.88	$58.04
Chicago-Joliet-Naperville, IL	2,870	0.79	$61.25
Boston-Cambridge-Quincy, MA	2,140	1.25	$85.69
Washington-Arlington-Alexandria, DC-VA-MD-WV	2,030	0.87	$78.58
Atlanta-Sandy Springs-Marietta, GA	1,960	0.87	$92.93
Phoenix-Mesa-Glendale, AZ	1,630	0.94	$81.13
Dallas-Plano-Irving, TX	1,590	0.76	$104.52

(1)Does not include self-employed. Source: Bureau of Labor Statistics, 2012

EMPLOYMENT AND OUTLOOK

Dentists held about 160,000 jobs nationally in 2012. More than one-fourth of dentists were self-employed, and almost all dentists were in private practice. Employment of dentists is expected to grow faster than the average for all occupations through the year 2020, which means employment is projected to increase 20 percent to 28 percent. As members of the baby-boom generation advance into middle age, a large number will need complicated dental work, such as bridges. In addition, elderly people are more likely to retain their teeth than were their predecessors, so they will require much more care than in the past. The younger generation will continue to need preventive checkups despite treatments such as fluoridation of the water supply, which decreases the incidence of tooth decay. However, employment of dentists is not expected to grow as rapidly as the demand for dental services. As their practices expand, dentists are likely to hire more dental hygienists and dental assistants to handle routine services. Dentists will increasingly provide care and instruction aimed at preventing the loss of teeth, rather than simply providing treatments such as fillings. Improvements in dental technology also will allow dentists to offer more effective and less painful treatment to their patients.

Employment Trend, Projected 2010–20

Health Diagnosing and Treating Practitioners: 26%

Dentists: 21%

Total, All Occupations: 14%

Note: "All Occupations" includes all occupations in the U.S. Economy. Source: U.S. Bureau of Labor Statistics, Employment Projections Program

Related Occupations
- Physician
- Surgeon

Related Military Occupations
- Dentist
- Physician & Surgeon

Conversation With . . .
ANGELA P. MOSS, DDS
Dentist, 18 years

1. What was your individual career path in terms of education, entry-level job, or other significant opportunity?

In high school, the idea was there – healthcare or dentistry. Then I got a Bachelor of Science degree in college. I liked working with my hands. I hesitated working with dying people. I interviewed with three dental schools, then went to dental school for four years. I did an additional hospital-based residency, recommended by one of the doctors at the practice where I'm now a partner. I had kept in touch with him during college and dental school and came into the practice as an associate for two years. I was very focused; I kept my eye on the goal.

2. Are there many job opportunities in your profession? In what specific areas?

A lot of dental students graduate every year; there's a major dental school in every state, some have two. There's general dentistry and a lot of people go into specialties: orthodonistry, pediadontistry, surgery, root canals, crowns. A lot of people go in to teaching. I do general dentistry but specialize in IV sedation. The decision to specialize often doesn't happen until dental school because the first two years you don't even see patients. So you get in there, see what it's about, and find out if you like a particular specialty.

3. What do you wish you had known going into this profession?

How challenging it would be, both mentally and physically. I sometimes have three hours of focus, maybe four. There was a point I had to switch my operating chair because I'd had some mid-back pain. I see a physical therapist occasionally. You need to keep your core pretty strong. With mental focus, I talk to other dentists; I also don't work full-time on purpose to raise my kids. Finally, learning the business aspect of dentistry was a challenge; we didn't go to business school.

4. How do you see your profession changing in the next five years and how what role does technology play?

Everything is going digital – the chart, the X-rays, even the impressions. Fortunately, a more computer-savvy generation is coming in to the field. But you'll need the training. A lot of manufacturers do the training on equipment. Also, the dental field has exploded with continuing education. Maryland requires 30 hours every two years, but many people do more.

5. Do you have any general advice or additional professional insights to share with someone interested in your profession?

If you think about general dentistry, it's such a melding of art and science. Most of what's going on in dentistry now is aesthetic, and it helps to have an artistic sensibility. You have to see the end before you start. If you don't have an aesthetic sense, dentistry is going to be difficult for you. For example, I'm a good sculptor, with fine hand-eye coordination. Arts and crafts were with me as a child. A lot of dentists I know are good at sculpting; they know how to create teeth. A lot of us are perfectionists, and that's a lot of the stress. But I think most dentists tend to be caring people. They're helpers.

6. Can you suggest a valuable "try this" for students considering a career in your profession?

Generally, by high school people know if they're artistic. But take an art class. Also, who's your general dentist? Why don't you go in, spend a day, and see what they do? Dentistry is problem-solving, science, business, and people skills. It's precise. We work in millimeters, and tenths of millimeters.

SELECTED SCHOOLS

Harvard University
188 Longwood Avenue
Boston, MA 02115
617.432.1443
hsdm.harvard.edu

Tufts University
1 Kneeland Street
Boston, MA 02111
617.636.6828
dental.tufts.edu

University of Maryland, Baltimore
650 W. Baltimore Street
Baltimore, MD 21201
410.706.7101
www.dental.umaryland.edu

University of Michigan, Ann Arbor
1011 N. University Avenue
Ann Arbor, MI 48109
734.763.6933
dent.umich.edu

University of North Carolina, Chapel Hill
Manning Drive & Columbia Street, CB#7450
Chapel Hill, NC 27599
919.537.3737
www.dentistry.unc.edu

University of Pennsylvania
240 S. 40th Street, #122
Philadelphia, PA 19104
215.898.8943
www.dental.upenn.edu

University of Nebraska
42nd & Emil
Omaha, NE 68198
402.559.4000
www.unmc.edu/dentistry

University of the Pacific
2155 Webster Street
San Francisco, CA 94155
415.929.6400
dental.pacific.edu

University of Texas, Austin
702 Colorado, Suite 620
Austin, TX 78701
512.399.4785
www.uthscsa.edu

University of Washington
1959 NE Pacific Street
Seattle, WA 98195
206.543.5982
www.dental.washington.edu

MORE INFORMATION

Academy of General Dentistry
211 East Chicago Avenue, Suite 900
Chicago, IL 60611
888.243.3368
www.agd.org

Academy of Gp Orthodontics
509 East Boydstun Avenue
Rockwall, TX 75087
800.634.2027
www.academygportho.com

American Academy of Pediatric Dentistry
211 East Chicago Avenue, Suite 1700
Chicago, IL 60611
312.337.2169
www.aapd.org

American Association of Endodontists
211 E. Chicago Avenue, Suite 1100
Chicago, IL 60611-2691
800.872.3636
www.aae.org

American Association of Orthodontists
401 North Lindbergh Boulevard
St. Louis, MO 631418
800.424-2841
www.braces.org

American Association of Public Health Dentistry
3085 Stevenson Drive, Suite 200
Springfield, IL 62703
217.529.6941
www.aaphd.org

American Association of Women Dentists
216 W. Jackson Boulevard, Suite 625
Chicago, IL 60606
800.920.2293
www.aawd.org

American Dental Association
211 East Chicago Avenue
Chicago, IL 60611-2678
312.440.2500
www.ada.org

American Dental Education Association
1400 K Street, NW, Suite 1100
Washington, DC 20005
202.289.7201
www.adea.org

National Dental Association
3517 16th Street, NW
Washington, DC 20010
202.588.1697
www.ndaonline.org

Michael Auerbach/Editor

Dietitian & Nutritionist

Snapshot

Career Cluster: Health Science, Food Science, Human Services
Interests: Science, Health & Wellness, Food
Earnings (Yearly Average): $56,445
Employment & Outlook: Faster Than Average Growth Expected

OVERVIEW

Sphere of Work

Dietitians and nutritionists are responsible for assessing patients' nutritional needs and planning healthy food regimens that help prevent and treat medical conditions. They manage institutional food programs, oversee meal preparation, recommend dietary modifications, and provide education to individuals and groups of all ages. Increased interest in public nutrition means that there is a growing demand for dietitians and nutritionists who analyze food products and report information on nutritional content and vitamin supplements, among other issues of concern, to the public. The primary difference

between a dietitian and a nutritionist is education: a dietitian must have academic credentials and clinical experience, while a nutritionist typically does not.

Work Environment

Dietitians and nutritionists work in medical clinics, nursing homes, sports centers, hospitals, correctional facilities, schools, and corporations such as food manufacturing companies. Many travel to see patients who need at-home care. Some dietitians and nutritionists are consultants. This profession offers flexible hours in a variety of work settings, including kitchens, laboratories, and bright, organized offices. Kitchens can often be hot, crowded, fast-paced environments.

Profile

Working Conditions: Work Indoors
Physical Strength: Light Work
Education Needs: Bachelor's Degree
Master's Degree
Licensure/Certification: Required
Physical Abilities Not Required: No
Heavy Labor
Opportunities Or Experience: Military
Service, Volunteer Work, Part-Time
Work
Holland Interest Score*: ISR, SEI, SIE

* See Appendix A

Occupation Interest

Individuals who wish to be dietitians and nutritionists should find satisfaction in working with people, educating patients, and making a positive impact on the nutritional status of individuals and communities. Those who excel in science and math may be well suited to the work. Dietitians and nutritionists tend to be patient, well organized, and detail oriented. They can listen attentively, express themselves clearly and articulately, analyze data to solve problems, and make sound decisions. Other valuable qualities include teamwork, initiative, and compassion for others.

A Day in the Life—Duties and Responsibilities

During a typical workday, dietitians and nutritionists visit patients, assess patients' or clients' nutritional needs, design and coordinate nutrition programs, evaluate and report results, and confer with other health professionals to balance patients' food needs with their medical needs. Dietitians and nutritionists encourage patient compliance with nutrition plans by teaching them how foods interact with specific medications or clinical treatments. In schools, hospitals, and other institutional settings, they may also meet with the clinical manager and dietetic technician for updates, provide medical nutrition therapy, or oversee food preparation. Those who are employed as consultants often suggest specific diet modifications for their clients.

Dietitians and nutritionists frequently work in a public health capacity by regulating food serving sizes, giving presentations on nutrition, or teaching the aging population how to shop for food. They may prepare and distribute a variety of educational materials on subjects related to health and nutrition. Many are involved in conducting nutrition research and enacting public policies that relate to food processing, consumer information about food, and national dietary guidelines and recommendations.

Duties and Responsibilities

- Selecting, training, and directing food-service workers
- Providing diet counseling services
- Coordinating dietary services with those of other departments
- Acting as a consultant to management
- Preparing records and reports
- Promoting sound eating habits through education and research
- Supervising the planning, preparation, and service of meals

OCCUPATION SPECIALTIES

Clinical Dietitians

Clinical Dietitians plan and direct the preparation and service of diets in consultation with physicians. They create both individualized and group nutritional programs based on the health needs of patients or residents.

Management Dietitians

Management Dietitians plan general meal programs. They work in food service settings such as cafeterias, hospitals, and food corporations. They may be responsible for buying food and for carrying out other business-related tasks.

Community Dietitians

Community Dietitians plan, develop, administer and coordinate nutrition programs and services as part of the health care services for an organization.

Research Dietitians

Research Dietitians conduct, evaluate and interpret research to improve the nutrition of healthy and sick people.

WORK ENVIRONMENT

Physical Environment

Dietitians and nutritionists tend to work in facilities that are clean, bright, and well ventilated. In offices, they sit at desks for extended periods. In kitchens and laboratories, they may be required to stand for a significant part of the day.

Relevant Skills and Abilities

Analytical Skills
- Analyzing information
- Solving problems

Communication Skills
- Speaking and writing effectively

Interpersonal/Social Skills
- Cooperating with others
- Providing support to others
- Working as a member of a team

Organization & Management Skills
- Coordinating tasks
- Managing people/groups
- Performing duties that change frequently

Planning & Research Skills
- Creating and laying out a plan
- Researching information

Technical Skills
- Performing scientific, mathematical, or technical work

Human Environment

Dietitians and nutritionists interact with patients and their families, and with fellow staff members such as doctors, nurses, and dietetic technicians.

Technological Environment

Dietitians and nutritionists take measurements using scales, calorimeters, glucose meters, skinfold calipers, and bioelectric impedance machines. Financial and medical software, databases, and office suites help them track patient information such as weight, diet, medications, protein supplements, and lab results.

EDUCATION, TRAINING, AND ADVANCEMENT

High School/Secondary

High school students interested in becoming dietitians and nutritionists should focus on math, science, health, and communication courses. In addition, students should prepare themselves by participating in relevant extracurricular activities. To learn what dietitians and nutritionists do each day, interested students may find it useful to seek an internship. High school career counselors often have lists of internship opportunities. Aspiring dietitians and nutritionists should apply to college or university programs.

Suggested High School Subjects
- Applied Biology/Chemistry
- Applied Communication
- Applied Math
- Biology
- Chemistry
- College Preparatory
- Computer Science
- English
- Family & Consumer Sciences
- Food Service & Management
- Foods & Nutrition
- Health Science Technology
- Mathematics
- Physiology
- Science
- Sociology

Famous First

The first nationwide food labeling standards for nutritional information appeared in 1992, the result of the Nutrition Labeling and Education Act. According to the act, packaged foods were required to bear labels identifying their ingredients, nutritional values, and serving sizes, among other information. Also newly regulated was the use of promotional terms such as "low fat" and "light."

College/Postsecondary

A college degree provides the best opportunities for employment or advancement. College and university students looking to enter the field should study biology, food sciences, math, chemistry, medicine, physiology, administration and institution management, education, psychology, and counseling, in pursuit of an undergraduate degree in dietetics, nutrition, food service, or a related discipline. Students may gain experience and build connections through internships and co-ops that integrate clinical work with university-level coursework. Many dietitians and nutritionists choose to pursue a graduate degree after completing their undergraduate studies.

Related College Majors

- Dietetics/Human Nutritional Services
- Foods & Nutrition Science
- Foods & Nutrition Studies, General
- Human & Animal Physiology

Adult Job Seekers

Adults with a bachelor's or master's degree will have better job opportunities in this field. By joining professional associations such as the American Dietetic Association, adult job seekers can benefit from ongoing networking, professional development services, food and nutrition information, and mentorships to establish career and educational options. These professional organizations generally maintain job lists and advertise open dietitian and nutritionist positions.

Professional Certification and Licensure

For dietitians and nutritionists, licensure, certification, and registration requirements vary by state; therefore, candidates need to determine what the requirements are in the state or states where they want to work. Some states require that all practitioners of dietetics and nutrition be licensed, a process which entails doing specific coursework, passing an exam, and completing a supervised internship. Where certification is mandatory, those without it can still practice but cannot use certain titles.

The Commission on Dietetic Registration provides voluntary certification that is completely distinct from state licensure or certification. Registered dietitians (RDs) must fulfill education and work experience requirements in order to qualify for the certifying exam.

Additional Requirements

Dietitians and nutritionists must be resourceful and always willing to research the latest information, as the state of medical knowledge is frequently changing. Specializing in a particular body system or age group may be helpful for advancement in this field.

EARNINGS AND ADVANCEMENT

Earnings depend on the geographic location and size of the employer and the community and the employee's education, specialty area, and number of years in practice. Median annual earnings of dietitians and nutritionists were $56,445 in 2012. The lowest ten percent earned less than $35,330, and the highest ten percent earned more than $80,009.

Dietitians and nutritionists may receive paid vacations, holidays, and sick days; life and health insurance; and retirement benefits. These are usually paid by the employer.

Metropolitan Areas with the Highest Concentration of Jobs in this Occupation

Metropolitan area	Employment(1)	Employment per thousand jobs	Hourly mean wage
New York-White Plains-Wayne, NY-NJ	2,970	0.58	$29.11
Los Angeles-Long Beach-Glendale, CA	1,740	0.45	$32.00
Chicago-Joliet-Naperville, IL	1,430	0.39	$24.38
Minneapolis-St. Paul-Bloomington, MN-WI	1,170	0.67	$26.75
Philadelphia, PA	1,050	0.57	$25.58
Boston-Cambridge-Quincy, MA	910	0.53	$29.62
Pittsburgh, PA	720	0.64	$20.67
Washington-Arlington-Alexandria, DC-VA-MD-WV	700	0.30	$29.54

(1)Does not include self-employed. Source: Bureau of Labor Statistics, 2012

EMPLOYMENT AND OUTLOOK

Dietitians and nutritionists held about 58,000 jobs in 2012. More than half of all jobs were in hospitals, nursing care facilities, outpatient care centers or offices of physicians. Employment of dietitians and nutritionists is expected to grow faster than the average for all occupations through the year 2020, which means employment is projected to increase 20 percent. This is due to increased emphasis on the prevention of disease by improved dietary habits. A growing and aging population will increase demand for meals and nutritional counseling in nursing homes, schools, prisons, community health programs and home health care agencies.

Employment Trend, Projected 2010–20

Health Diagnosing and Treating Practitioners: 26%

Dietitians and Nutritionists: 20%

Total, All Occupations: 14%

Note: "All Occupations" includes all occupations in the U.S. Economy. Source: U.S. Bureau of Labor Statistics, 2012.

Related Occupations
- Cook/Chef
- Food Service Manager

Related Occupations
- Dietitian
- Food Service Manager

Conversation With . . .
JESSICA WAGNER
Nutritionist/Health Coach, 6 years

1. What was your individual career path in terms of education, entry-level job, or other significant opportunity?

Eight years prior to my nutrition and health counseling education, I had obtained a Bachelor's degree in East Asian Studies from Wittenberg University. There's a huge connection between how to live a healthy lifestyle and the philosophy of East Asian Studies. Then I worked for 10 years in international education, advising and counseling individuals, and learned that one-on-one counseling is my thing. During this time, I also realized I was not healthy in the workplace and other people weren't either. We weren't getting the basics, like fresh air and sunlight every day, in our cubicles. We were eating cafeteria food, or too busy to cook dinner. I got very sick, and wanted to cure myself naturally. So I received a post-bachelor's certificate in Health Counseling through The Center for Educational Outreach and Innovation at Teacher's College Columbia University and The Institute for Integrative Nutrition (IIN) in New York City. For nine months, I traveled there once a month for intensive study all day Saturday and Sunday and, quite often, Monday. Upon graduation, I was prepared to open my own health and nutritional counseling practice. A year later, I completed the Integrative Nutrition Immersion Graduate Program.

2. Are there many job opportunities in your profession? In what specific areas?

The most valuable opportunity in this profession is to open your own practice. I have created my own niche. I do workshops, I've done group programs, and I do one-on-one counseling, which is where I think my talent is. I offer one-on-one relationships to clients who need serious help. They can email or text me between sessions. I'm holding them by the hand and I think that's really needed. In addition to operating a business, there are opportunities in doctors' offices, yoga studios, gyms, chiropractic or other wellness practices. Corporations regularly look for health and nutrition coaches to provide workshops and counseling to employees.

3. What do you wish you had known going into this profession?

Only hands-on experience could prepare me to work effectively with people. Each person, depending on their personality and fears, will respond differently to your guidance. Most people are afraid to break old habits and will try to hold onto unhealthy patterns. With sensitivity, care, and respect, you can learn how to guide even the most fearful people. Nutritional knowledge alone doesn't make you a good health and nutrition coach. You need to be a good listener and a patient teacher.

4. How do you see your profession changing in the next five years?

I see this profession becoming much more mainstream. The public interest in conventional medicine is shifting to holistic-based approaches and preventative services. Doctors simply don't have the time to counsel their clients on how to make healthy lifestyle changes. I see every doctor's office having a health and nutrition coach. I also see health insurance coverage for this kind of preventive wellness service.

5. What role will technology play in those changes, and what skills will be required?

Technology is already playing a large role in this field. Many health and nutrition coaches provide counseling services over the phone and Internet, as I do. In addition, webinars are provided regularly for groups of clients. Being so easily accessible means clients are more apt to hire me.

6. Do you have any general advice or additional professional insights to share with someone interested in your profession?

If you want the flexibility of creating your own work hours and having an important impact on the lives of people, no other career that I know of can provide that in quite the same way that this profession does. Transforming the health and happiness of people is truly the best job anyone could have.

7. Can you suggest a valuable "try this" for students considering a career in your profession?

Call an admission's counselor at a school that offers training in this field and ask to sit in on a class. If you feel inspired, take it a step further by reading a good book recommended by the professor. If you still feel inspired, try out a healthy nutritional lifestyle for a good year or so, following the recommendations in the book. During this time, practice talking to people about your experiences. Offer tips to people looking for answers. Practice having simple conversations with individuals and being a mentor and advocate for their health. .

SELECTED SCHOOLS

Many colleges and universities offer programs in health and nutrition; some
have degree programs in dietetics. Interested students are advised to consult
with a school guidance counselor or research area postsecondary schools. The
website of the Commission on the Academy of Nutrition and Dietetics (see
below) allows users to search for accredited programs in their stateeld.

MORE INFORMATION

Academy of Nutrition & Dietetics
120 South Riverside Plaza,
Suite 2000
Chicago, IL 60606
800.877.1600
www.eatright.org

**American Association for
Nutritional Consultants**
400 Oakhill Drive
Winona Lake, IN 46590
888.828.2262
www.aanc.net

**American Society for Nutritional
Sciences**
9650 Rockville Pike, Suite 4500
Bethesda,MD 20814
301.634.7050
www.nutrition.org

**Association for Healthcare
Foodservice**
455 S. 4th Street, Suite 650
Louisville, KY 40202
888.528.9552
info@healthcarefoodservice.org
www.healthcarefoodservice.org

Dietary Managers Association
406 Surrey Woods Drive
St. Charles, IL 60174
800.323.1908
www.dmaonline.org

Susan Williams/Editor

Emergency Medical Technician (EMT)

Snapshot

Career Cluster: Health Care, Public Safety & Security
Interests: First Aid, Medical Technology, Patient Care
Earnings (Yearly Average): $32,182
Employment & Outlook: Faster Than Average Growth Expected

OVERVIEW

Sphere of Work

An emergency medical technician (EMT) is responsible for providing emergency medical services and administering lifesaving techniques to people who have suffered an injury or have been suddenly stricken ill. EMTs generally work in teams of two and may be employed by hospitals, fire departments, police departments, or private firms. EMTs often work long and erratic hours, in addition to being "on call." As "first responders" to an accident or emergency scene, they use their extensive abilities in first aid, CPR, and other forms of medical care to stabilize the victim and transfer him or her

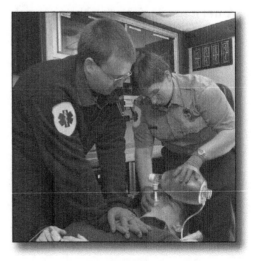

via ambulance to the nearest hospital or medical center for further treatment.

Work Environment

EMTs generally work in a team of two individuals, one of whom drives the ambulance while the other cares for the patient while in transit. The work of an EMT is physically very challenging, as he or she must administer to a patient in all types of weather and locations. They may also be exposed to communicable diseases. Although the job of an EMT is very challenging both physically and psychologically, many EMTs are willing to overlook these risks to work in an exciting field while helping people.

Profile

Working Conditions: Work Both Indoors And Outdoors
Physical Strength: Medium Work
Education Needs: High School Diploma Or G.E.D., Technical/Community College Apprenticeship
Licensure/Certification: Required
Physical Abilities Not Required: N/A
Opportunities For Experience: Apprenticeship, Military Service, Volunteer Work
Holland Interest Score*: ESI

* See Appendix A

Occupation Interest

EMTs experience a fast-paced, exciting career that offers them a chance to save lives. EMTs are quick thinkers and capable of handling high-stress situations. Although they receive a great deal of training in the medical arts, their level of formal training is not nearly as extensive as a nurse or doctor. Additionally, they are typically strong and emotionally stable, which helps them when they transport a victim from an accident scene to the hospital.

A Day in the Life—Duties and Responsibilities

An EMT is generally on call during the course of his or her shift. This means that he or she is either on the road in an ambulance or at the station where he or she is based. When a call is received, the EMT travels to the scene to assess a patient's medical condition, coordinating with the police, fire, and other officials on site. The EMT must carefully analyze the victim's symptoms, often speaking with witnesses and relatives to get a better understanding of the patient and to determine what kind of treatment should be administered. Based on that assessment, he or she either treats the patient at the site or transports the victim to the nearest hospital or urgent care clinic.

If the patient must be removed from the scene immediately, an EMT must provide the best possible care to stabilize the victim while the ambulance is in transit. He or she must therefore be balanced and strong as well as quick thinking. During transportation and upon arrival at the hospital, the EMT coordinates with the emergency room staff to alert them about the patient's symptoms and status. After the patient is brought into the hospital, the EMT must file reports and then return to his or her base of operations to restock and clean the ambulance.

An EMT's day is often long and almost always unpredictable. EMTs must deal with the both the patient and any witnesses to the incident or accident. Such situations are stressful and require a sense of tact. Furthermore, EMTs should also be prepared tohandle victims who may have communicable diseases or an accident or crime scene situated in a dangerous location.

Duties and Responsibilities

- Responding to emergency calls received by dispatchers
- Determining the nature and extent of illness or injury
- Establishing priorities for emergency medical care
- Covering patients, placing them on stretchers, and lifting them into the ambulance
- Determining the best route for the emergency vehicle to travel
- Watching patients constantly and communicating with the hospital on patient's condition during transporting
- Following step-by-step direction of medical staff

OCCUPATION SPECIALTIES

Basic EMTs

Basic EMTs, also known as EMTs, care for patients at the scene and while taking patients by ambulance to a hospital. An EMT-Basic has the emergency skills to assess a patient's condition and manage respiratory, cardiac, and trauma emergencies.

Intermediate EMTs

Intermediate EMTs, also known as Advanced EMTs, have completed the training required at the EMT-Basic level as well as training for more advanced skills, such as the use of intravenous fluids and some medications.

Paramedics

Paramedics provide more extensive prehospital care than do EMTs. In addition to carrying out the procedures that EMTs use, paramedics can give medications orally and intravenously, interpret electrocardiograms (EKGs)—used to monitor heart function—and use other monitors and complex equipment.

WORK ENVIRONMENT

Physical Environment

The work environment of an EMT revolves around an ambulance and the site of an accident or health emergency. Tensions and emotions are often high at accident and emergency scenes. Physical dangers are numerous, and include the presence of blood, answering calls in high-crime neighborhoods, vehicle stability and passenger extrication, and accident debris. EMTs also work at a base of operations at a hospital, fire station, or private garage.

Relevant Skills and Abilities

Communication Skills
- Speaking effectively

Interpersonal/Social Skills
- Ability to remain calm under pressure
- Being sensitive to others
- Cooperating with others
- Having good judgment
- Working as a member of a team

Organization & Management Skills
- Following instructions
- Managing people/groups
- Performing duties that change frequently
- Performing routine work

Technical Skills
- Working with your hands

Other Skills
- Ability to withstand scenes of medical trauma
- General physical fitness

Human Environment

EMTs must work as a team, not only with their partners but also with police, firefighters, and security personnel at the scene of an incident. They must work with doctors, nurses, and other hospital personnel to ensure that the patient is well cared for upon arrival. They must deal with the patients and their loved ones as well.

Technological Environment

Depending on their level of training, EMTs use a wide range of medical devices. These items include stretchers, defibrillators, surgical tools, needles, bandages, and heart monitors. They should also be familiar with driving an ambulance and using telecommunication devices and medical computer technology.

EDUCATION, TRAINING, AND ADVANCEMENT

High School/Secondary

High school students interested in becoming an emergency medical technician are encouraged to take courses that will help them learn many of the disciplines required in this field. These include biology, chemistry, anatomy, and first aid training (such as CPR). Furthermore, they should take courses that enable them to communicate clearly and sensitively with patients and medical staff, such as English and sociology. Many school systems also offer EMT training and disaster management organizations.

Suggested High School Subjects
- Applied Biology/Chemistry
- Applied Math
- Biology
- Chemistry
- Driver Training
- English
- First Aid Training
- Health Science Technology
- Sociology

Famous First

The first hospital ambulance service appeared in Cincinnati, Ohio, around 1865. Emphasis was placed on swift transportation, not patient treatment. The first ambulance driver received an annual salary of $360.

Postsecondary

As EMTs obtain more training, their designation as an EMT is elevated. Aspiring EMTs should continue their educations after receiving basic technical training. Coursework in anatomy, physiology, and related subjects may be completed at junior, technical, and community colleges or at undergraduate colleges and universities.

Related College Majors
- Emergency Medical Technology

Adult Job Seekers

EMT positions continue to grow in number, both in private companies and for local police and firefighters. Adults can enter this field at the most basic level (First Responders, such as police officers and firefighters) through the highest level (Paramedic). Adults seeking to become EMTs should take advantage of any training courses available as well as networking opportunities available through national EMT and first responder organizations.

Professional Certification and Licensure

Every state requires that EMTs become certified, especially when the EMT is at an Intermediate level or higher. This process of certification varies from state to state. Additionally, most states require that EMTs register with the National Registry of Emergency Medical Technicians, usually once every two years. Interested individuals should check the certification requirements of their home state.

Additional Requirements

Because of the heavy lifting and strenuous activity that is involved in the job of an emergency medical technician, such individuals should remain in excellent physical condition. They should also demonstrate a calm demeanor, especially in crisis situations. In addition, they should communicate clearly, maintain a clean (and therefore safe) appearance, and be sensitive to others.

EARNINGS AND ADVANCEMENT

Earnings depend on the type and geographic location of the employer and the individual's level of training and experience. Emergency medical technicians working in areas where there is a heavy volume of calls usually earn the highest salaries. Emergency medical technicians are employed by private ambulance services, hospitals and fire departments.

Median annual earnings of emergency medical technicians were $32,182 in 2012. The lowest ten percent earned less than $20,893, and the highest ten percent earned more than $54,452.

Emergency medical technicians may receive paid vacations, holidays, and sick days; life and health insurance; and retirement benefits. These are usually paid by the employer.

Metropolitan Areas with the Highest
Concentration of Jobs in this Occupation

Metropolitan area	Employment	Employment per thousand jobs	Hourly mean wage
Chicago-Joliet-Naperville, IL	8,510	2.34	$27.48
New York-White Plains-Wayne, NY-NJ	8,300	1.61	$20.19
Los Angeles-Long Beach-Glendale, CA	4,610	1.19	$13.60
Atlanta-Sandy Springs-Marietta, GA	4,230	1.87	$15.34
Philadelphia, PA	3,720	2.04	$18.43
Boston-Cambridge-Quincy, MA	3,470	2.03	$19.24
Pittsburgh, PA	3,310	2.94	$14.87
Baltimore-Towson, MD	3,200	2.54	$20.09

Source: Bureau of Labor Statistics, 2012

EMPLOYMENT AND OUTLOOK

Emergency medical technicians held about 233,000 jobs nationally in 2012. About one-third worked more than full-time. Employment of emergency medical technicians is expected to grow much faster than the average for all occupations through the year 2020, which means employment is projected to increase 30 percent or more. Population growth and urbanization will increase the demand for emergency medical technicians. In addition, a growing elderly population will further spur demand for EMT services as they become more likely to have medical emergencies. Competition for jobs will be strong in fire, police and rescue squad departments because of attractive pay and benefits and good job security.

Employment Trend, Projected 2010–20

Emergency Medical Technicians and Paramedics: 33%

Health Technologists and Technicians: 26%

Total, All Occupations: 14%

Note: "All Occupations" includes all occupations in the U.S. Economy. Source: U.S. Bureau of Labor Statistics, Employment Projections Program

Related Occupations
- Athletic Trainer
- Firefighter
- Licensed Practical Nurse (LPN)
- Nursing Aide
- Registered Nurse (RN)

Related Military Occupations
- Cardiopulmonary & EEG Technician
- Medical Service Technician

Conversation With . . . JAKE MILES

Emergency Medical Technician, 10 years

1. What was your individual career path in terms of education, entry-level job, or other significant opportunity?

I started my career as a lifeguard. There I learned CPR, First Aid, and other life saving skills. I always enjoyed helping people as a lifeguard, so becoming an EMT was an easy step to take. I took my EMT course at Northeastern University. A year later I joined the Boston Fire Department as a firefighter. About five years later, I got hurt at work and was on crutches for about six months. I couldn't work. Someone suggested I look into nursing school. I took nursing classes during the day and worked nights and weekends as a firefighter/EMT. Now I work two 24-hours on-call as a PICC-line (Peripherally Inserted Central Catheter) nurse and two 24-hour shifts at the firehouse.

2. Are there many job opportunities in your profession? In what specific areas?

There are many opportunities in the field as an EMT. You could work for a private ambulance company, or you could work for the city or town where you live. In some places, the fire departments handle 911 calls or has an Emergency Medical Services (EMS) department. Some EMTs work in emergency rooms as technicians that help the nurses.

An EMT-B, or Basic, does basic first responder work. Once you become an EMT-Basic, you can move on to be an EMT-P, or paramedic. Paramedics can give different medicines, they can intubate, they can give IVs. That's another six-month course; three months in class and three months in the ER, practicing putting in IVs and other skills. It's a pretty intensive course. Usually they like you to have a few years as an EMT-Basic before becoming a paramedic.

Being an EMT can lead to many opportunities in the health care field. I know about nine guys in the fire department who have gotten their nursing degrees.

3. What do you wish you had known going into this profession?

I wish I had known that the private companies do more transporting of patients from home to the hospital versus doing more emergency work. I thought as an ambulance EMT, I'd be doing all 911 calls. It's not. You might take dialysis patients to appointments. It was boring. As a paramedic, you do strictly 911 calls. Every now and then, if you're working for a private ambulance company, an emergency call might be dispatched through if there are a lot of calls, but it's rare. At least that's how it is in Boston, where the city provides EMS.

4. How do you see your profession changing in the next five years?

EMT-Paramedics are going to become more prevalent in the future because they can do more. EMT-Ps will probably do all emergency responses. They have a higher level of training and companies are going to want higher skilled personnel. In Boston, the fire department might actually merge with EMS eventually. Then everyone on an ambulance be a paramedic.

5. What role will technology play in those changes, and what skills will be required?

Much of the paperwork and reports is usually still handwritten, but that's changing. I know Boston EMS does everything on the computer, on a tablet/laptop. Some of the equipment, the EKG machines and things like that, will become more advanced. As technology advances, you need to be able to adapt to the changes.

6. Do you have any general advice or additional professional insights to share with someone interested in your profession?

If you like to help people and you're not too squeamish about blood and other aspects of people being sick and injured, then becoming an EMT might be a good choice for you. The emotional part of dealing with tragedy can be tough. For the fire department specifically, we have a Stress Management Team that, when you do deal with something tragic, you can talk to them. You develop a little bit of an emotional block, but still, sometimes calls do bother you. I've had a few that took me a while to get over. I think on my third shift, I did CPR and the lady ended up dying in the ER. It was awful. Now I can kind of separate myself from it.

Working as an EMT, you will get an adrenaline rush, but it's better if you are a calm person and can remain calm under pressure.

7. Can you suggest a valuable "try this" for students considering a career in your profession?

One thing that you could do to see if you would enjoy being an EMT is to take some classes. CPR and First Aid classes would be the best.

SELECTED SCHOOLS

Many technical and community colleges across the United States offer programs leading to certification as an EMT. Interested students are advised to consult with a school guidance counselor or research area postsecondary schools. The website of the National Registry of Emergency Medical Technicians (see below) allows users to search for accredited EMT programs in their state. The website of the National Association of Emergency Medical Technicians (see below) lists accredited bachelor's degree programs in emergency medical services.

MORE INFORMATION

EMS1.com
200 Green Street, 2nd Floor
San Francisco, CA 94111
866.431.5367
www.ems1.com

EMS World
www.emsworld.com

National Association of Emergency Medical Technicians
P.O. Box 1400
Clinton, MS 39060-1400
601.924.7744
www.naemt.org

National Highway Traffic Safety Administration
Office of Emergency Medical Services
1200 New Jersey Avenue SE
Washington, DC 20590
888.327.4236

www.nhtsa.gov/Driving+Safety/gency+Medical+ServicesNational Registry of Emergency Medical Technicians
Rocco V. Morando Building
6610 Busch Blvd., P.O. Box 29233
Columbus, OH 43229
614.888.4484
www.nremt.org

Michael Auerbach/Editor

Home Health Aide

Snapshot

Career Cluster: Health Care

Interests: Patient Care, Health Care

Earnings (Yearly Average): $21,794

Employment & Outlook: Faster Than Average Growth Expected

OVERVIEW

Sphere of Work

Home health aides provide patient care in patient homes and in residential facilities such as nursing homes and rehabilitation centers. The range of services provided by home health aides includes preventative care, personal hygiene, cooking and household chores, routine medical care, medical appointment transportation, and socio-emotional support. Home health aides are generally paid hourly and are employed by individuals, insurance companies, social service agencies, public health agencies, hospitals, and residential facilities.

Work Environment

Home health aides spend their workdays seeing patients in a wide variety of settings, including patient homes, nursing homes, rehabilitation centers, and adult daycare facilities. Home health aides may work with one patient at a time or travel each day to care for multiple patients in their homes or medical facilities. Given the diverse demands of the home health aide profession, home health aides may work days, evenings, nights, weekends, and on-call hours to meet patient or caseload needs.

Profile

Working Conditions: Work Indoors
Physical Strength: Light Work, Medium Work
Education Needs: High School Diploma Or G.E.D. Licensure/Certification Required
Licensure/Certification: Usually Not Required
Physical Abilities Not Required: No Strenuous Labor
Opportunities For Experience: Volunteer Work
Holland Interest Score*: SRI

* See Appendix A

Occupation Interest

Individuals drawn to the profession of home health aide tend to be physically strong, nurturing, competent, patient, and intelligent people who have the ability to quickly assess situations, demonstrate caring, and solve problems. Those who succeed as home health aides tend to exhibit traits such as empathy, patience, resourcefulness, responsibility, time management, and concern for individuals. Home health aides should find satisfaction in improving the quality of life for a wide range of people, including the disabled, the elderly, and the terminally ill.

A Day in the Life—Duties and Responsibilities

The daily occupational duties and responsibilities of home health aides will be determined by the individual's job specialization. Home health aides may specialize in pediatric care, elder care, management of chronic illness, psychiatric care, Alzheimer or dementia care, or hospice or end-of-life care. The range of possible duties and responsibilities is wide, but some experiences are common to all, such as care in the patient's home, assistance with basic tasks relative to personal care, nutrition, and daily medication.

Some home health-care aids may assist in housekeeping, transportation to the grocery store or medical visits, and physical therapy or exercise. They will be an integral member of the patient care team, which may include family members, social workers, medical professionals, and other home health aides.

For home-bound patients, home health-care workers may do the shopping and meal preparation, as well as track routine medical information such as blood pressure and pulse rate and coordinate in-home medical care. For those home health aides who work with social service agencies or long-term-care facilities, more regulatory tasks may be required, such as conducting background interviews with patients to record their health history, educating clients about public health services and resources, providing emotional support, teaching them practical life skills, and providing patient updates to agency supervisors and client families.

In addition to the range of responsibilities described above, home health aides may also be responsible for completing patient charts and required documentation on a daily basis.

Duties and Responsibilities

- Assisting clients with daily needs
- Bathing and shampooing clients
- Helping clients with dressing and grooming
- Helping clients to move around their homes
- Checking client blood pressure, respiration, and temperature
- Helping clients with exercises
- Assisting clients with medication and artificial limbs
- Helping clients transfer between chairs, wheelchairs, and beds
- Helping elderly or disabled clients with toileting as needed
- Doing cleaning and laundering in client homes or rooms
- Shopping for food and preparing meals for clients
- Attending to bed-bound clients as needed
- Providing moral support

OCCUPATION SPECIALTIES

Home Health Aides

Home Health Aides typically work for certified home health or hospice agencies that receive government funding and therefore must comply with regulations. They work under the direct supervision of a medical professional, usually a nurse. These aides keep records of services performed and of the client's condition and progress. They report changes in the client's condition to the supervisor or case manager. Aides also work with therapists and other medical staff.

Personal Care Attendants

Personal Care Attendants, also called homemakers, caregivers, and companions—provide clients with companionship and help with daily tasks in a client's home. They are often hired in addition to other medical health workers, such as hospice workers, who may visit a client's home. Personal care aides do not provide any type of medical service.

WORK ENVIRONMENT

Physical Environment

The immediate physical environment of home health aides varies based on their caseload and employer. Home health aides spend their workdays seeing patients in patient homes, social service agencies, public health agencies, hospitals, and residential facilities such as assisted living residences, nursing homes, and rehabilitation centers.

Human Environment

Home health aides work with a wide variety of people and should be comfortable caring for children, the elderly, the chronically ill, the terminally ill, the disabled, and mentally ill people, as well as communicating with patient families, colleagues, and physicians.

Relevant Skills and Abilities

Communication Skills
- Speaking effectively
- Listening attentively

Interpersonal/Social Skills
- Being able to remain calm in stressful situations
- Being persistent
- Being sensitive to others
- Cooperating with others
- Providing support to others
- Working as a member of a team

Organization & Management Skills
- Adhering to a schedule
- Planning daily actions

Other Skills
- Preparing food
- Being comfortable with people who are ill or disabled

Technological Environment

Home health aides use activity logs (often in paper form) and other record-keeping forms to keep track of client status for supervising nurses or other medical personnel. They may sometimes use computers and telecommunication tools to perform their jobs. In addition, home health aides use medical equipment, such as glucose monitors, wheelchair lifters, and blood pressure cuffs, to care for patients.

EDUCATION, TRAINING, AND ADVANCEMENT

High School/Secondary

High school students interested in pursuing a career as a home health aide should prepare themselves by developing good study habits. High school-level study of psychology and biology will provide a strong foundation for work as a home health aide or college-level work in the field. Due to the diversity of home health aide duties, high school students interested in this career path will benefit from seeking internships or part-time work that expose the students to the nursing community and people facing physical and mental challenges. High school students may be able to secure employment as a home health aide directly out of high school.

Suggested High School Subjects
- Applied Biology/Chemistry
- Applied Communication
- Child Care
- English
- First Aid Training
- Foods & Nutrition
- Health Science Technology
- Medical Assisting
- Nurse Assisting
- Psychology
- Sociology
- Speech

Famous First

The first visiting nurse service was established by Lillian Wald (pictured), pioneering nurse and humanitarian, in New York City's Lower East Side tenement district in 1893. Wald and another nurse rented a room in the district to be closer to their patients. The service soon drew the attention of donors and public officials and eventually grew large enough to operate in all five boroughs plus Nassau and Westchester counties.

Library of Congress
photograph by Harris & Ewing

Postsecondary

Generally, postsecondary education is not necessary for a career in home health care. Those students interested in pursuing an associate's degree may consider focusing their course of study in the areas of nursing or a related field such as psychology or gerontology. Coursework in nutrition, anatomy, physiology, and psychology may also prove useful in their future work. Postsecondary students can gain work experience and potential advantage in their future job searches by securing internships or part-time employment as home health aides or nursing assistants.

Related College Majors
- Home Health Aide Training
- Human Anatomy & Physiology
- Pre-Nursing Training

Adult Job Seekers

Adults seeking employment as home health aides should have, at a minimum, a high school degree. Adult job seekers in the home health or nursing field will benefit from joining professional associations to help with networking and job searching. Professional home health associations, such as the National Association for Home Care and Hospice, generally offer career workshops and maintain lists and forums of available jobs.

Professional Certification and Licensure

The federal government has guidelines for home health aides whose employers receive reimbursement from Medicare. Federal law requires home health aides to pass a competency test covering basic subjects related to patient care. Home health aides may receive training before taking the competency test. Federal law suggests at least 75 hours of classroom and practical training, supervised by a registered nurse. Training and testing programs may be offered by the employing agency, but must meet the standards of the Center for Medicare and Medicaid Services. Training programs vary with state regulations.

Professional certification and licensure of home health aides is voluntary in some states. Home health aides may choose to pursue certification as certified nurse assistants (CNAs). The CNA certification, which is earned through a state-based competency exam and completed state-approved training program, will provide increased work opportunities in residential facilities, a higher salary, and greater opportunities for advancement. Other home health aide certification options include programs administered by local chapters of the American Red Cross and the Visiting Nurse's Association of America.

Additional Requirements

Individuals who find satisfaction, success, and job security as home health aides will be knowledgeable about the profession's requirements, responsibilities, and opportunities. Integrity, empathy, patience, and personal and professional ethics are required of home health aides as they interact with vulnerable people and have access to patient's personal information and their homes. Home health aides should generally have a driver's license and be sufficiently strong to lift and move patients as needed.

EARNINGS AND ADVANCEMENT

Home health aides and personal care attendants receive slight pay increases with experience and added responsibility. Usually, they are paid only for the time worked in the home; normally, they are not paid for travel time between jobs. Median annual earnings of aides and attendants were $21,794 in 2012. The lowest ten percent earned less than $17,278, and the highest ten percent earned more than $31,153. Depending on full-time or part-time status, home health aides and personal care attendants may receive paid vacations, holidays, and sick days; life and health insurance; and retirement benefits.

Metropolitan Areas with the Highest
Concentration of Jobs in this Occupation
(Home Health Aide)

Metropolitan area	Employment (1)	Employment per thousand jobs	Hourly mean wage
New York-White Plains-Wayne, NY-NJ	96,340	18.68	$9.74
Chicago-Joliet-Naperville, IL	30,940	8.50	$11.10
Philadelphia, PA	20,580	11.29	$10.68
Minneapolis-St. Paul-Bloomington, MN-WI	16,690	9.54	$11.65
Cleveland-Elyria-Mentor, OH	15,830	15.92	$9.87

(1) Does not include Nursing Aides or self-employed. Source: Bureau of Labor Statistics, 2012

Metropolitan Areas with the Highest
Concentration of Jobs in this Occupation
(Personal Care Attendant)

Metropolitan area	Employment (1)	Employment per thousand jobs	Hourly mean wage
New York-White Plains-Wayne, NY-NJ	79,770	15.47	$10.80
Minneapolis-St. Paul-Bloomington, MN-WI	33,540	19.17	$11.46
McAllen-Edinburg-Mission, TX	20,730	91.05	$8.15
Dallas-Plano-Irving, TX	18,520	8.83	$8.37
San Antonio-New Braunfels, TX	17,900	20.76	$8.20

(1) Does not include Nursing Aides or self-employed. Source: Bureau of Labor Statistics, 2012

EMPLOYMENT AND OUTLOOK

Home health aides held about 840,000 jobs nationally in 2012. Another 985,000 jobs were held by personal care attendants. Most aides and attendants are employed by home health services agencies, homemaker assistance agencies, visiting nurse associations, residential care facilities with home health departments, hospitals, public health and welfare departments, community volunteer agencies, and temporary help firms. Self-employed home health aides work with no agency affiliation and accept clients, set fees, and arrange work schedules on their own.

Employment of home health aides and personal care attendants is expected to grow much faster than the average for all occupations through the year 2020, which means employment is projected to increase as much as 70 percent. This is a result of both growing demand for home health-care services from an aging population and efforts to contain health-care costs by moving patients out of hospitals and nursing care facilities as quickly as possible. In addition, a preference by most people for care in the home and improvements in medical technologies for in-home treatment will contribute to job growth.

Employment Trend, Projected 2010–20

Personal Care Aides: 70%

Home Health Aides: 69%

Other Personal Care and Service Workers: 35%

Health-Care Support Occupations: 34%

Total, All Occupations: 14%

Note: "All Occupations" includes all occupations in the U.S. Economy. Source: U.S. Bureau of Labor Statistics, Employment Projections Program

Related Occupations
- Childcare Worker
- Licensed Practical Nurse (LPN)
- Medical Assistant
- Nursing Aide

> # *Conversation With . . .*
> # *BAILEY McDONALD,*
> ## Home Health Aide, 18 months

1. What was your individual career path in terms of education, entry-level job, or other significant opportunity?

I began nursing school at Quincy College. During my first semester there, I started getting clinical experience where I was able to put my skills to use.

During that time, I completed the Certified Nursing Assistant/Home Health Aide course offered by the Red Cross, and passed the written and practical CNA exam to be licensed by the Commonwealth of Massachusetts. A few months after that, I started my job with Right at Home.

2. Are there many job opportunities in your profession? In what specific areas?

There are quite an extensive amount of jobs for Certified Nursing Assistants (CNAs) in the industry because they are certified in the skills required to work in a hospital setting, nursing home, acute care rehab or home care. Home Health Aides are certified to work in long-term care facilities or provide home care, but not to work in hospitals. Having the CNA license gives you many more opportunities for jobs A lot of home health care clients only want a licensed person to care for them. A third type of job is Personal Care Assistant (PCA). Most home health agencies also offer homemaker/companion services to clients as well, and those services are provided by an unlicensed person.

3. What do you wish you had known going into this profession?

One thing someone should know about going into someone's home to care for them is that you need to be a patient, compassionate, professional person. You will need a lot of patience every day because you never know how a client will be feeling when you're with them and many times they cannot fully communicate. They may be in pain, but unable to communicate that to you. They may be upset about something, but unable to tell you why. You need to be professional in the sense that your own personal problems and issues need to be left at the door because the elderly can sense your mood quickly and it can easily influence their own mood negatively.

4. How do you see your profession changing in the next five years?

With the aging of the baby boomers, I anticipate that in the next five years the demand for Home Heath Aides and Certified Nursing Assistants will grow.

5. What role will technology play in those changes, and what skills will be required?

One interesting way my company is implementing technology in accordance with Massachusetts state law is paying Home Health Aides and Certified Nursing Assistants for travel time by tracking the mileage with new mapping software. In the past, they would give CNAs a flat stipend for travel time. I also foresee home health clients specifically requesting aides in their home who have at least basic computer skills. This way they can turn to their home health aides for help keeping in touch with their families, their grandchildren, and their friends. My best advice is to at least have a basic knowledge of computers because it can only help you with any career goal.

6. Do you have any general advice or additional professional insights to share with someone interested in your profession?

Being a Home Health Aide is a great job for a student in nursing school. It allows you to put into practice some of the things you learn in class, and applying the knowledge helps you remember what you learned in ways that you can't always achieve from reading a text book. You can also work a very flexible schedule as a Certified Nursing Assistant, and that's a plus for a student..

7. Can you suggest a valuable "try this" for students considering a career in your profession?

If someone is considering a career with home health care or wants to complete the HHA/CNA course, I would suggest volunteering at a local hospital or nursing home. They always need extra hands and being around the geriatric population is good exposure for what you can expect working in the industry. Another suggestion would be to contact either the Red Cross or another facility that offers training and request to observe a class before actually paying and signing up for the course.

SELECTED SCHOOLS

Many technical and community colleges offer programs in professional health
care or pre-nursing. Interested students are advised to consult with a school
guidance counselor or research area postsecondary schools. Also advisable
is contacting your state health department and/or local American Red Cross
along with hospitals, nursing homes, and residential care facilities to learn
first-hand about training opportunities—and CNA certification—in your area.

MORE INFORMATION

**American Health Care
Association**
1201 L Street NW
Washington, DC 20005
202.842.4444
www.ahcancal.org

**National Association for Home
Care and Hospice**
228 7th Street SE
Washington, DC 20003
202.547.7424
pubs@nach.org
www.nahc.org

**National Association of Health
Care Assistants**
501 E. 15th Street
Joplin, MO 64080
417.623.6049
www.nahcacares.org

**National Network of Career
Nursing Assistants**
3577 Easton Road
Norton, OH 44203
330.825.0342
cna-network.org

Briana Nadeau/Editor

Licensed Practical Nurse (LPN)

Snapshot

Career Cluster: Health Care

Interests: Health, Patient Care, Nursing

Earnings (Yearly Average): $42,803

Employment & Outlook: Faster Than Average Growth Expected

OVERVIEW

Sphere of Work

Licensed practical nurses (LPNs), also known as "licensed vocational nurses," provide personal care to patients and administrative assistance to medical professionals. LPNs document patient vital signs, prepare patients for injections, dress and re-dress bandages, clean wounds and sores, and give massages. Working under the supervision of doctors, nurse managers, and registered nurses (RNs), many LPNs perform routine medical tests and assist in medical procedures. They also ease the workloads of doctors and registered nurses by performing administrative tasks, such as

organizing, updating, and filing patient records. LPNs often work in retirement homes and rehabilitation centers, contributing to the cleanliness, nutrition, and comfort of the elderly, disabled, and convalescing.

Work Environment

LPNs typically work in medical facilities such as hospitals, medical office buildings, nursing and retirement homes, and health-care clinics. These settings are clean, well-organized, and busy. LPNs usually work with many patients during the course of a single day's shift. They normally work forty hours per week (as dictated by an established schedule), although in some facilities, they may work longer hours or on nights, weekends, and/or holidays. They may also work different shifts on different days. LPNs must also stay on their feet during a long shift, sometimes lifting patients, and handle stress caused by high caseloads, emergency situations, and uncooperative patients.

Profile

Working Conditions: Work Indoors
Physical Strength: Medium Work
Education Needs: Technical/ Community College
Licensure/Certification: Required
Physical Abilities Not Required: No Strenuous Labor
Opportunities For Experience: Apprenticeship, Military Service, Volunteer Work, Part-Time Work
Holland Interest Score*: SAC

* See Appendix A

Occupation Interest

LPNs play an important role in providing comfort and personal care to patients. LPNs lighten the workloads of doctors and registered nurses by performing administrative tasks and basic medical procedures. Prospective LPNs tend to be helpful, patient, and concerned about the well-being of others. They should demonstrate good judgment, work well in team settings, and thrive under stress. The educational training required for LPNs is not as lengthy or intensive as that of a registered nurse, and work as an LPN can lead to more advanced health-care positions.

A Day in the Life—Duties and Responsibilities

LPNs have varied duties and responsibilities based largely on the state restrictions and type of employer. Generally, LPNs carefully monitor patients, log medications and intravenous fluids on patient charts, track patient nutrition and waste elimination, report changes in patient condition, take vital signs, dress and re-dress wounds, and collect blood and urine samples for analysis. They also perform tasks relative to the patient's comfort, which may include helping with meals and dressing, providing alcohol rubs and sponge baths, treating bedsores, administering enemas, and giving massages. LPNs are also responsible for sterilizing, organizing, and assembling medical equipment for use on a patient. In some states, LPN may be qualified to administer medications and participate in more intensive medical procedures, such as delivering infants.

Additionally, LPNs serve as information resources for the patients and their families. They take part in conversations between doctors, registered nurses, and other medical professionals regarding patient care and relay the plan of action in simple, intelligible terms. They frequently help patients or patient families to fill out insurance forms, medical authorizations, and other important documents. LPNs also educate patients on the steps necessary to improve their health, such as taking medications on time, adhering to special diets, and adjusting their lifestyles. Furthermore, LPNs help train family members on

Duties and Responsibilities

- Taking and recording temperature, blood pressure, pulse, and respiration rate
- Dressing wounds
- Giving injections
- Administering preoperative and postoperative care
- Assisting patients in activities of daily living
- Providing irrigations (tissue cleansings) and catheterizations (tube insertions/removals)
- Applying compresses, ice bags, and heat packs
- Administering prescribed medication
- Observing patients' conditions and reporting reactions to the medical personnel in charge
- Recording fluid intake and output
- Monitoring intravenous therapy

how to care for their loved ones by providing diets, exercise regimens, medication schedules, and other useful guidelines.

WORK ENVIRONMENT

Physical Environment

LPNs generally work in medical settings such as hospitals, nursing homes, clinics, rehabilitation centers, and medical offices. These facilities are typically very busy, clean, and orderly. Owing to the nature of their work, LPNs may be exposed to contagious illnesses, toxic chemicals and radiation, sharp medical instruments, and blood and other bodily fluids. Because LPNs are on their feet for most of their shifts and may be required to lift patients, muscle strains and related injuries are common.

Relevant Skills and Abilities

Communication Skills
- Speaking effectively
- Listening carefully

Interpersonal/Social Skills
- Providing support to others
- Working as a member of a team

Organization & Management Skills
- Following instructions
- Paying attention to and handling details
- Performing duties that may change frequently

Technical Skills
- Performing technical work

Other Skills
- Being comfortable with people who are ill or disabled

Human Environment

In addition to patients and their families, LPNs interact with medical students, medical technicians, emergency personnel (such as emergency medical technicians), volunteers, and administrative staff. LPNs must take direction from RNs, nurse managers, physicians, and hospital administrators. Experienced LPNs may act as supervisors to nursing assistants, aides, and interns.

Technological Environment

LPNs must use a wide range of medical equipment, including hypodermic and intravenous needles, catheterization tubes, fetal heart monitors, enema kits, nebulizers, spirometers, stethoscopes, blood pressure cuffs, and thermometers. To fulfill their administrative tasks, they must use electronic medical record (EMR) software as well as office management and calendar programs. monitors, wheelchair lifters, and blood pressure cuffs, to care for patients.

EDUCATION, TRAINING, AND ADVANCEMENT

High School/Secondary

High school students are encouraged to take biology, chemistry, physics, anatomy and physiology, and other science courses. They should also study mathematics as well as nutrition, child development, psychology, and first aid. Courses that develop communication skills, such as English, are also very useful.

Suggested High School Subjects
- Algebra
- Applied Math & Physics
- Biology
- Chemistry
- Child Growth & Development
- English
- First Aid Training
- Foods & Nutrition
- Health Science Technology
- edical Assisting
- Nurse Assisting
- Physical Science
- Physiology
- Psychology
- Science

Famous First

The first formal training course in practical nursing was developed by the Young Women's Christian Association (YWCA) in New York City in 1892. The course focused on the care of infants, children, and the elderly and disabled. Students were also taught the basics of cooking and nutrition.

Library of Congress

College/Postsecondary

Aspiring LPNs must complete a state-approved nursing program through accredited junior and community colleges and vocational schools. Such programs last about a year, although associate's degree programs in this field are two-year programs. In addition to intensive study in patient care, LPN candidates enrolled in these programs must have practical training in a medical setting.

Related College Majors
- Anatomy & Physiology
- Health Science
- Home Health Aide Training
- Nursing (L.P.N.)

Adult Job Seekers

Qualified LPNs may find employment by applying directly to open positions at hospitals and other health-care facilities. Some may also obtain assistance through nursing school job sites. LPNs may find it helpful to join and network through professional practical nursing organizations, such as the National Federation of Licensed Practical Nurses, or associations that focus on a particular field of health care, such as geriatrics or oncology. Others first obtain a job as a Certified Nursing Assistant (CNA) and, as their skills and experience grow, receive promotions to LPN posts. Experienced LPNs may move into supervisory roles, enroll in registered nurse training programs, or specialize in a particular type of care or population.

Professional Certification and Licensure

All licensed practical nurses must obtain a state license prior to beginning practice. Licensure requirements may differ between states. Although some states have reciprocal licensure agreements, LPNs should expect to obtain new state licensure if they move. In general, LPN candidates must have a high school diploma and pass the National Council Licensure Examination (NCLEX-PN). This lengthy, computer-based test focuses on four core areas of nursing: safe and effective care environment, health promotion and maintenance, psychosocial integrity (emotional stability and social balance), and physiological integrity. Continuing education is usually required for periodic licensure renewal.

Additional Requirements

LPNs should be sympathetic, sensitive observers and communicators. They must manage multiple tasks simultaneously and demonstrate sound organizational skills. Furthermore, they should be level-headed, able to handle stressful situations calmly and effectively. Members of professional nursing associations must comply with their organization's code of ethics.

Fun Fact

Of various professionals, nurses were ranked first for honesty and ethical standards.
Source: Gallup Poll

EARNINGS AND ADVANCEMENT

Earnings of licensed practical nurses depend primarily on the type and geographic location of the employer. Median annual earnings of licensed practical nurses were $42,803 in 2012. The lowest ten percent earned less than $31,461, and the highest ten percent earned more than $59,371.

Licensed practical nurses may receive paid vacations, holidays, and sick days; life and health insurance; and retirement benefits. These are usually paid by the employer. Licensed practical nurses are usually required to purchase their own uniforms, shoes, and watch with a second hand, although some employers provide reimbursement of these costs.

Metropolitan Areas with the Highest Concentration of Jobs in this Occupation

Metropolitan area	Employment (1)	Employment per thousand jobs	Hourly mean wage
New York-White Plains-Wayne, NY-NJ	19,950	3.87	$24.08
Los Angeles-Long Beach-Glendale, CA	19,700	5.09	$24.18
Dallas-Plano-Irving, TX	13,150	6.27	$22.27
Houston-Sugar Land-Baytown, TX	13,050	4.94	$22.18
Chicago-Joliet-Naperville, IL	10,800	2.97	$22.17
Philadelphia, PA	10,020	5.50	$22.94
Atlanta-Sandy Springs-Marietta, GA	9,550	4.22	$19.12
Minneapolis-St. Paul-Bloomington, MN-WI	8,650	4.95	$20.67

[1] Does not include self-employed. Source: Bureau of Labor Statistics, 2012

EMPLOYMENT AND OUTLOOK

There were approximately 720,000 licensed practical nurses employed
nationally in 2012. About three-fourths worked full time. Employment
is expected to grow faster than the average for all occupations through
the year 2020, which means employment is projected to increase about
22 percent. This is in response to the long-term care needs of a rapidly
growing and aging population and the overall growth of the health-care
industry. Applicants for jobs in hospitals may face competition as the
number of hospital jobs for licensed practical nurses declines due to
more procedures being performed in physicians' offices and outpatient
clinics. Rapid employment growth is projected in other health-care
industries, with the best job opportunities occurring in nursing care
facilities and in home health-care services.

Employment Trend, Projected 2010–20

Health Technologists and Technicians: 26%

Licensed Practical Nurses: 22%

Total, All Occupations: 14%

Note: "All Occupations" includes all occupations in the U.S. Economy. Source: U.S. Bureau of Labor
Statistics, Employment Projections Program

Related Occupations
- Emergency Medical Technician
- Home Health Aide
- Medical Assistant
- Nurse Practitioner
- Nursing Aide
- Registered Nurse (RN)

Related Military Occupations
- Medical Care Technician

Conversation With . . .
DENISE WHITMAN
Licensed Practical Nurse, 30 years

1. What was your individual career path in terms of education, entry-level job, or other significant opportunity?

I always wanted to be a nurse, and after high school I went into an LPN nursing program. Back then it was a ten-month program – now it's fourteen – and if you were a resident of Northampton (Mass.) and under 21, you could go for free. I was 17, took a placement test, and got in. I got a job right away after graduation; I was hired on a medical surgical floor. Back then, they hired nurses before they took the LPN nursing board exam so I started working in September and didn't go for the boards until the end of October.

I did long-term care for many years when my girls were small. Then I worked for a primary care doctor for ten years and then I came here, to the surgical care group.

2. Are there many job opportunities in your profession? In what specific areas?

I would suggest anybody today go for their RN and not their LPN. Hospitals are not hiring LPNs nearly as much as they used to. There are employment opportunities in nursing homes and doctor's offices. If you want more job opportunities, then further schooling to become an RN is needed.

3. What do you wish you had known going into this profession?

I wish I'd gone for my RN. LPNs do so many of the same things but they get paid less. In a nursing home setting, for example, often an LPN and RN do the same thing.

4. How do you see your profession changing in the next five years?

We're already seeing it: more triage and less job availability. You're going to be seeing a lot more medical assistants doing the hands-on work with patients that LPNs have always done – the vital signs, transferring patients. I like being hands-on. My job in the next six months to 12 months will be phone triage. Currently, I bring patients in the examining room and obtain vital signs, current medications and allergies, assist with procedures and do phone triage.

5. **What role will technology play in those changes, and what skills will be required?**

You're definitely going to need computer skills to access electronic medical records.

6. **Do you have any general advice or additional professional insights to share with someone interested in your profession?**

What they go over in school with you is very different than real life. Usually we're short-staffed and it's busy. What you're taught at school is idealistic and that's not the real world.

I have lots of empathy and I feel like that works to my benefit as a nurse. I feel like I understand the pain they're going through – the fear, the loneliness – and I feel like it makes me a better nurse. If you see something very upsetting, you might share with a co-worker or a doctor, but after awhile, it's all part of life. You do what you can for them when they are with you in your care.

7. **Can you suggest a valuable "try this" for students considering a career in your profession?**

If you're looking and seriously thinking about being a nurse, I would suggest working as a volunteer. Try to get yourself into the area of nursing you'd like to do.

SELECTED SCHOOLS

Many technical and community colleges offer programs in practical nursing. Interested students are advised to consult with a school guidance counselor or research area postsecondary schools. Some of the professional organizations listed in the "More Information" section, below, provide lists of selected schools and other educational resources.

MORE INFORMATION

American Association of Colleges of Nursing
1 Dupont Circle NW, Suite 530
Washington, DC 20036
202.463.6930
www.aacn.nche.edu

American Health Care Association
1201 L Street, NW
Washington, DC 20005
202.842.4444
www.ahcancal.org

American Nurses Association
8515 Georgia Avenue, Suite 400
Silver Spring, MD 20910
800.274.4262
nursingworld.org

National Association for Practical Nurse Education and Service
1940 Duke Street, Suite 200
Alexandria, VA 22314
703.933.1003
www.napnes.org

National Council of State Boards of Nursing
111 East Wacker Drive, Suite 2900
Chicago, IL 60601-4277
312.525.3600
www.ncsbn.org

National Federation of Licensed Practical Nurses
111 W. Main Street, Suite 100
Garner, NC 27529
919.779.0046
nflpn@mgmt4u.com
www.nflpn.org

National League for Nursing
61 Broadway, 33rd Floor
New York, NY 10006
212.363.5555
www.nln.org

National Student Nurses Association
45 Main Street, Suite 606
Brooklyn, NY 11201
718.210.0705
www.nsna.org

Michael Auerbach/Editor

Medical Assistant

Snapshot

Career Cluster: Health Care, Business Administration

Interests: Health Care, Record Keeping, Office Management, Clinical Assistance

Earnings (Yearly Average): $30,592

Employment & Outlook: Faster Than Average Growth Expected

OVERVIEW

Sphere of Work

Medical assistants perform administrative and clinical support tasks that contribute to the efficient operation of a medical office. Administrative medical assistants handle paperwork and logistics for the offices where they work. Clinical medical assistants assist physicians with patient consultations, which may entail a variety of patient interactions as well as sample collection and cleaning responsibilities. Some medical assistants perform both administrative and clinical work. Others are charged with additional clinical activities related to a medical specialty.

Work Environment

Medical assistants work in medical office environments. Medical offices are sterile, highly organized, brightly lit, and very busy environments. Medical assistants generally work a standard forty hours per week. Part-time, evening, or weekend hours may also be available. Managing high levels of activity and multiple tasks as well as interacting with impatient or rude patients make for a stressful work environment for medical assistants. Medical assistants must follow strict procedures regarding patient information, treatments, safety, and time management.

Profile

Working Conditions: Work Indoors
Physical Strength: Light Work
Education Needs: Technical/
Community College
Licensure/Certification:
Recommended
Physical Abilities Not Required: No
Heavy Labor
Opportunities For Experience:
Apprenticeship, Military Service,
Volunteer Work, Part-Time Work
Holland Interest Score*: SCR

* See Appendix A

Occupation Interest

Medical assistants play an important role in the efficient, effective, and safe operation of a physician's office. Timeliness, impeccable record keeping, and strong organizational and social skills are essential in the administrative medical assistant. The work of clinical medical assistants helps physicians to diagnose and treat their patients' ailments as well as to ensure patients' continued physical wellbeing. They should demonstrate caring and concern for others. The need for medical services, and thus, medical assistants remains strong. Medical assistants who perform their jobs well are likely to earn promotions.

A Day in the Life—Duties and Responsibilities

Medical assistants serve two purposes, providing both administrative and clinical support for physicians. The size and type of employer determines whether a medical assistant has administrative or clinical duties or a combination of the two. Facilities with fewer staff tend to have a single medical assistant who functions in both roles. In larger institutions, there are usually several medical assistants working in niche roles.

From the reception area of a medical office, administrative medical assistants answer phones, schedule appointments and laboratory procedures, and greet patients and provide necessary forms to complete patient files. These medical assistants file and maintain patient and financial records, complete and process insurance forms using the proper codes, manage mail and supply orders, and maintain a patient database. Some administrative medical assistants call in prescriptions, prepare correspondence from physicians to patients, and arrange hospital admissions and referrals. In some cases, they may handle patient billing and other bookkeeping.

Clinical medical assistants facilitate the diagnosis and treatment of patients. Their exact duties depend on the state in which they work. They interview patients, recording their symptoms, histories, and vital signs. They also assist physicians with examinations and minor surgical procedures. Clinical medical assistants occasionally perform and assist in routine lab, electrocardiogram (EKG), x-ray, and other tests and procedures. They follow up with patients, changing dressings, removing stitches, and providing patients with information about medications, treatments, and special diets. Medical assistants are responsible for sterilizing instruments, disposing of used needles

Duties and Responsibilities

- Answering the phone, handling mail, greeting patients, and filing records
- Keeping patient data and medical histories
- Arranging for hospital admission and laboratory services
- Checking and ordering office and medical supplies
- Typing dictation, correspondence, and reports
- Filling in Medicare, Medicaid, and other insurance forms
- Sending bills and doing bookkeeping
- Giving information to patients about preparation necessary for tests, x-rays, and laboratory examinations
- Assisting physicians during patient examinations, treatments, minor surgeries, and emergencies

and other hazardous waste, and ordering and restocking supplies as needed.

Some medical assistants specialize in a particular field of medicine and, as such, have duties specific to that field. For example, optometric medical assistants may help patients try on new contact lenses or assist optometrists in conducting eye tests in addition to the typical clinical medical assistant duties. Podiatric assistants, meanwhile, take casts of patients' feet, prepare equipment, and provide some patient treatments, as required.

OCCUPATION SPECIALTIES

Chiropractor Assistants

Chiropractor Assistants aid chiropractors during physical examination of patients, give specified office treatments, and keep patients' records.

Optometric and Ophthalmic Assistants

Optometric and Ophthalmic Assistants perform any number of tasks to assist optometrists and ophthalmologists, including preparing patients for vision and eye examinations, assisting in testing patients, and instructing patients in care and use of glasses and contact lenses or treatment of an eye condition. Ophthalmic Medical Assistants may also help an ophthalmologist in surgery.

Podiatric Assistants

Podiatric Assistants assist podiatrists in patient care by preparing patients for treatment, sterilizing equipment, preparing dressings, administering treatments, and developing x-rays.

WORK ENVIRONMENT

Physical Environment

Medical assistants work in medical offices. These environments are clean, highly organized, and brightly lit. Offices often have many patients seeking assistance at the same time—medical assistants may experience some stress as a result of such demanding conditions. Additionally, assistants work with needles, surgical tools, blood, and other bodily fluids during the course of their daily responsibilities, which increases their risk of exposure to viruses and other communicable illnesses.

Relevant Skills and Abilities

Communication Skills
- Speaking effectively
- Recording and reporting information

Interpersonal/Social Skills
- Cooperating with others
- Having good judgment
- Working as a member of a team

Organization & Management Skills
- Following instructions
- Paying attention to and handling details
- Performing duties that change frequently

Technical Skills
- Working with data or numbers
- Working with machines, tools, or other objects
- Working with your hands

Other Skills
- Working in a medical setting

Human Environment

Medical assistants work with a large number of individuals within the office, including physicians, nurses and nursing assistants, medical technicians, medical students, and phlebotomists (blood-work specialists). Besides their co-workers, medical assistants interact with patients and their families, medical suppliers and vendors, insurance company representatives, and pharmacists.

Technological Environment

Medical assistants must be familiar with a variety of medical and office technologies. When working directly with patients, they may use blood pressure units, stethoscopes, hypodermic needles, ophthalmoscopes, spirometers, and nebulizers. To fulfill their clerical duties, medical assistants must use many types of computer software, including patient management, calendaring and scheduling, accounting, and office management systems.

EDUCATION, TRAINING, AND ADVANCEMENT

High School/Secondary

High school students are encouraged to take biology, chemistry, nutrition, and health courses. Additionally, classes that build accounting and bookkeeping skills, such as math and business courses, are useful. Future medical assistants should take computer science classes to build their applied knowledge of databases and software. Some vocational high schools teach medical assistance courses as well.

Suggested High School Subjects
- Applied Biology/Chemistry
- Applied Math
- Biology
- Bookkeeping
- Business
- Business & Computer Technology
- Chemistry
- English
- First Aid Training
- Foods & Nutrition
- Health Science Technology
- Mathematics
- Medical Assisting
- Shorthand

Famous First

The first medical clinic to serve a wide array of outpatients opened in 1889 and was affiliated with the Johns Hopkins Medical School in Baltimore, Md. Prior to that time there were a few small, specialized clinics in selected cities but none that served the general populace and that was prepared to handle a broad range of common medical needs.

Library of Congress

College/Postsecondary

Although many medical assistants receive on-the-job training, most medical assistants pursue postsecondary training either through an accredited one-year medical assisting certificate or diploma program from a vocational school or an associate's degree at a community or technical college. Interested individuals should be sure to enroll in programs accredited by the Commission on Accreditation of Allied Health Education Programs (CAAHEP) or the Accreditation Bureau of Health Education Schools (ABHES). Training programs include both classroom and laboratory components and cover subjects such as life sciences, medical law, patient relations, basic medical procedures and pharmacology, medical terminology and codes, and accounting

Related College Majors
- Anatomy & Physiology
- Health-Care Administration
- Health Sciences
- Medical Assistant Training
- Medical Laboratory Assistant Training
- Pharmacy Technical Assistant Training

Adult Job Seekers

Medical assistant candidates may pursue open positions by applying directly to the physicians or medical centers that post them. Medical assistants may also find job placement through their postsecondary schools or by consulting job websites dedicated to medical assistants, such as Medical Assistant Net. In addition, medical assistants may join and network through a trade association, such as the American Medical Association or the American Association of Medical Assistants (AAMA). Experienced medical assistants may advance to related health-care positions or supervisory administrative roles.

Professional Certification and Licensure

Certification is not required by every state for work as a medical assistant, although some states do require it and voluntary certification can, in any case, enhance a candidate's credentials. To become a nationally recognized Certified Medical Assistant (CMA) from the American Association of Medical Assistants or the Association of Medical Technologists, a candidate must complete training in an accredited program, have relevant work experience, and pass a written examination. Current CPR certification and continued education typically are required for CMA recertification.

Additional Requirements

Medical assistants must be well organized, able to multitask, and demonstrate strong administrative and communications skills. Furthermore, they must be quick to learn new concepts and terminology. Successful medical assistants work well with the public, keeping a professional appearance and maintaining a courteous, polite demeanor at all times.

EARNINGS AND ADVANCEMENT

Earnings of medical assistants depend on the type and location of the employer and the employee's education, experience and skill level. Median annual earnings of medical assistants were $30,592 in 2012. The lowest ten percent earned less than $22,059, and the highest ten percent earned more than $42,601.

Medical assistants may receive paid vacations, holidays, and sick days. They may have health insurance through the physician's office.

Metropolitan Areas with the Highest
Employment Level in this Occupation

Metropolitan area	Employment	Employment per thousand jobs	Hourly mean wage
Los Angeles-Long Beach-Glendale, CA	22,670	5.86	$15.96
New York-White Plains-Wayne, NY-NJ	14,390	2.79	$16.22
Houston-Sugar Land-Baytown, TX	12,550	4.75	$14.77
Chicago-Joliet-Naperville, IL	12,530	3.44	$15.05
Dallas-Plano-Irving, TX	10,200	4.86	$15.09
Atlanta-Sandy Springs-Marietta, GA	10,010	4.43	$14.40
Phoenix-Mesa-Glendale, AZ	8,460	4.89	$15.60
Boston-Cambridge-Quincy, MA NECTA Division	7,930	4.63	$18.74

Source: Bureau of Labor Statistics, 2012

EMPLOYMENT AND OUTLOOK

Nationally, there were approximately 553,000 medical assistants employed in 2012. Nearly two-thirds worked in physicians' offices. Employment is expected to grow much faster than the average for all occupations through the year 2020, which means employment is projected to increase 30 percent or more. Employment growth will be driven by technological advances in medicine, an increase in the number of health practitioners, and the growth and aging of the population. Job prospects should be very good for medical assistants with formal training or experience, particularly those with formal certification.

Employment Trend, Projected 2010–20

Medical Assistants: 31%

Other Health-Care Support Occupations: 25%

Total, All Occupations: 14%

Note: "All Occupations" includes all occupations in the U.S. Economy. Source: U.S. Bureau of Labor Statistics, Employment Projections Program

Related Occupations
- Administrative Assistant
- Dental Assistant
- Executive Secretary
- Licensed Practical Nurse (LPN)
- Medical Laboratory Technician
- Medical Records Administrator
- Nursing Aide
- Secretary

Related Military Occupations
- Medical Care Technician
- Medical Record Technician
- Medical Service Technician
- Optometric Technician
- Radiologic (X-Ray) Technician

Conversation With . . .
RENEE LEFEBVRE
Medical assistant, X-ray and MRI technologist
3 years

1. **What was your individual career path in terms of education, entry-level job, or other significant opportunity?**

When I went to college, I started out pursuing a degree in biology. Then I decided to specialize in the medical field. I thought I would study to be a physician's assistant, but when I shadowed different professions, I discovered I was interested in radiology. After I graduated from college with a bachelor's degree in medical biology, I went to a two-year program to learn to be an X-ray technologist. I worked as an X-ray tech for six months, then moved to the West Coast and found a job working as an X-ray tech and a medical assistant.

2. **Are there many job opportunities in your profession? In what specific areas?**

There seem to be lots of medical assistant jobs. They're in every doctor's office you can imagine; everything from orthopedics to ear, nose and throat practices. There are medical assistants in hospital settings, too. In the emergency room, medical assistants will often triage patients and take their history before a doctor sees them.

3. **What do you wish you had known going into this profession?**

I wish I knew how much I would be dealing with insurance companies. Most people go into this because they want to interact with patients and have lots of hands-on experiences. You do that, but you also spend a lot of time doing paperwork and talking on the phone to insurance companies trying to get this test or that test approved.

The best advice for anyone going into this profession, or any profession in the medical field, is to be open minded. You never know what you're going to get. If you keep an open mind, you'll be less stressed and you'll be better at problem solving.

4. How do you see your profession changing in the next five years?

The development of different technologies, and the high emphasis and reliance on computers and technology in general, is causing everything to speed up. We need to slow down and remember that we're dealing with patients. We need to talk with them and not just hurry up and put everything in the computer.

5. What role will technology play in those changes, and what skills will be required?

You need to have a basic, if not advanced, knowledge of computers. You need to learn to use a variety of different programs. Most facilities use electronic medical records (EMRs) as opposed to paper medical records. You're constantly adding to those records, entering in prescriptions and sending them out electronically to be filled; entering in MRI imaging and lab orders. It's an intense program and can be overwhelming, but as long as you have good typing skills, are not afraid of technology, and have a good memory, you'll be fine.

6. Do you have any general advice or additional professional insights to share with someone interested in your profession?

Really consider what area you want to work in. Do you want to work with families? Do you want to work in orthopedics with people who have broken bones or need hip replacements? Do you want to work in cardiology? People go into the field and then get a job and it's not what they expected. If you're working in a family practice, you'll be ordering tests, sending patients to specialists, giving vaccinations. When I started as a medical assistant in orthopedics, I had no experience in taking off casts and removing staples because not every office requires that.

7. Can you suggest a valuable "try this" for students considering a career in your profession?

You should have really good communication skills and be able to interact with people well because it's all based on that. From the second you get the patient from the waiting room until the doctor sees them, you're it.

A lot of time you get patients who want to tell you everything and you have to be sympathetic and listen, but also get your job done in a timely manner. You don't want to come off as rushing them or as inconsiderate or unsympathetic.

Sometimes you get someone who won't tell you why they're there. Maybe they're shy or maybe they're scared. You've got to consider what they might be going through. Don't make any assumptions. They may not want to tell you, they may want to tell the doctor. Practice talking with people, especially if it's medically related in some way. Watch some shows on the Discovery Channel. If you get faint at the sight of blood or are a germaphobe, then being a medical assistant is probably not for you.

SELECTED SCHOOLS

Many technical and community colleges offer programs in medical assistant training. Interested students are advised to consult with a school guidance counselor or research area postsecondary schools. Some of the professional organizations listed in the "More Information" section, below, provide search tools for locating schools in your state.

MORE INFORMATION

Accrediting Bureau of Health Education Schools
7777 Leesburg Pike, Suite 314
North Falls Church, VA 22043
703.917.9503
www.abhes.org

American Association of Medical Assistants
20 North Wacker Drive, Suite 1575
Chicago, IL 60606
312.899.1500
www.aama-ntl.org

Commission on Accreditation of Allied Health Education Programs
1361 Park Street
Clearwater, FL 33756
727.210.2350
www.caahep.org

Health Professions Network
P.O. Box 112
Shillington, PA 19607
678.200.2619
www.healthpronet.org

Medical Assistant Net
107 Rimmon Avenue
Chicopee, MA 01013
www.medicalassistant.net

Michael Auerbach/Editor

Medical Laboratory Technician

Snapshot

Career Cluster: Health Science, Medicine

Interests: Medicine, Science, Medical Technology

Earnings (Yearly Average): $38,457

Employment & Outlook: Faster Than Average Growth Expected

OVERVIEW

Sphere of Work

Medical laboratory technicians work in laboratories performing medical tests used for the diagnosis and treatment of diseases. They use manual and automated equipment to prepare specimens, examine specimens under microscopes, identify bacteria, record blood counts, perform urinalysis, and carry out automated tests. Specialized medical laboratory technicians, such as orthotic and prosthetic technicians and medical appliance technicians, may also craft, produce, and service medical equipment that helps individuals live improved and independent lives.

Work Environment

Medical laboratory technicians spend their workdays in medical laboratories located in hospitals, doctors' offices, medical technology businesses, educational facilities, and independent medical laboratories. Human interaction in medical labs tends to be limited to laboratory staff, doctors, and patients. Medical laboratory technicians generally work forty hours or more each week. A medical laboratory technician's shifts may include days, evenings, weekends, and holidays to meet the medical community's need for test results.

Profile

Working Conditions: Work Indoors
Physical Strength: Light Work
Education Needs: Technical/ Community College
Licensure/Certification: Recommended
Physical Abilities Not Required: No Heavy Labor
Opportunities For Experience: Internship, Military Service, Part-Time Work,
Holland Interest Score*: RIE

* See Appendix A

Occupation Interest

Individuals drawn to the profession of medical laboratory technician tend to be intelligent, analytical, and detail oriented. Those most successful as medical laboratory technicians display traits such as good eyesight, hand-eye coordination, focus, problem-solving skills, manual dexterity, responsibility, effective time management, and concern for others. Medical laboratory technicians should enjoy spending time in laboratory settings and have a strong background in science.

A Day in the Life—Duties and Responsibilities

A medical laboratory technician's daily occupational duties and responsibilities are determined by the individual's area of job specialization and work environment. Medical laboratory technician specialties include chemistry, microbiology, urinalysis, cytotechnology (cells), histotechnology (tissues), immunology, hematology (blood), orthotics and prosthetics, and medical appliances.

Most medical laboratory technicians run medical tests and assist in the analysis of test results. Some technicians, commonly known as phlebotomists, draw blood from patients in accordance with required safety protocols. Medical laboratory technicians often perform qualitative and quantitative analysis of bodily fluids such as blood, spinal fluid, and urine using microscopes and automated analysis equipment. They screen slides of cells for evidence of cancers or abnormalities, prepare slides of human tissues for pathologists, and test batches of donated blood prior to its use in transfusions. Recording blood counts, incubating bacteria, preparing vaccines, and maintaining cultures at set temperatures to encourage growth are other common duties. Medical laboratory technicians may prepare vaccines and conduct safety tests to ensure that they are sterile and contain the intended active or inactive virus.

Regardless of the specific testing procedure, the medical laboratory technician must prepare the solutions and reagents that will be used in laboratory tests, and once a test has been completed, review the results to check for procedure and specification conformity. He or she then translates test data into charts and narratives that doctors can use to help explain results to patients. The technician must document all testing procedures performed and report any and all abnormal findings or unusual test results to pathologists. In addition, medical laboratory technicians are responsible for setting up, calibrating, and sterilizing all medical laboratory equipment and materials on an ongoing basis.

Technicians who specialize in orthotics and prosthetics or medical appliances assist in the fabrication and maintenance of medical devices that treat patient conditions. They may help develop, craft, and produce assistive and adaptive medical devices according to prescription specification. These technicians may also help fit, repair, and service these devices or teach patients how to use them.

Duties and Responsibilities

- Collecting blood samples and body fluids
- Performing manual or automated testing using a variety of instruments
- Cleaning and sterilizing laboratory equipment
- Preparing solutions
- Keeping records of tests

OCCUPATION SPECIALTIES

Cytotechnologists

Cytotechnologists are medical laboratory technicians who screen slides of human cells to detect evidence of cancer or hormonal abnormalities.

Histotechnologists

Histotechnologists prepare sections of tissue for examination by a doctor or pathologist. They use different techniques which prepare the tissue to be studied for the diagnosis of body dysfunction and malignancy.

Immunology and Microbiology Technologists

Immunology Technologists examine elements of the human immune system and its response to foreign bodies. Microbiology Technologists examine and identify bacteria and other microorganisms.

Orthotic and Prosthetic Technologists

Orthotic and Prosthetic Technologists craft, produce, and service assistive and adaptive medical devices that help individuals live improved and independent lives.

Phlebotomists

Phlebotomists collect and analyze blood samples.

WORK ENVIRONMENT

Physical Environment

Medical laboratory technicians spend their workdays in laboratory settings located in hospitals, doctors' offices, medical businesses, educational facilities, and independent medical laboratories. Technicians frequently handle hazardous biological material and must therefore take safety precautions to avoid exposure to infection.

Relevant Skills and Abilities

Analytical Skills
- Analyzing data

Communication Skills
- Speaking effectively

Organization & Management Skills
- Making decisions
- Managing time
- Meeting goals and deadlines
- Paying attention to and handling details

Planning & Research Skills
- Solving problems
- Researching information

Technical Skills
- Performing scientific, mathematical, and technical work
- Using technology to process information
- Working with machines, tools, or other objects

Human Environment

Medical laboratory technicians have limited human interaction at work, but they should be comfortable meeting with laboratory staff, pathologists, physicians, and patients. Medical laboratory technicians are usually supervised by a medical technologist or laboratory manager. Orthotics and prosthetics technicians work for orthotists, prosthetists, and podiatrists.

Technological Environment

Medical laboratory technicians use computers and laboratory instruments, such as microscopes and automated analyzers, for hematology and urinalysis. Technicians should also be comfortable using the equipment necessary for collecting thin section tissue samples as well as those for preserving and growing tissue samples, vaccines, and viruses. They may need to use software for accounting, databases, patient records, and medical testing. Medical appliance technicians and orthotics and prosthetics technicians must be familiar with power tools, laboratory ovens, and computer-aided design (CAD) software.

EDUCATION, TRAINING, AND ADVANCEMENT

High School/Secondary

High school students interested in becoming medical laboratory technicians should prepare themselves by developing good study habits. High school–level study of biology, chemistry, computer science, and mathematics will provide a strong foundation for college-level work in the medical laboratory field. Drafting and mechanical classes are beneficial for those who intend to become medical appliance technicians. Owing to the diversity of a medical laboratory technician's responsibilities, high school students interested in this career path will benefit from seeking internships or part-time jobs that expose students to laboratory and medical settings and procedures.

Suggested High School Subjects
- Algebra
- Applied Biology/Chemistry
- Applied Math
- Biology
- Chemistry
- Computer Science
- English
- Health Science Technology
- Laboratory Technology
- Mathematics
- Medical Assisting
- Physical Science
- Physiology
- Science

Famous First

The first public health laboratory was established in Providence, R.I., in 1888. It was followed a few years later by two health laboratories in New York City, one for Pathology, Bacteriology, and Disinfection (1892) and the other specifically for Tuberculosis (1893).

College/Postsecondary

Postsecondary students interested in becoming medical laboratory technicians should work toward a certificate or an associate's degree in medical laboratory technology, clinical sciences, applied technology, or a related field. Those who complete an accredited training program will find it easier to become certified. Medical laboratory technology programs can be accredited by one of several organizations: the National Accrediting Agency for Clinical Laboratory Sciences (NAACLS), Commission on Accreditation of Allied Health Education Programs (CAAHEP), or the Accrediting Bureau of Health Education Schools (ABHES).Orthotic and prosthetic technician training programs are accredited by the National Commission on Orthotic and Prosthetic Education (NCOPE). Postsecondary students can gain work experience and potential advantage in their future job searches by securing internships or part-time employment in laboratory and medical settings.

Related College Majors
- Clinical Laboratory Science
- Medical Laboratory Technology

Adult Job Seekers

Adults seeking employment as medical laboratory technicians should have, at a minimum, a certificate or an associate's degree from an accredited program. A bachelor's degree in science may be necessary for some positions. Adult job seekers should educate themselves about the educational and professional licensure requirements of their home states and the organizations with which they seek employment. Adult job seekers may benefit from joining professional associations to help with networking and job searching. Professional medical associations, such as American Association of Bioanalysts (AAB) and American Society for Clinical Pathology (ASCP), generally offer job-finding workshops and maintain lists and forums of available jobs.

Professional Certification and Licensure

Professional certification may be a condition of employment. ASCP and the American Medical Technologists (AMT) offer voluntary certifications for medical laboratory technicians. The Medical Laboratory Technician (MLT) designation and others may be earned by passing national exams offered by the ASCP Board of Registry and the AAB Board of Registry. Candidates must meet a combination of education and work experience requirements to qualify for these exams. As with any voluntary certification process, it is beneficial to consult credible professional associations within the field and follow professional debate as to the relevancy and value of any certification program.

State certification and licensing requirements for medical laboratory technicians vary. In general, state-level licensure for medical laboratory technicians requires successfully completing both a national exam and an associate's degree or a one-year training program in medical technology. License renewal is often contingent on the completion of ongoing continuing education. Specific state-level certification and licensing requirement information should be sought directly from state departments of health.

Additional Requirements

Individuals who find satisfaction, success, and job security as medical laboratory technicians will be knowledgeable about the profession's requirements, responsibilities, and opportunities. Medical laboratory technicians must be honest and ethical as professionals in this role have access to private medical information. Membership in professional medical associations is encouraged among all medical laboratory technicians as a means of building professional community and networking.

EARNINGS AND ADVANCEMENT

Medical laboratory technicians may advance to supervisory positions in laboratory work or become chief medical technologists or laboratory managers in hospitals through additional education and experience. Graduate education in medical technology, one of the biological sciences, chemistry, management, or education usually speeds advancement. A doctoral degree is needed to become a medical laboratory director.

Medical laboratory technicians had median annual earnings of $38,457 in 2012. The lowest ten percent earned less than $25,663, and the highest ten percent earned more than $59,402.

Medical laboratory technicians may receive paid vacations, holidays, and sick days; life and health insurance; and retirement benefits. These are usually paid by the employer

Metropolitan Areas with the Highest Employment Level in this Occupation

Metropolitan area	Employment	Employment per thousand jobs	Hourly mean wage
Los Angeles-Long Beach-Glendale, CA	5,730	1.48	$19.21
Atlanta-Sandy Springs-Marietta, GA	4,680	2.07	$17.99
Philadelphia, PA	3,860	2.12	$19.54
New York-White Plains-Wayne, NY-NJ	3,720	0.72	$23.02
Chicago-Joliet-Naperville, IL	3,350	0.92	$18.80
Boston-Cambridge-Quincy, MA	3,230	1.89	$19.80
Phoenix-Mesa-Glendale, AZ	2,630	1.52	$20.63
Houston-Sugar Land-Baytown, TX	2,580	0.98	$17.45

Source: Bureau of Labor Statistics, 2012

EMPLOYMENT AND OUTLOOK

Medical laboratory technicians held about 158,000 jobs nationally in 2012. More than half worked in hospitals. Most others worked in medical laboratories and physicians' offices. Employment is expected to grow about as fast as the average for all occupations through the year 2020, which means employment is projected to increase approximately 15 percent. Technological advances will continue to have two opposing effects on employment. The growing number of elderly persons and the increasing use of more powerful medical laboratory procedures to detect and diagnose disease imply a need for more medical technologists, while automation of laboratory equipment implies that fewer positions will be necessary.

Employment Trend, Projected 2010–20

Health Diagnosing and Treating Practitioners: 26%

Medical Laboratory Technicians: 15%

Total, All Occupations: 14%

Medical Laboratory Technologists: 11%

Note: "All Occupations" includes all occupations in the U.S. Economy. Source: U.S. Bureau of Labor Statistics, Employment Projections Program

Related Occupations
- Clinical Laboratory Technician
- Science Technician

Related Military Occupations
- Medical Laboratory Technician

Conversation With . . .
DANIELLE WHITNEY
Medical Laboratory Technician, 5 years

1. What was your individual career path in terms of education, entry-level job, or other significant opportunity?

I have an associate's degree in clinical laboratory science from Bristol Community College, which is a two-year program in Fall River, Massachusetts. I got a temporary job working in the lab at Cape Cod Hospital the summer right after graduation. When a 24-hour per week chemistry tech job opened up, I took that and later was able to pick up another eight hours a week. Now I work 32 hours per week, which is considered full time and comes with benefits.

2. Are there many job opportunities in your profession? In what specific areas?

There are a lot of job opportunities, and different places where you can work when you have a lab degree. In addition to hospitals, there are private labs and research labs, or you can get into teaching. Also, some veterinary practices employ lab techs to look at the animals' blood work. There are also different departments within the labs, so you have chemistry, hematology, microbiology, and blood bank techs. There always seem to be openings.

3. What do you wish you had known going into this profession?

I didn't realize a lot of the jobs require you to do phlebotomy. Where I work, they don't require us to do that, but at all of the other hospitals around here, the techs are required to draw the blood and actually do the testing on it.

A really good piece of advice for anyone going into this profession is don't be afraid to ask questions if you're not sure about something. Things are always changing, so even if you've been working somewhere for a really long time, there are always going to be questions that pop up.

4. How do you see your profession changing in the next five years?

I've been here for five years and I know that during that time, things have changed a lot. I think that will only continue for the next five years. Already, the lab is less hands-on and more automated. When I first came here, we would be capping and de-capping all of the specimens—manually removing and replacing the caps on the specimen tubes. Now we have a robot that does that. We have hundreds of tubes that come in here every day. With the automation, there's less chance of having the serum or plasma spill or of contaminating the specimens. I see the lab becoming even more automated in the future. Newer, faster testing will become available so the ER is able to get their results more quickly than they do now.

5. What role will technology play in those changes, and what skills will be required?

Obviously the technology will get even better. Computer skills are an absolute must. The tests are analyzed by the computer and all of the results go out through the computer to the doctors' offices. The lab where I work just got a new computer system, so everyone had to learn how to use it

6. Do you have any general advice or additional professional insights to share with someone interested in your profession?

For this job, you can do a two-year program and get an associate's degree, but there are also four-year programs where you get a bachelor's degree. Definitely look into the different schooling options to see what will fit better with your plans. If you want to be a department head or a lab manager at some point, you'll need a four-year degree. You can also do two years of school, get a job in a lab, then continue your education to get the four-year degree.

It's important to research the different departments within the lab to find the best fit for you. You may decide that you don't like microbiology work, but you can have a clinical laboratory science degree and never have to do microbiology work. You can work in chemistry or in blood banks.

7. Can you suggest a valuable "try this" for students considering a career in your profession?

See if you can shadow a medical lab worker to get a feel for the job. Contact your local hospital and tell them that you're thinking of going into that field and ask if you can get a tour of the lab or follow a tech.

Often hospitals will have students working in the lab. Ask to talk with one of the students. Find out from that person what it's like to study to be a lab tech and what it's like to actually work in the lab.

SELECTED SCHOOLS

Many technical and community colleges offer programs in medical laboratory training. Interested students are advised to consult with a school guidance counselor or research area postsecondary schools. Some of the professional organizations listed in the "More Information" section, below, provide search tools for locating schools in your state.

MORE INFORMATION

American Association of Bioanalysts
906 Olive Street, Suite 1200
St. Louis, MO 63101-1448
314.241.1445
www.aab.org

American Medical Technologists
10700 West Higgins, Suite 150
Rosemont, IL 60018
800.275.1268
www.amt1.com

American Society for Clinical Laboratory Science (ASCLS)
2025 M Street NW, Suite 800
Washington, DC 20036
www.ascls.org

American Society for Cytopathology (ASC)
100 West Tenth Street, Suite 605
Wilmington, DE 19801
www.cytopathology.org

American Society of Clinical Pathologists
Career Information
33 West Monroe Street, Suite 1600
Chicago, IL 60603
312.738.1336
www.ascp.org

Clinical Laboratory Management Association (CLMA)
401 North Michigan Avenue, Suite 2200
Chicago, IL 60611
312.321.5111
www.clma.org

National Accrediting Agency for Clinical Laboratory Sciences
8410 W. Bryn Mawr Avenue, Suite 670
Chicago, IL 60631
773.714.8880
www.naacls.org

Simone Isadora Flynn/Editor

Medical Records Administrator

Snapshot

Career Cluster: Health Care, Business Administration

Interests: Record Keeping, Information Management, Business Administration

Earnings (Yearly Average): $89,326

Employment & Outlook: Faster Than Average Growth Expected

OVERVIEW

Sphere of Work

Medical records administrators, also called health information administrators or health information managers, are responsible for overseeing the privacy, safety, and accessibility of medical records. They build, implement, and maintain medical information systems for use by physicians, nurses, patients, medical researchers, hospitals, medical offices and clinics, government inspectors or regulatory agencies, and insurance companies. Medical records administrators also prepare budgets, head committees, manage work teams, and train and supervise health information

technicians who enter patient data into the medical information system.

Work Environment

Medical records administrators work in the medical records or health information offices of hospitals and other medical facilities, insurance and pharmaceutical companies, government health agencies, and medical laboratories, among others. They generally work forty-hour weeks, often with occasional overtime or evening hours to meet increased workload or troubleshoot problems related to the medical records system.

Profile

Working Conditions: Work Indoors
Physical Strength: Light Work
Education Needs: Technical/ Community College, Bachelor's Degree
Licensure/Certification: Usually Not Required
Physical Abilities Not Required: No Heavy Labor
Opportunities For Experience: Internship, Part-Time Work,
Holland Interest Score*: SIE

* See Appendix A

Occupation Interest

Individuals drawn to the profession of medical records administrator tend to be organized and detail oriented. Those most successful at the job of medical records administrator display traits such as accuracy, initiative, and thoroughness, as well as the ability to problem solve. Medical records administrators should have training in management and record keeping.

A Day in the Life—Duties and Responsibilities

On a typical day, a medical records administrator may have to prepare a budget for his or her department, attend a seminar on advances in record-keeping software, or respond to an emergency related to the system, such as a loss of records or an unauthorized user gaining access. Chief among an administrator's responsibilities is ensuring the security of all medical records. Administrators are in charge of training and supervising staff, and may oversee health information technicians as they enter patient data into medical information system, or review medical records for accuracy and completeness. They also liaise with insurance companies and other department heads as needed.

In addition to the range of responsibilities described above, all medical records administrators are responsible for educating themselves and their staff about the administrative, physical, and technical patient privacy safeguards included in HIPAA (Health Insurance Portability and Accountability Act).

Duties and Responsibilities

- Maintaining records regarding patients, their illnesses, diagnoses, and treatments
- Overseeing the work of medical records staff
- Communicating with insurance companies and medical staff
- Training the medical records staff for specialized jobs
- Gathering medical statistics for governmental health agencies
- Updating the information management system as necessary
- Developing and working with budgets
- Ensuring patient privacy and the confidentiality of medical records

OCCUPATION SPECIALTIES

Health Information Technicians

Health Information Technicians document patients' health information, including the medical history, symptoms, examination and test results, treatments, and other information about healthcare provider services.

Medical Coders

Medical Coders review patient records and assign classification codes to represent the diagnosis and treatment of medical conditions for administrative, statistical, and insurance purposes.

Medical Transcriptionists

Medical transcriptionists listen to voice recordings that physicians and other health professionals make and convert them into written reports. They interpret medical terminology and abbreviations in preparing patients' medical histories, discharge summaries, and other documents.

WORK ENVIRONMENT

Immediate Physical Environment

Medical records administrators generally work in well-lit and temperature-controlled offices. They may, however, sometimes be at risk for job-related injuries such as eyestrain and backache.

Relevant Skills and Abilities

Analytical Skills
- Assessing needs and providing solutions

Communication Skills
- Speaking and writing effectively

Interpersonal/Social Skills
- Cooperating with others
- Working as a member of a team

Organization & Management Skills
- Coordinating tasks
- Making decisions
- Managing people/groups
- Organizing information or materials
- Paying attention to and handling details

Technical Skills
- Performing technical work

Human Environment

Medical records administrators should be comfortable interacting with patients, physicians, insurance representatives, government inspectors, and laboratory and office staff. Due to the private nature of medical records, medical records administrators should act with confidentiality and tact.

Technological Environment

Medical records administrators use a wide variety of tools and equipment to complete their work, including computers, electronic medical records software, medical coding charts, insurance rate charts and books, printers, calculators, photocopying machines, telephones, word processing software, fax machines, and scanners

EDUCATION, TRAINING, AND ADVANCEMENT

High School/Secondary

High school students interested in pursuing a career as a medical records administrator should study business administration, computers, communications, and science and math. Classes in typing and bookkeeping are also recommended, as are classes in health science.

Suggested High School Subjects
- Applied Communication
- Business
- Business & Computer Technology
- Business Law
- College Preparatory
- Computer Science
- English
- Health Science Technology
- Keyboarding
- Mathematics
- Science
- Sociology

Famous First

The first radio fax transmission of medical records occurred in 1925, when AT&T transmitted stethogram (heartbeat) and electrocardiogram (heart electrical activity) pictures from its New York City office to a physician in Chicago.

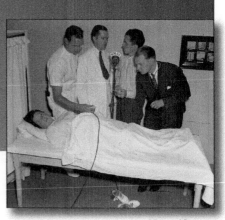

Library of Congress

College/Postsecondary

Prospective medical records administrators should work toward an associate's or bachelor's degree in medical records administration, health information administration, or a related field from a program accredited by the CAAHEP (Commission on Accreditation of Allied Health Education Programs). Coursework in medical terminology, mathematics, and business may also prove useful. Students looking for work experience should apply for administrative internships or part-time clerical employment with local hospitals or medical offices.

Related College Majors
- Business Administration & Management, General
- Medical Records Administration

Adult Job Seekers

Adults seeking employment as medical records administrators should have at least an associate's degree from a medical records administrator training program accredited by the CAAHEP. Some senior medical records administrator jobs require extensive experience and bachelor's degrees. Adult job seekers should join professional associations such as the American Health Information Management Association (AHIMA), as these organizations often provide job-finding workshops and information about available jobs.

Professional Certification and Licensure

Certification and licensure is not legally required for medical records administrators but may be required as a condition of employment, salary increase, or promotion. The American Health Information Management Association, or AHIMA, offers the Registered Health Information Administrator (RHIA) designation to individuals who have completed a medical records administrator training program and passed a national examination.

Additional Requirements

High levels of integrity and professional ethics are required of medical records administrators, as professionals in this role have access to confidential medical records.

Fun Fact

Forty-four percent of hospitals reported having at least a basic electronic health records system in 2012, nearly triple the number that had the basic EHR in 2011.

Source: Robert Wood Johnson Foundation report, Health Information Technology in the United States, 2013

EARNINGS AND ADVANCEMENT

Earnings are based on the individual's level of education and experience. Median annual earnings of medical records administrators were $89,326 in 2012. The lowest ten percent earned less than $54,357, and the highest ten percent earned more than $153,573.

Medical records administrators may receive paid vacations, holidays, and sick days; life and health insurance; and retirement benefits. These are usually paid by the employer

Metropolitan Areas with the Highest Employment Level in this Occupation

Metropolitan area	Employment	Employment per thousand jobs	Hourly mean wage
Chicago-Joliet-Naperville, IL	5,010	1.38	$18.65
Los Angeles-Long Beach-Glendale, CA	4,990	1.29	$19.18
New York-White Plains-Wayne, NY-NJ	4,560	0.88	$21.30
Houston-Sugar Land-Baytown, TX	3,860	1.46	$19.30
Phoenix-Mesa-Glendale, AZ	3,570	2.06	$17.12
Boston-Cambridge-Quincy, MA NECTA Division	3,390	1.98	$20.93
Dallas-Plano-Irving, TX	3,320	1.58	$17.45
Philadelphia, PA	2,670	1.46	$17.27

Source: Bureau of Labor Statistics, 2012

EMPLOYMENT AND OUTLOOK

Medical records administrators held about 182,000 jobs in 2012. Most worked in hospitals, offices of physicians or in nursing and residential care facilities. Employment is expected to grow faster than the average for all occupations through the year 2020, which means employment is projected to increase 20 percent or more. This is due to rapid growth in the number of medical tests, treatments and procedures, and because medical records will be increasingly scrutinized by providers, insurance companies and consumers.

Employment Trend, Projected 2010–20

Health Technologists and Technicians: 26%

Medical Records Administrators: 21%

Total, All Occupations: 14%

Note: "All Occupations" includes all occupations in the U.S. Economy. Source: U.S. Bureau of Labor Statistics, Employment Projections Program

Related Occupations
- Bookkeeper and Accounting Clerk
- Computer & Information Systems Manager
- Computer Operator
- Information Technology Project Manager

Conversation With . . .
CORRINA HALLORAN
Health Information Director/Privacy Officer
20 years

1. What was your individual career path in terms of education, entry-level job, or other significant opportunity?

A community health center saved my son's life. My son didn't have health insurance and I was a cosmetologist. It was a Catch-22. When we went to the community health center, on our first or second visit while I was waiting, I applied for a job as a managed care coordinator. I gave it a shot and they hired me. After that, I started taking classes at night and on weekends. Over time, I earned a certificate in Public Health Management and then, after working there for a decade, a grant opportunity from the Massachusetts League of Community Health Centers allowed me to use my years at the community health center as credits. I was able to directly to graduate school at Suffolk University. I have an undergraduate degree in business administration and a Master's degree in Public Administration (MPA).

2. Are there many job opportunities in your profession? In what specific areas?

Yes, absolutely. You need to learn new skills and know medical terminology and understand various applications. With the Electronic Records Act and the Health Insurance Portability and Accountability Act (HIPAA), jobs aren't going away but there are higher standards. Ten years ago, medical records was an entry level job. Now, it's not; you need to know insurance policies and government applications. In my department, instead of a medical records clerk we now have four roles: a medical records supervisor, two coordinators, and someone who can perform very technical audits.

3. How do you see your profession changing in the next five years?

The federal government mandates patient rights and privacy rights and they are very different. Patient rights are everywhere: you must treat everybody with dignity and respect. These rights are expanding every day and have policies and procedures attached to them that need to be managed as part of medical records work. There are federal and state laws that attach to the protection of patients' confidentiality. Privacy rights go more to HIPAA – for example, you have a right to restrict medical records. Health care providers will want or need a specialist in the area of the Health Insurance Accountability Act (HIPAA) to protect patients as well as employees from any liability that may arise.

4. What role will technology play in those changes, and what skills will be required?

HIPAA and the HITECH Act (the federal Health Information Technology Act) required some health care facilities to transfer paper records to electronic records. A whole lot of new regulations were attached to the transfer of paper to electronic records. Once the process has been implemented successfully, there are a lot of training and policy changes that come into play. Once you have electronic records, you will need an effective IT team to assist in glitches as this progresses.

For example, our system just added a fourth application, so now we have a scanning department to bring in records from the outside; practice management, which schedules appointments; EMR, which is the actual medical record, and QSI, for dental electronic records.

5. Do you have any general advice or additional insights to share with someone interested in your profession?

I have worked in the private sector and in public health. I find working in community health centers and serving the under-served to be far more rewarding than working in the private sector. There are days that are quite challenging but it is a great feeling when you can help someone who just got lost in the health care system, even if it is as easy as explaining a procedure or process to help them navigate their way to the high quality care we all deserve. I still love my job! It feels like I'm giving back to the community what the community gave me.

You do have to have a strong mind, empathy, compassion and attention to detail to really make a difference in this area. The medical records staffs work with a variety of people such as patients, providers and administrators so they do need "people skills." It is not likely you will be working alone!

6. Can you suggest a valuable "try this" for students considering a career in your profession?

Many medical records offices no longer take on volunteers due to the highly sensitive nature of the position.

SELECTED SCHOOLS

Many technical and community colleges offer programs in medical records administration. Interested students are advised to consult with a school guidance counselor or research area postsecondary schools. The Commission on Accreditation for Health Informatics and Information Management Education (see below) provides a search tool for locating training programs in your state.

MORE INFORMATION

American Academy of Professional Coders
2480 South 3850 West, Suite B
Salt Lake City, UT 84120
801-236-2200
www.aapc.com

American Association of Healthcare Administrative Management
11240 Waples Mill Road, Suite 200
Fairfax, VA 22030
703.281.4043
www.aaham.org

American College of Health Care Administrators
1321 Duke Street, Suite 400
Alexandria, VA 22314
202.536.5120
www.achca.org

American Health Information Management Association
233 North Michigan Avenue, Suite 2150
Chicago, IL 60601-5800
312.233.1100
www.ahima.org

Association for Healthcare Documentation
4230 Kiernan Avenue, Suite 170
Modesto, CA 95356
209.527.9620

www.ahdionline.orgAssociation of Records Managers & Administrators
11880 College Boulevard, Suite 450
Overland Park, KS 66210
800.422.2762
www.arma.org

Commission on Accreditation for Health Informatics and Information Management
233 N. Michigan Avenue, 21st Floor
Chicago, IL 60601
312.233.1100
www.cahiim.org

Professional Association of Healthcare Coding Specialists
218 E. Bearss Avenue #354
Tampa, FL 33613
888.708.4707
www.pahcs.org

Simone Isadora Flynn/Editor

Neurologist

OVERVIEW

Sphere of Work

Neurologists are physicians who specialize in treating patients with neurological disorders. Neurology is a branch of medicine concerned with the human nervous system, which includes the brain, spinal cord, and outlying nerves. Neurologists are highly trained and are able to test, diagnose, and treat patients with a wide variety of neurological disorders. They can prescribe medicine based on results of blood work, x-rays, and other tests. Some neurologists, known as neurosurgeons, specialize in performing related surgeries.

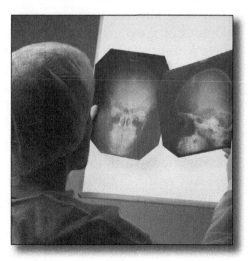

Work Environment

Neurologists work in a variety of inpatient and outpatient medical facilities. Some work out of private offices or clinics, while many others work out of group practices, health-care organizations, or hospitals. At larger institutions, neurologists share patients with other physicians and nurses. These facilities are frequently well lit and sterile. Neurologists may be required to stand for extended periods of time and work long and irregular hours.

Profile

Working Conditions: Work Indoors
Physical Strength: Light Work
Education Needs: Medical Degree
Licensure/Certification: Required
Physical Abilities Not Required: No Heavy Labor
Opportunities For Experience: Military Service
Holland Interest Score*: ISR

* See Appendix A

Occupation Interest

Like many professionals in the medical field, neurologists come from a broad range of medical backgrounds, but the majority of them have made neurology the focus of their education. They need to be very empathetic and understanding, as they must frequently interact with patients who are sick or injured. Neurologists must also be very detail oriented and ensure that their patients are receiving the proper treatment and diagnosis. This also requires excellent problem-solving skills.

A Day in the Life—Duties and Responsibilities

Like other physicians, neurologists are primarily responsible for examining, diagnosing, and treating the injuries or ailments of their patients. While these procedures can lead to similar day-to-day activities, each patient is unique. A neurologist will also record a patient's medical history, prescribe appropriate medications, and perform or order diagnostic tests. These tests may include blood tests, x-rays, and computed axial tomography (CAT) scans. Neurologists also examine patients' reflexes, vision, strength, sensations, and coordination, which are all related to the nervous system. Nurses typically assist in the administration of these tests. Other duties of the profession may include making hospital rounds, filling out paperwork, and teaching, usually at the college level.

Some neurologists specialize in certain areas of the field, such as research, clinical trials, or neurosurgery. All of these specializations require additional training. They can also specialize in diagnosing and treating specific disorders, such as dementia, epilepsy, or insomnia. Neurologists also spend a great amount of time educating their patients and patients' families about appropriate precautions, treatments, and medications. It is common for a neurologist to see a dozen or more patients per day.

Research can also be a part of a neurologist's day. Many neurologists publish articles in medical and scientific journals and present findings of case studies throughout their careers. It is common for neurologists to travel to related conferences to network, present findings, and compare research.

Duties and Responsibilities

- **Examining patients**
- **Diagnosing diseases and conditions of the brain and nervous system**
- **Ordering or performing various tests and procedures**
- **Prescribing and administering medications and treatments**
- **Teaching patients about preventative medicine**
- **Keeping abreast of research in the field**

WORK ENVIRONMENT

Physical Environment

Neurologists work in health facilities alongside others in the profession. These facilities include hospitals, group practices, health-care organizations, clinics, and private practices.

Relevant Skills and Abilities

Analytical Skills
- Analyzing data

Communication Skills
- Speaking and writing effectively
- Listening attentively
- Expressing thoughts and ideas clearly

Interpersonal/Social Skills
- Being able to remain calm under pressure
- Being able to work independently
- Cooperating with others
- Providing support to others
- Working as a member of a team
- Being sensitive to others
- Being patient
- Having good judgment
- Being objective

Organization & Management Skills
- Handling challenging situations
- Making decisions
- Managing people/groups
- Paying attention to and handling details
- Performing duties that may change frequently
- Managing time
- Demonstrating leadership

Planning & Research Skills
- Developing evaluation strategies
- Using logical reasoning
- Identifying problems
- Identifying resources
- Gathering information
- Solving problems

Technical Skills
- Performing scientific, mathematical, and technical work

Other Skills
- Being comfortable working in a medical setting

Human Environment

Neurologists work with a variety of professionals as well as patients. They frequently communicate and collaborate with others in the medical field, including other neurologists, surgeons, and researchers. The nature of their work requires them to make physical contact with and be very close to patients with various ailments throughout the day.

Technological Environment

Neurologists use a broad range of tools, from small instruments to large, sophisticated medical apparatuses. Basic instruments include digital thermometers, eye charts, and stethoscopes. To examine a patient's neurological system further, a neurologist may use functional magnetic resonance imaging (MRI), lumbar punctures, and electrodiagnostic tests. Neurologists must follow safety procedures when operating medical machinery.

EDUCATION, TRAINING, AND ADVANCEMENT

High School/Secondary

A high school diploma is required in order to enroll in the postsecondary courses required of a neurologist. At the high school level, basic and advanced courses in subjects such as biology, chemistry, and mathematics would greatly benefit an individual interested in pursuing a career in the field.

Suggested High School Subjects

- Algebra
- Biology
- Chemistry
- College Preparatory
- English
- Geometry
- Health Science Technology
- Humanities
- Mathematics
- Physics
- Physiology
- Psychology
- Science
- Sociology
- Statistics
- Trigonometry

Famous First

The first brain surgery for mental illness to gain wide acceptance was the prefrontal lobotomy. It was first performed in Europe in the early 1930s, and first performed in the United States in 1936 by Dr. Walter Freeman and Dr. James W. Watts of George Washington University. The procedure entailed severing the connections between the prefrontal cortex (the forwardmost portion of the brain) and the rest of the brain. By the 1950s lobotomy was a fairly common procedure; Freeman himself performed over 3,000 of them. Eventually, however, the scientific basis for the procedure along with the negative effects seen in patients (extreme lack of emotion) led to calls for its termination.

College/Postsecondary

Neurologists typically complete four years of undergraduate schooling followed by four years of medical school. Depending on a neurologist's specialty, further education may be required. Undergraduates planning to continue on to medical school are typically not required to major in a specific subject, but they should excel in courses such as biology, chemistry, and physics. Undergraduates are also encouraged to volunteer at local hospitals or medical facilities. This is an effective way to gain valuable experience and observe experienced professionals.

To enroll in medical school, an individual must submit transcripts and letters of recommendation and pass the Medical College Admission Test (MCAT). Medical schools are very competitive, so undergraduate students should do their best to excel in all aspects of their education. An applicant will typically have to interview with an admissions board, which will also consider extracurricular activities, volunteer work, and various qualities of the applicant's personality.

The first two years of medical school typically combine instruction in classrooms and laboratories. Courses required for neurologists include anatomy, medical ethics, biochemistry, and, since their work involves the human brain, psychiatry. They are also instructed in necessary skills such as how to record a patient's medical history, examine a patient, and diagnose problems.

For the final two years of medical school, students are given hands-on instruction alongside experienced professionals in hospitals or other medical facilities. Students are observed throughout the examination, diagnosis, and treatments of patients. After completing medical school, students then enter an internship or a residency program, which can last three to eight years. These take place in hospitals or other medical facilities.

Related College Majors
- Anatomy & Physiology
- Biochemistry
- Medicine (M.D.)
- Neuroscience
- Osteopathic Medicine
- Pre-Medicine Studies

Adult Job Seekers

Adult job seekers interested in pursuing careers in neurology should take into account the length and cost of medical school as well as the irregular hours required of many medical professionals. Neurologists usually pursue their careers immediately after leaving high school, so if an adult is considering this profession, he or she is encouraged to contact a local medical school and inquire how to begin the process.

Professional Certification and Licensure

All neurologists must be licensed by the states in which they wish to practice medicine. The requirements for this license vary by state but typically involve taking written and practical exams. After receiving the license, a neurologist can test to become a board-certified doctor in neurology. This can be done through the American Board of Medicinal Specialties, which offers a test incorporating both written and oral sections.

Additional Requirements

Neurologists must be able to communicate with
patients and their families compassionately. To
examine and diagnose patients accurately, neurologists
must be very detail oriented and be good problem
solvers. They should also be persistent, as some patients require extra
attention, treatment, and monitoring. Neurologists who own their own
practices should be very organized.

EARNINGS AND ADVANCEMENT

Neurologists have among the highest earnings of any occupation.
Earnings depend on geographic location, whether the neurologist
is salaried or in private practice, number of years in practice,
skill, personality and professional reputation. According to Allied
Physicians, Inc., median annual earnings of neurologists were
$264,090 in 2012.

Neurologists may receive paid vacations, holidays, and sick days;
life and health insurance; and retirement benefits. Self-employed
neurologists must arrange for their own health insurance and
retirement programs. Some employers provide for paid educational
leave.

Metropolitan Areas with the Highest
Employment Level in this Occupation

Metropolitan area	Employment (1)	Employment per thousand jobs	Hourly mean wage
New York-White Plains-Wayne, NY-NJ	26,080	5.06	$73.84
Chicago-Joliet-Naperville, IL	12,140	3.33	$72.56
Los Angeles-Long Beach-Glendale, CA	7,740	2.00	$94.73
Atlanta-Sandy Springs-Marietta, GA	6,210	2.75	$97.02
Nassau-Suffolk, NY	6,110	5.00	$97.38
Bethesda-Rockville-Frederick, MD	5,910	10.56	$78.24
Boston-Cambridge-Quincy, MA	5,750	3.36	$62.33
Washington-Arlington-Alexandria, DC-VA-MD-WV	5,170	2.21	$81.05

(1)Does not include family and general physicians. Source: Bureau of Labor Statistics, 2012

EMPLOYMENT AND OUTLOOK

Neurologists held about 20,000 jobs nationally in 2012. Employment of neurologists is expected to grow faster than the average for all occupations through the year 2020, which means employment is projected to increase 20 percent or more. This is due to the continued growth of the health-care industry. Demand for all physicians will continue to increase as consumers are looking for high levels of care using the latest technologies, tests and therapies.

Employment Trend, Projected 2010–20

Health Diagnosing and Treating Practitioners: 26%

Physicians and Surgeons: 24%

Total, All Occupations: 14%

Note: "All Occupations" includes all occupations in the U.S. Economy. Source: U.S. Bureau of Labor Statistics, Employment Projections Program

Related Occupations
- Cardiologist
- Neuropsychologist
- Pediatrician
- Psychiatrist

Related Military Occupations
- Physician & Surgeon

Conversation With . . .
CATHERINE PHILLIPS
Neurologist, 25 years

1. What was your individual career path in terms of education, entry-level job, or other significant opportunity?

I was a chemistry major at Oberlin College. During the summers, I worked as a nurse's aide in a nursing home. I loved being with the older patients and I enjoyed being part of a team. I also worked in a laboratory in my college and while I enjoyed working hard, I realized that I didn't want to stay up late for test tubes. If I was going to work hard, I wanted to do it with people. After college, I went to the University of California at San Francisco School of Medicine, then I did three years of residency training, then two years of fellowship. I decided to go into neurology when I took a neurology rotation and realized that I really liked it. I did my neurology residency and epilepsy fellowship at the University of Pennsylvania in Philadelphia. When you do neurology, you're solving puzzles. When someone comes in and they're dizzy, you have to think of all the different parts of the brain and the nerves that can contribute to someone being dizzy. I'm an epilepsy specialist. I tried all different things and realized I love this one area.

2. Are there many job opportunities in your profession? In what specific areas?

There's a shortage in the country of neurologists, so yes, there are tremendous opportunities in the field. In particular, there's a shortage of neurosurgeons because there is such a long training period.

3. What do you wish you had known going into this profession?

I wish I had known how many years of training were required. But I'm not sure I would have done anything differently had I known. When you come out, you're in a job where you have excellent job security and a very livable wage. I learned from my parents to always try to do a job where you can try to help other people. My father was a minister and a university professor. I really believe in getting to know people in different fields and talking with them and understanding what they do and what drives them. You can learn so much and you can get an idea of what you might want to do.

4. **How do you see your profession changing in the next five years?**

I think there will be a lot more restrictions, less autonomy, and less freedom in some ways. There will be salary reductions.

Also, everything is becoming much more electronic. We spend a lot of time in front of a computer. The good thing about it is that online learning has made it easier to keep up with our education and to prepare for the recertifying exams that all physicians have to take. Technology has also improved patient care. I can pull up medical notes, X-rays, or MRIs of any patient in our health care system, whereas in the old days, I had to go get the actual films. It's also much easier to look up illnesses with my patients. I can Google things with the patient right there.

5. **What role will technology play in those changes, and what skills will be required?**

You have to be willing to be flexible and open to change, particularly where health care reform is taking us. Doctors have to learn how to be part of a team that consists of many different people: the pharmacist, the nurse, the medical student, the physician.

6. **Do you have any general advice or additional professional insights to share with someone interested in your profession?**

You don't start off being a neurologist. You break it up into pieces. The first thing is to decide whether you're interested in medicine. You can be a physician's assistant or a nurse practitioner working within a neurologist's office. When you practice with your neurologist, you learn. You can go to medical school later. You don't have to go right out of college. Medical schools are actually happier to admit people who have experience under their belt.

7. **Can you suggest a valuable "try this" for students considering a career in your profession?**

I think that getting some experience in the field will help you determine whether you're well suited. In neurology, there is a certain amount of bookishness to the field, so you have to be willing to keep up with new developments. The hardest hurdle to jump is to figure out if you like the health care field enough to spend the years of training, and whether you have the discipline that requires.

SELECTED SCHOOLS

Many medical schools have programs in neurology. Below are listed some of the more prominent institutions in this field.

**Columbia University
School of Medicine**
630 W. 168th Street
New York, NY 10032
212.305.2862
www.cumc.columbia.edu

**Emory University
School of Medicine**
201 Dowman Drive
Atlanta, GA 30322
404.727.6123
www.med.emory.edu

**Icahn School of Medicine at
Mount Sinai**
1428 Madison Avenue
New York, NY 10029
212.241.6500
icahn.mssm.edu

Johns Hopkins University
School of Medicine
733 N. Broadway
Baltimore, MD 21205
410.955.3182
www.hopkinsmedicine.org

**University of California, Los
Angeles**
David Geffen School of Medicine
10833 Le Conte Avenue
Los Angeles, CA 90095
310.825.6774
healthsciences.ucla.edu

**University of California, San
Francisco**
UCSF School of Medicine
513 Parnassus Avenue
San Francisco, CA 94143
415.476.9000
meded.ucsf.edu

University of Pennsylvania
Perelman School of Medicine
3620 Hamilton Walk
Philadelphia, PA 19104
215.662.4000
www.med.upenn.edu

University of Rochester
School of Medicine and Dentistry
601 Elmwood Avenue, Box 601A
Rochester, NY 14642
585.275.8762
www.urmc.rochester.edu

University of Washington
School of Medicine
1959 N.E. Pacific Street
Seattle, WA 98195
206.685.9232
www.uwmedicine.org

Weill Cornell Medical College
445 E. 69th Street, Room 104
New York, NY 10021
212.746.1067
weill.cornell.edu

MORE INFORMATION

American Academy of Neurology
1080 Montreal Avenue
Saint Paul, MN 55116
800.879.1960
www.aan.com

**American Board of Medical
Specialties**
222 North LaSalle Street, Suite 1500
Chicago, IL 60601
312.436.2600
www.abms.org

American Medical Association
515 N. State Street
Chicago, IL 60654
800.621.8335
www.ama-assn.org

**American Neurological
Association**
5841 Cedar Lake Road, Suite 204
Minneapolis, MN 55416
952.545.6284
www.aneuroa.org

**Federation of State Medical
Boards**
400 Fuller Wiser Road, Suite 300
Euless, TX 76039
817.868.4000
www.fsmb.org

Patrick Cooper/Editor

Nurse Practitioner

Snapshot

Career Cluster: Health Science

Interests: Health Care, Medicine, Patient Care

Earnings (Yearly Average): $81,701

Employment & Outlook: Faster Than Average Growth Expected

OVERVIEW

Sphere of Work

Nurse practitioners work in the medical field, providing health care to people from infants to the elderly. Nurse practitioners have completed licensure as registered nurses (RNs) as well graduate-level training and additional certification, which enables them to perform health assessments and other specialized tasks. They are able to provide more autonomous, specialized, and advanced medical care than those with just a registered-nurse degree. There are proposals under consideration that would require nurse practitioners to complete a doctoral degree starting in 2015.

Nurse practitioners conduct physical examinations, manage chronic illnesses, order diagnostic tests, and interpret those tests in order to provide the appropriate medical treatment to patients. Some states require that nurse practitioners perform these duties under the supervision of a physician. The utilization of nurse practitioners is an effective use of staffing resources, as it frees physicians to focus on more serious issues and results in improved medical care for patients.

Work Environment

Nurse practitioners work with other health professionals such as physicians, certified nursing assistants (CNAs), registered nurses (RNs), and a variety of other support personnel. They can work in private physician practices, hospitals, health clinics, schools, health-maintenance organizations (HMOs), nursing homes, and government health-care organizations. Nurse practitioners often work long and irregular hours, and the job requires them to be on their feet for the majority of the workday.

Profile

Working Conditions: Work Indoors
Physical Strength: Light Work
Education Needs: Bachelor's Degree
  Master's Degree
Licensure/Certification: Required
Physical Abilities Not Required: No
  Heavy Labor
Opportunities For Experience:
  Nursing Background, Volunteer Work
Holland Interest Score*: ISA

* See Appendix A

Occupation Interest

Nurse practitioners can specialize in a variety of specific areas, such as family practice, women's health, pediatrics, geriatrics, oncology, psychiatry, and acute care. The goal is to provide each patient with appropriate, individualized care, so nurse practitioners should be perceptive, flexible, patient, and sensitive to changes in their patients' conditions. Nurse practitioners also benefit from strong communication and organizational skills, which help them keep abreast of changes in their fast-paced and high-stakes work environment.

A Day in the Life—Duties and Responsibilities

Nurse practitioners use their advanced education, diagnostic skills, and training to provide an accurate analysis of patients' symptoms and test results. Once they have thoroughly assessed a patient, nurse practitioners prescribe the appropriate treatment for the patient's acute or chronic illnesses. Nurse practitioners meet with a variety of patients on a daily basis, discussing their conditions, symptoms, and treatment options. They also conduct physical examinations and patient interviews to obtain their patients' medical histories in order to provide the appropriate individualized care. This may involve using simple diagnostic tools in the examination room, or it may require the nurse practitioner to order laboratory testing by medical technicians and then interpret the test results.

Nurse practitioners must also educate patients and their families on preventative health-care measures and health-maintenance techniques that will help patients better manage their illness and their recovery. In addition to patient appointments, nurse practitioners regularly communicate with physicians, medical technicians, social workers, RNs, and other health-care and office personnel to coordinate multiple aspects of patient care. Nurse practitioners also operate in an office setting, documenting patient recommendations, diagnoses, and treatment outcomes.

Duties and Responsibilities

- Assessing the health of individual patients
- Checking for problems that need to be referred to physicians or other resources
- Treating acute and chronic illnesses
- Teaching health maintenance to patients and their families
- Consulting and coordinating all phases of a patient's health care
- Taking health histories
- Performing physical examinations
- Requesting and interpreting laboratory studies
- Developing and implementing therapeutic and preventive health-care plans
- Offering counseling
- Keeping abreast of developments in the field

OCCUPATION SPECIALTIES

Adult Nurse Practitioners

Adult Nurse Practitioners treat adolescents and adults, focusing on disease prevention, health promotion, and the management of patients with health problems. Most adult nurse practitioners practice in primary care settings.

Family Nurse Practitioners

Family Nurse Practitioners treat patients ranging from infants to elder adults, focusing on health care in the context of the family unit and the community. Most family nurse practitioners practice in ambulatory care settings such as outpatient clinics.

Gerontology Nurse Practitioners

Gerontology Nurse Practitioners treat elderly adults, including those who are frail or hospitalized. Most gerontology nurse practitioners practice in clinics or in acute- or long-term care facilities.

Pediatric Nurse Practitioners

Pediatric Nurse Practitioners treat newborns, infants, and children, focusing on child health and wellness and prevention/management of common pediatric illnesses and conditions. They practice in variety of primary care settings.

Women's Health Nurse Practitioners

Women's Health Nurse Practitioners provide primary care to women across the life cycle, focusing on conditions unique to women and in the context of interpersonal relationships, the family, and the community. They practice in a variety of care settings.

WORK ENVIRONMENT

Physical Environment

Nurse practitioners work in a variety of diverse environments, including examination rooms, patient homes, and testing and diagnostic rooms. They primarily work in medical offices and hospitals, though they may also work in other environments, such as schools and private homes. Their work with patients may involve contact with human blood and other biohazardous materials, so safety practices must be observed.

Relevant Skills and Abilities

Analytical Skills
- Analyzing data

Communication Skills
- Speaking and writing effectively

Interpersonal/Social Skills
- Cooperating with others
- Providing support to others

Organization & Management Skills
- Making decisions
- Managing people/groups
- Paying attention to and handling details

Technical Skills
- Working with data or numbers
- Working with your hands

Human Environment

Nurse practitioners must have strong interpersonal skills, as they work and interact with physicians, medical assistants, medical technicians, nursing assistants, RNs, licensed practical nurses, and patients and their families. Nurse practitioners may work in a general or family practice, where they will work with patients who are diverse in age and gender. Alternatively, they may focus on a specific medical field, such as pediatrics or orthopedics, which could limit the scope of their patients in terms of gender, age, or medical condition.

Technological Environment

Nurse practitioners work with a variety of medical technologies. They may be responsible for ordering and interpreting laboratory test results and other medical exams, such as x-rays and computed axial tomography (CAT) scans. Nurses also use electrodes and other monitors to track their patients' heart rate, blood pressure, and other vital information. They rely heavily on electronic medical records to track their patients' medical histories, treatment preferences, and other information. Nurses are responsible for regularly updating this information in order to coordinate patient care with other medical professionals.

EDUCATION, TRAINING, AND ADVANCEMENT

High School/Secondary

High school students can prepare for a career as a nurse practitioner by taking courses in biology, chemistry, and other science-related subjects. Classes in computers and communication are also helpful. A student interested in becoming a nurse practitioner can also volunteer at a health-care organization to gain practical experience at an early age.

Suggested High School Subjects
- Applied Biology/Chemistry
- Applied Communication
- Applied Math
- Biology
- Chemistry
- Child Growth & Development
- English
- Foreign Languages
- Health Science Technology
- Nurse Assisting
- Physical Science
- Physiology
- Science

Famous First

The first nurse practitioner was Loretta Ford, who with pediatrician Dr. Henry Silver founded the first nurse practitioner training program at the University of Colorado in 1965. Initially, the program was limited to pediatric nursing but later it expanded into other areas such as family nursing and gerontology.

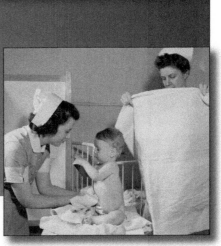

Library of Congress

College/Postsecondary

Students interested in becoming nurse practitioners should enroll in an accredited nursing program to earn a bachelor of science in nursing (BSN) degree. Course work typically includes classes in anatomy, physiology, microbiology, psychology, emergency care, and ethics. Aspiring nurse practitioners should then complete a period of residency in order to obtain their licensure as a registered nurse.

A licensed nurse must complete additional course work and gain clinical experience in order to become a nurse practitioner. This is typically achieved by completing a two-year master of science in nursing (MSN) program and obtaining certification from the American Association of Nurse Practitioners (AANP). At this stage in their education, aspiring nurse practitioners may choose to specialize in a particular area, such as obstetrics and gynecology, psychiatry, or pediatrics. Nurses who have completed their certification as a nurse practitioner will be able to work with more autonomy and increased responsibilities than RNs.

Related College Majors
- Anatomy & Physiology
- Microbiology
- Nursing (R.N.)

Adult Job Seekers

Because extensive knowledge, training, and certification are required to become a nurse practitioner, adult job seekers should be sure that they have the appropriate education and experience. Interested individuals with no experience in the field should consider enrolling in a program to complete an associate of science in nursing (ASN) or BSN degree; these programs typically take three to five years to complete.

Professional Certification and Licensure

Nurse practitioners are required to obtain certification and licensing in their respective states. All nurse practitioners must first obtain their nursing license by passing the National Council Licensure Examination before completing graduate-level training and receiving certification from the AANP.

Additional Requirements

Nurse practitioners must be willing to commit themselves to ongoing professional development and continuing education in order to maintain their certification and to stay abreast of technological and medical advances in this fast-paced field.

EARNINGS AND ADVANCEMENT

Nurses with additional education who become nurse practitioners can expect increases in both salary and responsibility. Administrative or teaching positions are also alternative promotional positions. Nurse practitioners had median annual earnings of $81,701 in 2012.

Nurse practitioners may receive paid vacations, holidays, and sick days; life and health insurance; and retirement benefits. These are usually paid by the employer.

Metropolitan Areas with the Highest
Employment Level in this Occupation

Metropolitan area	Employment	Employment per thousand jobs	Hourly mean wage
New York-White Plains-Wayne, NY-NJ	4,130	0.80	$49.75
Boston-Cambridge-Quincy, MA	2,620	1.53	$51.03
Los Angeles-Long Beach-Glendale, CA	2,370	0.61	$43.03
Atlanta-Sandy Springs-Marietta, GA	1,680	0.74	$40.04
Washington-Arlington-Alexandria, DC-VA-MD-WV	1,630	0.69	$37.88
Nassau-Suffolk, NY	1,540	1.26	$54.62
St. Louis, MO-IL	1,470	1.15	$38.31
Minneapolis-St. Paul-Bloomington, MN-WI	1,400	0.80	$45.75

Source: Bureau of Labor Statistics, 2012

EMPLOYMENT AND OUTLOOK

Nurse practitioners held about 106,000 jobs nationally in 2012. Employment is expected to grow faster than the average for all occupations through the year 2020, which means employment is projected to increase 25 percent or more. This is primarily due to technological advances in patient care, which permit a greater number of medical problems to be treated, and increasing emphasis on preventive care. In addition, the number of elderly people, who are more likely to need medical care, is projected to grow very rapidly. This particular field is growing rapidly because nurse practitioners provide some care previously offered only by physicians and in most states have the ability to prescribe medications.

Employment Trend, Projected 2010–20

Health Diagnosing and Treating Practitioners: 26%

Registered Nurses: 26%

Total, All Occupations: 14%

Note: "All Occupations" includes all occupations in the U.S. Economy. Source: U.S. Bureau of Labor Statistics, Employment Projections Program

Related Occupations
- Licensed Practical Nurse (LPN)
- Registered Nurse (RN)

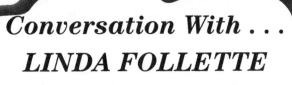

Conversation With . . . *LINDA FOLLETTE*

Registered Nurse, 37 years

Women's Health Nurse Practitioner, 6 years

1. What was your individual career path in terms of education, entry-level job, or other significant opportunity?

I am that person who always knew I wanted to be a nurse. I was a "candy striper" starting at age 15. I was lucky enough to be able to attend a four-year school and earned my Bachelor of Science in Nursing (BSN).

When I graduated, I started working at the same local hospital where I had volunteered. The first four years I worked in orthopedics, then a friend talked me into transferring to the maternity department. I was very hesitant and thought it would be boring. I was wrong! Over the next 10 years, I worked in maternity, labor and delivery, and nursery, and became a certified childbirth educator.

I decided that wasn't enough for me and accepted a job on a high-risk antepartum unit at a very busy medical center. Over the next 14 years, I was in charge of a growing and thriving unit. We opened a unit for obstetrical triage that served about 200 to 250 patients a month. Eventually I was accepted into the Masters in Nursing Women's Health Nurse Practitioner program at Stony Brook University in New York, and worked full-time and went to school part-time. I was lucky enough to have almost all my tuition reimbursed. I interviewed with the doctor I work for now and she accepted me. She took a chance on a new graduate. It is challenging and I learn something new every day.

Throughout my career, I have done administration, education, and direct patient care. I always came back to the patients. It was where I was the happiest and felt that I was at my best.

2. Are there many job opportunities in your profession? In what specific areas?

The nurse practitioner field is exploding. NPs, within their scope of practice, are qualified to diagnose medical problems, order treatments, prescribe medications, and make referrals. They can serve as a patient's primary care provider and see patients of all ages, depending on their specialty. NPs can specialize in all areas of medicine, such as family, pediatrics, women's health, cardiology, dermatology, pain management, orthopedics, acute care and rehabilitations services—to name a few.

The core philosophy is individualized care that focuses on patients' conditions as well as the effects of illness on the life of the patient and his/her family. NPs make prevention, wellness, and patient education their priority. NPs tend to focus more on holistic care: mind, body and soul, and spend time counseling and educating patients and their families.

NPs may conduct research or teach, and often are active in patient advocacy services and the development of health care policy at the local, state, and national levels. They can own and manage their practices.

3. What do you wish you had known going into this profession?

When you are taking care of patients day after day, they take a small piece of you. It is a tough lesson to learn to be compassionate and empathize with them and not take it home with you.

4. How do you see your profession changing in the next five years?

Our role is expanding as more people realize how economical it is to employ us. Patients feel that we have more time and are willing to listen more than our physician counterparts.

Our education requirements are changing as well. Currently the process begins with a Bachelor of Science degree, preferably in nursing. There are programs that allow other BS graduates entrance into the Master of Science degree in nursing. It is a two-to-four-year program that involves advanced coursework and clinical rotations. There is currently an initiative to require a Doctor of Nursing Practice degree for nurse practitioners. This will be an additional one to three years of advanced coursework and will include a project/dissertation and practicum.

5. What role will technology play in those changes, and what skills will be required?

The EMR, or electronic medical record, is here. Hospital systems, emergent care settings, and medical offices are slowly converting to the EMR. Any person who participates in the healthcare field, either as a provider or as a patient, needs to know how to access medical records.

6. Do you have any general advice or additional professional insights to share with someone interested in your profession?

You have to love it. Nursing is a wonderful, challenging, rewarding, frustrating field. The highs are incredibly high and the lows can be heartbreaking.

7. Can you suggest a valuable "try this" for students considering a career in your profession?

I recommend getting into a hospital setting and volunteering. Working with people is an excellent way to know if this field is for you. It helps to know if you have a "strong stomach."

SELECTED SCHOOLS

A number of nursing schools offer programs for students interested in becoming nurse practitioners. Below are listed some of the more prominent institutions in this field.

Johns Hopkins University
School of Nursing
525 N. Wolfe Street
Baltimore, MD 21205
410.955.4766
nursing.jhu.edu

Oregon Health and Science University
School of Nursing
3455 S.W. U.S. Veterans Hospital Road
Portland, OR 97239
503.494.7725
www.ohsu.edu/xd/education/schools/school-of-nursing/

Rush University
School of Nursing
600 S. Paulina Street, Suite 1080
Chicago, IL 60612
312.942.7117
www.rushu.rush.edu

University of California, San Francisco
School of Nursing
2 Koret Way
UCSF Box 0602
San Francisco, CA 94143
415.476.1435
nursing.ucsf.edu

University of Michigan, Ann Arbor
School of Nursing
400 N. Ingalls
Ann Arbor, MI 48109
734.763.5985
nursing.umich.edu

University of North Carolina, Chapel Hill
School of Nursing
Carrington Hall, CB#7640
Chapel Hill, NC 27599
919.966.4260
nursing.unc.edu

University of Pennsylvania
School of Nursing
418 Curie Boulevard
Philadelphia, PA 19104
215.898.8281
www.nursing.upenn.edu

University of Pittsburgh
School of Nursing
3500 Victoria Street
Pittsburgh, PA 15261
412.624.4586
www.nursing.pitt.edu

University of Washington
School of Nursing
1959 N.E. Pacific Street
Box 357260
Seattle, WA 98195
206.543.8736
nursing.uw.edu

Yale University
School of Nursing
P.O. Box 27399
West Haven, CT 06516
203.785.2389
nursing.yale.edu

MORE INFORMATION

American Association of Colleges of Nursing
1 Dupont Circle NW, Suite 530
Washington, DC 20036
202.463.6930
www.aacn.nche.edu

American Association of Nurse Practitioners
P.O. Box 12846
Austin, TX 78711
512.442.4262
www.aanp.org

American College of Nurse Practitioners
10024 S.E. 240th Street, Suite 102
Kent, WA 98031
253.852.9042
www.nurse.org

American Health Care Association
1201 L Street, NW
Washington, DC 20005
202.842.4444
www.ahcancal.org

American Nurses Association
8515 Georgia Avenue, Suite 400
Silver Spring, MD 20910
800.274.4262
nursingworld.org

National Association of Pediatric Nurse Practitioners
5 Hanover Square, Suite 1401
New York, NY 10004
917.746.8300
www.napnap.org

National League for Nursing
61 Broadway, 33rd Floor
New York, NY 10006
212.363.5555
www.nln.org

National Student Nurses Association
45 Main Street, Suite 606
Brooklyn, NY 11201
718.210.0705
www.nsna.org

Nurse Practitioner Associates for Continuing Education
209 W. Central Street, Suite 228
Natick, MA 01760
508.907.6424
www.npace.org

Chuck Goodwin/Editor

Nursing Aide

Snapshot

Career Cluster: Health Care

Interests: Health, Patient Care, Nursing

Earnings (Yearly Average): $25,451

Employment & Outlook: Faster Than Average Growth Expected

OVERVIEW

Sphere of Work

Nursing aides, also called nursing assistants or patient care assistants, provide basic health services and patient care to patients under the direct supervision of licensed medical professionals. The range of services provided by nursing aides includes preventive care, routine medical care, personal hygiene care, and medical appointment transportation. Nursing aides are generally paid hourly and are employed by hospitals, nursing homes, rehabilitation centers, insurance companies, social service agencies, public health agencies, and individuals.

Work Environment

Nursing aides spend their workdays seeing patients in various settings, including nursing homes, rehabilitation centers, hospitals, clinics, and patients' homes. Nursing aides may work with one patient at a time or care for multiple patients in medical facilities. Given the diverse demands of the health-care profession, nursing aides may need to work days, evenings, nights, weekends, and on-call hours to meet patient or caseload needs. Travel to visit housebound clients may be necessary as well.

Profile

Working Conditions: Work Indoors
Physical Strength: Medium Work
Education Needs: On-The-Job Training
High School Diploma With Technical
Education, Technical/Community
College
Licensure/Certification: Required
Physical Abilities Not Required: No
Strenuous Labor
Opportunities For Experience:
Internship, Volunteer Work, Part-Time
Work,
Holland Interest Score*: SER

* See Appendix A

Occupation Interest

Individuals drawn to the profession of nursing tend to be nurturing, competent, and intelligent people who have the ability to assess situations quickly, demonstrate caring, and solve problems. Those who succeed as nursing aides exhibit traits such as physical stamina, empathy, patience, resourcefulness, responsibility, strong communication skills, time management, and concern for others. Nursing aides should find satisfaction in or be comfortable with spending time with a wide range of people, including the elderly and the terminally ill.

A Day in the Life—Duties and Responsibilities

A nursing aide's specific daily duties and responsibilities are determined by the individual's job specialization. Nursing aides may specialize in pediatric care, elder care, management of chronic illness, psychiatric care, Alzheimer's or dementia care, or hospice (end-of-life) care.

Nursing aides help patients with their personal grooming and hygiene needs, administer prescription medications as needed, and respond to patients' calls for help or assistance. They assist patients with basic mobility tasks, including getting in and out of beds, wheelchairs, and vehicles, and activities such as showering. They may also accompany handicapped, mentally challenged, or elderly patients on medical appointments.

In some facilities, nursing aides may be more involved with patient exams and treatment. Some nursing aides perform routine medical exams, including measuring a patient's pulse, temperature, and respiration rate. Others supervise patients as they perform basic physical therapy exercises.

Depending on the facility's janitorial support, nursing aides may clean patient and exam rooms as well as sterilize and prepare medical materials required for exams or procedures. Those working in patient homes may be responsible for performing basic housecleaning chores, such as laundry and vacuuming.

Communication and teamwork are an important aspect of the nursing aide's job. Nursing aides participate in patient team meetings and provide patient updates to agency supervisors and client families. In addition, all nursing aides are responsible for completing patient charts and required documentation on a daily basis.

Duties and Responsibilities

- Answering signal lights and bells to determine patients' needs
- Measuring and recording patients' food and liquid intake and output
- Draping patients for examinations and treatments
- Setting up equipment
- Assisting with examinations
- Assisting patients in and out of bed
- Moving patients to and from treatment rooms using wheelchairs, wheeled carriages, or assisting them to walk
- Bathing, dressing and undressing patients and aiding them in other hygiene needs

OCCUPATION SPECIALTIES

Central Supply Nurse Aides

Central Supply Nurse Aides clean, sterilize, store, prepare, and issue treatment trays (medication, supplies, and instruments) and other supplies.

Delivery Nurse Aides

Delivery Nurse Aides prepare patients for childbirth and clean delivery rooms.

Nursery Nurse Aides

Nursery Nurse Aides bathe, weigh, dress, and feed newborn babies

Surgery Nurse Aides

Surgery Nurse Aides clean, sterilize, and assemble supplies and instruments used in surgery and maintain the cleanliness and order of operating rooms.

Orderlies

Orderlies may do some of the same tasks as nursing aides, although they do not usually provide healthcare services. They typically transport patients and clean equipment and facilities.

WORK ENVIRONMENT

Physical Environment

The immediate physical environment of nursing aides varies based on their caseload and employer. Nursing aides spend their workdays seeing patients in hospitals, private homes, social service agencies, public health agencies, and residential facilities such as nursing homes and rehabilitation centers.

Facilities where nursing aides work are usually clean and brightly lit. Nursing aides must avoid incurring injuries, illnesses, or exposure to harmful chemicals from performing patient care activities.

Relevant Skills and Abilities

Communication Skills
- Listening to others
- Speaking effectively

Interpersonal/Social Skills
- Being sensitive to others
- Cooperating with others
- Providing support to others
- Working as a member of a team

Organization & Management Skills
- Being prompt
- Following instructions
- Performing duties that may change frequently

Other Skills
- Being comfortable with people who are ill or disabled

Human Environment

Nursing aides work with a wide variety of people. They should be comfortable caring for children, the elderly, the disabled, and those with chronic, terminal, or mental illnesses. They must also communicate with patients' families, colleagues, and physicians.

Patients may be confused, discontented, or even violent at times. Nursing aides should be calm, patient, and emotionally strong to handle these situations effectively.

Technological Environment

Nursing aides use a variety of communication tools to perform their job. Nursing aides must also be comfortable using computers to access client records. In addition, nursing aides care for patients using medical equipment, such as glucose monitors, wheelchair lifters, and blood pressure cuffs.

EDUCATION, TRAINING, AND ADVANCEMENT

High School/Secondary

High school students interested in pursuing a career as a nursing aide should prepare themselves by developing good study habits. High school-level coursework in anatomy, psychology, and biology can provide a strong foundation for work as a nursing aide or for college-level work in the field. Given the diversity of nursing aide duties, interested high school students may benefit from seeking internships or part-time employment that exposes them to the nursing community and people in physical and mental need. High school students may be able to secure employment as a nursing aide directly following graduation. Most medical facilities provide on-the-job training for nursing aides.

Suggested High School Subjects
- Applied Biology/Chemistry
- Applied Communication
- English
- Health Science Technology
- Mathematics
- Medical Assisting
- Nurse Assisting
- Physical Education
- Science

Famous First

The first nurse midwifery service was founded by Mary Breckinridge (1881–1965) in the Appalachian region of Kentucky in 1925. Originally called the Kentucky Committee for Mothers and Babies, it later became the Frontier Nursing Service. The organization built a network of clinics and outposts staffed by nurse midwives who made home visits—on horseback, where necessary.

Library of Congress

College/Postsecondary

Postsecondary students interested in becoming nursing aides should work toward an associate's degree in nursing or a related field, such as psychology or gerontology. Nursing aide training programs provide instruction in beginning patient care, infection control, nutrition, psychology, anatomy, and physiology. Training programs also include a minimum of forty hours of clinical supervision in medical facilities. Postsecondary students can gain work experience and potential advantage in their future job searches by securing internships or part-time employment as nursing aides or patient care assistants.

Related College Majors
- Anatomy & Physiology
- Health Science
- Home Health Aide Training
- Pre-Nursing

Adult Job Seekers

Adults seeking employment as nursing aides should have, at a minimum, a high school diploma or an associate's degree in nursing or patient care. Adult job seekers in the nursing field may benefit from joining professional associations to help with networking and job searching. Professional nursing care associations, such as the National League for Nursing and the National Association of Health Care

Assistants, typically offer career workshops and maintain lists and forums of available jobs.

Professional Certification and Licensure

Nursing aides must complete the Certified Nurse Assistant (CNA) certification prior to beginning work as nursing aides. The CNA certification is earned by passing a state CNA competency exam and completing a state-approved CNA training program. Many community colleges, hospitals, and distance learning programs offer CNA training programs. CNA certification provides increased work opportunities in residential facilities, a higher salary, and greater opportunities for advancement. Voluntary nursing aide certification options include the National League of Nursing (NLN) Nursing Assistant Exam and State Health Department Nursing Aide Training Programs. Certification renewal typically requires continuing education.

Most states require prospective nursing aides to pass a physical examination and background check prior to beginning work. Medical facilities and individual states may have additional examination or certification requirements. Interested individuals should check the requirements of their home state and potential employer.

Additional Requirements

Individuals who find satisfaction, success, and job security as nursing aides will be knowledgeable about the profession's requirements, responsibilities, and opportunities. Nursing aides must have high levels of integrity and ethics, as they interact with vulnerable people and have access to personal information. Membership in nursing and health-care associations is encouraged among all nursing aides as a means of building status in a professional community and networking. Nursing aides need to find satisfaction in the work itself as the compensation offered nursing aides tends to be low and opportunities for professional advancement are few.

EARNINGS AND ADVANCEMENT

Earnings depend on the type and geographic location of the employer and the employee's experience and duties. Median annual earnings of nursing aides were $25,451 in 2012. The lowest ten percent earned less than $18,857, and the highest ten percent earned more than $36,655.

Nursing aides may receive paid vacations, holidays, and sick days; life and health insurance; and retirement benefits. These are usually paid by the employer. In addition, nursing aides may receive free or low cost meals, uniforms and uniform laundry service.

Metropolitan Areas with the Highest Employment Level in this Occupation

Metropolitan area	Employment (1)	Employment per thousand jobs	Hourly mean wage
New York-White Plains-Wayne, NY-NJ	56,810	11.02	$16.01
Chicago-Joliet-Naperville, IL	32,770	9.00	$12.18
Los Angeles-Long Beach-Glendale, CA	31,710	8.19	$13.29
Philadelphia, PA	24,710	13.55	$13.54
St. Louis, MO-IL	18,240	14.30	$11.25
Houston-Sugar Land-Baytown, TX	16,610	6.29	$11.76
Boston-Cambridge-Quincy, MA	16,420	9.59	$14.85
Atlanta-Sandy Springs-Marietta, GA	16,110	7.12	$11.14

(1)Does not include Home Health Aides. Source: Bureau of Labor Statistics, 2012

EMPLOYMENT AND OUTLOOK

There were approximately 1.4 million nursing aides employed nationally in 2012. Employment is expected to grow faster than the average for all occupations through the year 2020, which means employment is projected to increase 20 percent. This is due to increasing demand for health care of a growing and longer-living population. In addition, financial pressures on hospitals to discharge patients as soon as possible should produce more admissions to nursing care facilities. Modern medical technology also will increase the employment of nursing aides because, as the technology saves and extends more lives, it increases the need for long-term care provided by nursing aides.

Employment Trend, Projected 2010–20

Healthcare Support Occupations: 34%

Nursing Aides: 20%

Total, All Occupations: 14%

Note: "All Occupations" includes all occupations in the U.S. Economy. Source: U.S. Bureau of Labor Statistics, Employment Projections Program

Related Occupations
- Emergency Medical Technician
- Home Health Aide
- Licensed Practical Nurse (LPN)
- Medical Assistant
- Social and Human Services Assistant

Conversation With . . .
CAROLINE TRANFORD, CNA
Nursing Aide, 2 years

1. What was your individual career path in terms of education, entry-level job, or other significant opportunity?

To work at most facilities, you need to be in nursing school or otherwise have your Certified Nursing Assistant (CNA) license. I was on track to start nursing school, so I decided to go to the American Red Cross' CNA program.

2. Are there many job opportunities in your profession? In what specific areas?

Yes, there are various job opportunities in my profession. All inpatient facilities require direct patient care. This can vary from a large hospital, rehab facility, or small nursing home.

3. What do you wish you had known going into this profession?

I wish I was more prepared for how physically demanding the job is. This depends on where you work and the types of patients you are responsible for. I work on the traumatic brain injury floor. Most patients are completely dependent and require complete care, which means lifting and transferring these patients.

4. How do you see your profession changing in the next five years?

The Affordable Care Act includes funding for better training of Nursing Assistants and Home Health Aides, with the idea that these jobs can be the first step on a ladder progressing up into a nursing career. So while training may improve and become uniform across the country, the job itself will not change much.

My time as a nursing assistant has prepared me for a career in nursing more than I ever could have imagined. The small aspects of nursing that most people don't think about really end up being the most important. The most valuable skill I will be taking into my professional career is simply being comfortable and confident walking into a patient's room and talking to them. When I started as a Nursing Assistant, that was the most intimidating part of my job and the part I had the most trouble adjusting to.

Now I have worked with such a vast array of patients—with different backgrounds, health problems, and personalities—that I feel I will have a leg up over my peers going into nursing.

Person-to-person interaction is a crucial part of the Nursing Assistant's job, and I don't see that changing anytime soon.

5. What role will technology play in those changes, and what skills will be required?

Technology does not play a huge role in my current job. The hospital where I work has not yet gone digital when it comes to documentation. That will change soon, and nursing assistants will need to have the computer skills to transition from handwritten documentation to digital.

6. Do you have any general advice or additional insights to share with someone interested in your profession?

In order to go into this profession, you truly have to have a passion for it. The hard work and huge responsibilities are not exactly reflected in how much you are paid. Most people couldn't even imagine doing the majority of tasks that Nursing Aides perform on a daily basis when it comes to patient care. Even though we are at the bottom of the totem pole when it comes to education level, pay, and responsibilities, we are still a vital part of the health care team. I believe that we are one of the most important. We spend the most direct time with the patient. The patient's initial impression of the care they are receiving can help start off their rehabilitation experience on a positive note.

7. Can you suggest a valuable "try this" for students considering a career in your profession?

If you're thinking of going into this line of work, talk to an actual Nurse's Aide. Before starting my job, I felt like I had an idea of what it would be like. However, I was surprised by how important we were to every single patient. Empathy and patience are the two most necessary personality traits to be successful and happy in this career. Many times, I will have a patient close to my age, or a patient that reminds me of someone I love, and there is a fine line between caring about that patient and getting emotionally involved. But I also believe that how much I care about my patients and my determination to make their rehabilitation process as positive as possible sets me apart. That being said, working with brain-injured patients also has its more difficult moments, making patience a vital part of one's skill set. Patients are often agitated, restless, and even at times physically aggressive. Patience is key to making patients happy, while still being happy yourself when you go to work every morning.

SELECTED SCHOOLS

Many technical and community colleges offer programs in professional health care or pre-nursing. Interested students are advised to consult with a school guidance counselor or research area postsecondary schools. Also advisable is contacting your state health department and/or local American Red Cross along with hospitals, nursing homes, and residential care facilities to learn first-hand about training opportunities—and CNA certification—in your area.

MORE INFORMATION

National League for Nursing
61 Broadway, 33rd Floor
New York, NY 10006
212.363.5555
www.nln.org

National Association of Health Care Assistants
2709 West 13th Street
Joplin, MO 64801
800.784.6049
www.nahcacares.org

National Network of Career Nursing Assistants
3577 Easton Road
Norton, OH 44203
330.825.0342
cna-network.org

Simone Isadora Flynn/Editor

Pediatrician

Snapshot

Career Cluster: Health Science
Interests: Medicine, Health, Science, Working with Children
Earnings (Yearly Average): $203,677
Employment & Outlook: Faster Than Average Growth Expected

OVERVIEW

Sphere of Work

A pediatrician is a medical doctor who specializes in the health and wellbeing of children. Pediatricians work to prevent, diagnose, and treat infections, diseases, behavioral and developmental problems, and injuries in children. They also attempt to identify and/or prevent infant and child mortality, chronic conditions, and other dysfunctions. They strive to more fully understand the ways in which environmental and genetic factors contribute to illnesses in children. All pediatricians actively work toward defending children against a wide range of health and safety hazards. Lifelong learning is a job requirement, since pediatricians must be knowledgeable about constantly changing research

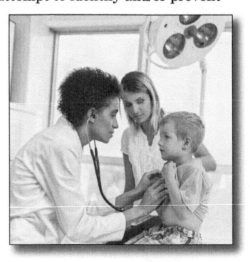

and treatment methods, as well as common diseases and behavioral problems.

Work Environment

Pediatricians usually work in private practice, and experience comfortable, clean, quiet working conditions. Those who operate out of a busy hospital or clinic often work in loud, bright, and hectic environments. Private-practice pediatricians generally maintain a standard forty-hour work week, while hospital pediatricians may work long shifts at night or on weekends, and may be on call. Pediatricians must be in good physical condition, as they may work long hours or stand for most of a work day. They should have excellent vision and hearing and good hand-eye coordination to perform exams and use instruments like stethoscopes.

Profile

Working Conditions: Work Indoors
Physical Strength: Light Work
Education Needs: Medical Degree
Licensure/Certification: Required
Physical Abilities Not Required: No Heavy Labor
Opportunities For Experience: Military Service, Volunteer Work
Holland Interest Score*: ISR

* See Appendix A

Occupation Interest

People interested in pursuing a career in pediatric medicine should possess a desire to help improve the lives of children through medical prevention and treatment, show good judgment, and be decisive as well as responsible and highly motivated. They should be good listeners, and they must be able to remain composed when interacting with anxious parents and family members or upset or unruly children. Pediatricians should be committed to seeking and finding medical solutions that will ultimately benefit the physical and mental development of infants, children, and young adults. They are well compensated for their work, but must undergo years of rigorous training and be willing to work extra hours as needed to resolve urgent medical issues.

A Day in the Life—Duties and Responsibilities

Pediatricians who practice general pediatrics see and evaluate infants, children, and teenagers with various medical conditions and illnesses on a daily basis. Once a pediatrician has thoroughly assessed and diagnosed a child's medical situation, he or she will decide how to proceed with treatment. Pediatricians are responsible for the general management of both serious and minor health problems, as well as acute and chronic illnesses. They conduct examinations and decide whether or not referral to a specialist is needed. They also consult with colleagues such as nurse practitioners, surgeons, and family practitioners to determine appropriate courses of action for the patients they see. They offer parents and patients advice on medical challenges and preventative measures, and they monitor the development of children with specific conditions. They document a patient's medical history, explain exam and lab results, and confer with patients about nutrition, diet, and how to achieve a healthy lifestyle. Sometimes they must prescribe appropriate medications and provide necessary immunizations and vaccinations. Because children are legal minors and require a guardian to make medical decisions, pediatricians must often deal extensively with parents, family members, and guardians of patients.

Duties and Responsibilities

- Examining patients
- Diagnosing diseases and conditions in infants, children, and adolescents
- Ordering or performing various tests and procedures
- Prescribing and administering medications and treatments
- Teaching patients and their parents or guardians about preventative medicine
- Keeping abreast of developments in the field

Some pediatricians choose to specialize in a particular area of children's medicine, such as adolescent medicine, pediatric surgery, pediatric radiology, pediatric cardiology, and others. These doctors assume many of the same responsibilities as general pediatricians, but narrow their focus to concentrate in depth on a specific health issue or category of issues.

WORK ENVIRONMENT

Physical Environment

Pediatricians who work in hospitals or clinics are subject to noisy, stressful, and busy environments. They must quickly react to shifting

Relevant Skills and Abilities

Analytical Skills
- Analyzing information

Communication Skills
- Speaking and writing effectively
- Listening attentively
- Expressing thoughts and ideas clearly

Interpersonal/Social Skills
- Being able to remain calm under pressure
- Being able to work independently
- Cooperating with others
- Providing support to others
- Working as a member of a team
- Being sensitive to others
- Being patient
- Having good judgment
- Being objective
- Being persistent

Organization & Management Skills
- Handling challenging situations
- Making decisions
- Managing people/groups
- Paying attention to and handling details
- Performing duties which change frequently
- Managing time
- Demonstrating leadership

Planning & Research Skills
- Developing evaluation strategies
- Using logical reasoning
- Identifying problems
- Identifying resources
- Gathering information
- Solving problems

Technical Skills
- Performing scientific, mathematical and technical work

Other Skills
- Working in a medical setting
- Working with children

priorities, numerous patients, and emergencies. Pediatricians who have their own practices usually work out of a clean, pleasant, and well-lit office.

Human Environment

Pediatricians interact with children, other physicians, nurses, medical assistants, and administrative staff members on a regular basis. They also interact with patients' family members and legal guardians. They may employ research assistants with whom they work closely to study the prevention of diseases.

Technological Environment

Pediatricians use a wide variety of tools and equipment to assist them in the examination, diagnosis, and treatment of young people. They use stethoscopes, otoscopes (to look into the ears), tongue depressors, blood pressure cuffs, forceps, laryngoscopes (to look down the throat), and other instruments. They must also use telephones, computers, the Internet, and email, as well as specialized medical software.

EDUCATION, TRAINING, AND ADVANCEMENT

High School/Secondary

High school students who wish to become pediatricians can prepare themselves by streamlining their studies to focus on the basic sciences, including organic and inorganic chemistry, biology, anatomy, psychology, and physics. They should also focus on mathematics, English, communications, nutrition, and physical education. Learning a commonly used foreign language, such as Spanish, is useful, as some pediatricians may have bilingual patients or patients who are English-language learners. High school students should make an effort to join extracurricular science clubs or school groups. On their own time, students can visit or volunteer at local hospitals, clinics, and family practices to become familiar with the duties and responsibilities of a pediatrician.

Suggested High School Subjects
- Algebra
- Biology
- Chemistry
- College Preparatory
- English
- Geometry
- Health Science Technology
- Humanities
- Mathematics
- Physics
- Physiology
- Psychology
- Science
- Sociology
- Statistics
- Trigonometry

Famous First

The first popular book on pediatrics was *The Care and Feeding of Children: A Catechism for the Use of Mothers and Children's Nurses* (1894), by Dr. Luther Emmett Holt, head of New York Babies Hospital (pictured). Although the book became a best seller and was widely used for decades, its author was an advocate of the science of eugenics, or improvement of the human race through selective breeding. As such, Holt discouraged reproduction by those deemed to be "unfit, diseased, degenerate, or defective."

Library of Congress

College/Postsecondary

After high school, prospective pediatricians go on to attend a college or university that will eventually award them a bachelor's degree in premedical studies. Candidates must then apply to a medical school. Most medical schools require applicants to have studied specific courses in medical sciences at the undergraduate level. In addition to these curriculum requirements, medical schools usually appreciate a student who is well rounded (meaning he or she has also taken liberal arts courses). Premed students should demonstrate practical experience in the sciences, such as biomedical research and volunteer work. They must also receive a passing score on the Medical College Admission Test (MCAT) in order to be accepted into medical school. Medical schools are highly selective, and the application process is extremely competitive; many students who apply to medical schools are rejected. However, many medical schools have been accepting more applicants because of the anticipated increase in demand for physicians.

Most medical programs focus on classroom and laboratory instruction in the sciences, particularly anatomy, physiology, biochemistry, pathology, and pharmacology. After pediatrics students complete a four-year graduate degree program, they must complete three to eight years of an internship or residency. Pediatric specialists may also complete additional training in their chosen field.

Related College Majors
- Anatomy & Physiology
- Bioscience
- Child Development
- Medicine (M.D.)
- Osteopathic Medicine
- Pre-Medicine Studies

Adult Job Seekers

People become pediatricians only after a total of at least twelve years of combined study and medical training. Once this training is complete and pediatricians obtain licensure, they often seek employment with the hospitals or clinics where they completed their residency or internship. Others may start private medical practices, either independently or with a small group of doctors. New pediatricians usually enter a competitive job market; however, those who choose to practice in medically underserved areas should have no trouble attracting new patients.

Professional Certification and Licensure

Pediatricians must graduate from an accredited medical school, successfully pass a licensing examination, and complete one to seven years of formal graduate medical training in order to become certified. Specific requirements concerning professional certification for pediatricians vary by state.

Additional Requirements

The study of medicine is a strenuous and time-consuming endeavor, and prospective pediatricians will need to be highly motivated, with the physical and emotional stamina necessary to successfully complete many years of education and training. A pediatrician's job can be especially challenging because he or she must work with young patients who cannot always properly communicate their health problems and conditions. Therefore, pediatricians must be extremely patient, friendly, and reassuring, and should enjoy spending time around adolescents, infants, children, and young adults.

EARNINGS AND ADVANCEMENT

Pediatricians have among the highest earnings of any occupation. Earnings depend on geographic location, whether the pediatrician is salaried or in private practice, number of years in practice, skill, personality and professional reputation. Median annual earnings of pediatricians (including specialists) were $203,677 in 2012.

Pediatricians may receive paid vacations, holidays, and sick days; life and health insurance; and retirement benefits. Self-employed pediatricians must arrange for their own health insurance and retirement programs. Some employers provide for paid educational leave.

Metropolitan Areas with the Highest Employment Level in this Occupation

Metropolitan area	Employment (1)	Employment per thousand jobs	Hourly mean wage
New York-White Plains-Wayne, NY-NJ	1,700	0.33	$78.99
Los Angeles-Long Beach-Glendale, CA	1,240	0.32	$90.12
Washington-Arlington-Alexandria, DC-VA-MD-WV	660	0.28	$61.19
Houston-Sugar Land-Baytown, TX	650	0.25	$78.28
Cleveland-Elyria-Mentor, OH	640	0.64	$55.19
Dallas-Plano-Irving, TX	610	0.29	$85.85
Atlanta-Sandy Springs-Marietta, GA	590	0.26	$82.78
Oakland-Fremont-Hayward, CA	460	0.48	$83.04

(1)Does not include specialists such as pediatric cardiologists or surgeons. Source: Bureau of Labor Statistics, 2012

EMPLOYMENT AND OUTLOOK

Pediatricians held about 35,000 jobs nationally in 2012. Employment of pediatricians is expected to grow faster than the average for all occupations through the year 2020, which means employment is expected to increase 20 percent or more. This is due to the continued growth of the health-care industry. Demand for all physicians will continue to increase as consumers are looking for high levels of care using the latest technologies, tests and therapies.

Newly trained pediatricians are likely to experience competition as they seek to begin a practice. Those who are willing to locate in inner cities, rural locations and other areas where doctors are not in oversupply should have the least difficulty

Employment Trend, Projected 2010–20

Health Diagnosing and Treating Practitioners: 26%

Physicians and Surgeons: 24%

Total, All Occupations: 14%

Note: "All Occupations" includes all occupations in the U.S. Economy. Source: U.S. Bureau of Labor Statistics, Employment Projections Program

Related Occupations
- Cardiologist
- Neurologist
- Physician
- Radiologist
- Surgeon

Related Military Occupations
- Physician & Surgeon

Conversation With . . . *DREW TOMENCHOK,*

Retired Pediatrician

1. What was your individual career path in terms of education, entry-level job, or other significant opportunity?

I did four years of undergraduate study at the University of Pennsylvania, where I received a Bachelor of Arts in genetics. I was interested in genetics, in working in a lab and doing research. An advisor said, 'Well, you can practice medicine and still do that,' and encouraged me to go into medicine. I did four years at the University of Medicine and Dentistry of New Jersey, receiving my medical degree. I also did four years of research at this time and received a Master's of Science in genetics. I did post- graduate training for two years at the University of Virginia and one year at Carolinas Medical Center. I have practiced as a hospitalist, in a pediatric emergency room, and in private practice.

2. Are there many job opportunities in your profession? In what specific areas?

There is, and will continue to be, a shortage of pediatricians. It's a lower paying specialty in medicine. All the primary care specialties are lowing paying, and have shortages.

There are opportunities in private practice, in ERs, and as a hospitalist, where pretty much you work in the hospital the whole time and you take care of other people's patients and patients who don't have a doctor. It's a growing field, but it's a rough schedule. I would work 24 hours, then have two days off. Twenty-four-hour shifts every three days can get pretty old after a while.

3. What do you wish you had known going into this profession?

The Golden Age of medicine was probably the 70s and 80s, when doctors did very well and were very well respected. Before, what the doctor said went. Today, the insurance companies have a protocol. That protocol may work for a lot of patients, but it doesn't work for all patients. Even when I know from my experience that it's not going to work, they tell us, 'You have to do it this way first.'

4. What role will technology play in those changes, and what skills will be required?

The practice of pediatrics–as well as many disciplines within medicine–is changing.

Paperwork required by the government and private insurance companies places a large burden on the practicing physician. Treatment decisions frequently are based on the patient's insurance plan, as opposed to what is optimal for the patient. Most physicians get into medicine to help people, but find a large amount of time is spent dealing with the government and insurance companies concerning reimbursement. Financial pressures also force medical doctors to see more patients in a day and spend less time with each patient.

In the future I believe most pediatricians will work in large groups with other MDs as well as nurse practitioners and physician assistants, with the latter seeing an increasing number of patients and the MDs seeing more complex patients and performing a supervisory role.

5. What role will technology play in those changes, and what skills will be required?

In pediatrics, I see it changing the way we interact with patients and creating new ways of communicating with the patient: email and Skype and things like that. But the fundamentals will remain the same.

6. Do you have any general advice or additional professional insights to share with someone interested in your profession?

As a pediatrician, you want to be friendly and outgoing. There are different parents out there who want different kinds of things. Some parents like somebody who is a straight shooter and some people want someone who is going to lie to them, quite frankly–which I never really understood.

I also worked in what was like a nursing home for children, where there were a lot of children who had a lot of disabilities, who were on ventilators and things like that. That was where I was most at home. There aren't many places like that. A lot of people find it very sad, and it is, but I was just able to deal with it. The families are very grateful. Working in an ER was probably the highest stress job. You're challenged constantly.

7. Can you suggest a valuable "try this" for students considering a career in your profession?

I worked in a hospital lab while I was in college. This was great a experience. I learned phlebotomy (blood drawing), and met many medical doctors and observed their practice.

Also think about being a nurse practitioner or physician's assistant. There's less training and less responsibility, so it's less hassle, and you still get to do a lot of the same things as a physician. If, after a few years, you decide you want to go to medical school, that's still an option.

SELECTED SCHOOLS

Many medical schools have programs in pediatrics. Below are listed some of the more prominent institutions in this field.

Baylor College of Medicine
1 Baylor Place
Houston, TX 77030
713.798.4951
www.bcm.edu

Harvard Medical School
25 Shattuck Street
Boston, MA 02115
617.432.1000
hms.harvard.edu

Johns Hopkins University
School of Medicine
733 N. Broadway
Baltimore, MD 21205
410.955.3182
www.hopkinsmedicine.org

Stanford University
School of Medicine
291 Campus Drive
Stanford, CA 94305
650.725.3900
med.stanford.edu

University of California, San Francisco
UCSF School of Medicine
513 Parnassus Avenue
San Francisco, CA 94143
415.476.9000
meded.ucsf.edu

University of Cincinnati College of Medicine
231 Albert Sabin Way
Cincinnati, OH 45229
513.558.4704
www.med.uc.edu

University of Colorado, Denver
School of Medicine
13001 E. 17th Place
Aurora, CO 80045
303.724.8025
www.ucdenver.edu/academics/
colleges/medicalschool

University of Pennsylvania
Perelman School of Medicine
3620 Hamilton Walk
Philadelphia, PA 19104
215.662.4000
www.med.upenn.edu

University of Pittsburgh
School of Medicine
3550 Terrace Street
Pittsburgh, PA 15261
412.648.9891
www.medschool.pitt.edu

University of Washington
School of Medicine
1959 N.E. Pacific Street
Seattle, WA 98195
206.685.9232
www.uwmedicine.org

MORE INFORMATION

American Academy of Pediatrics
141 Northwest Point Boulevard
Elk Grove Village, IL 60007
847.434.4000
www.aap.org

American Board of Medical Specialties
222 N. LaSalle Street, Suite 1500
Chicago, IL 60601
312.436.2600
www.abms.org

American Board of Pediatrics
111 Silver Cedar Court
Chapel Hill, NC 27514
919.929.0461
www.abp.org

American Medical Association
515 N. State Street
Chicago, IL 60654
800.621.8335
www.ama-assn.org

International Pediatrics Association
Saint Louis University
1465 S. Grand Boulevard
St. Louis, MO 63104
314.577.5642
www.ipa-world.org

Pediatric Professional Association
10600 Quivira Road, Suite 210
Overland Park, KS 66215
913.541.3300
www.ppadocs.com

Society for Adolescent Health and Medicine
111 Deer Lake Road, Suite 100
Deerfield, IL 60015
847.753.5226
www.adolescenthealth.org

Pharmacist

Snapshot

Career Cluster: Health Science

Interests: Chemistry, Medications, Patient Care

Earnings (Yearly Average): $118,264

Employment & Outlook: Faster Than Average Growth Expected

OVERVIEW

Sphere of Work

Pharmacists are skilled health-care professionals responsible for the accurate and safe distribution of prescription drugs. They advise patients and physicians and other health practitioners on selecting the right medicines and dosages, and help them to avoid harmful drug interactions. Pharmacists understand medication side effects and make recommendations to customers about how to cope with them if they arise. Many customers also rely on pharmacists to answer questions about new medications or for practical advice on how to handle everyday health problems that do not require prescription medication. Pharmacists may also

work for pharmaceutical companies, helping develop or market new medications.

Work Environment

Pharmacists generally work in retail drugstores or in health-care facilities such as hospitals. In both places, not only do they dispense medications but they also advise patients about diet, exercise, and stress management as it relates to medical products and home health-care supplies. Providing home health care is another option in the field of pharmacy.

Profile

Working Conditions: Work Indoors
Physical Strength: Light Work
Education Needs: Doctoral Degree
Licensure/Certification: Required
Physical Abilities Not Required: No Heavy Labor
Opportunities For Experience: Military Service
Holland Interest Score*: IES

* See Appendix A

Occupation Interest

Individuals interested in becoming pharmacists usually want to help people stay healthy or return to health by recommending or dispensing the right medication and by answering questions about medications and health conditions. Helping customers is the first priority for pharmacists, and they maintain a keen interest in drugs, drug therapy, and how drugs work. The specialized technical knowledge of pharmacists is an important resource for understanding the role of medications and how they work to help patients. Many pharmacists run their own businesses and/or manage a staff of pharmacy technicians.

A Day in the Life—Duties and Responsibilities

During a typical work day, pharmacists assist physicians with the selection, dosages, interactions, and side effects of medications. They monitor patient health and progress as it pertains to drug therapy, and they answer questions about prescription and over-the-counter drugs to help patients manage conditions such as diabetes, high blood pressure, and asthma. Frequently they coordinate with physicians via telephone about a particular patient's needs.

Although physicians prescribe a patient's medications, pharmacists often possess more comprehensive information about other medications a patient is taking for existing and past conditions. Pharmacists specialize in the study of medications and are sometimes able to offer more in-depth information to the patient about his or her prescriptions. In addition, pharmacists must be well-versed in pharmacy law and the many government regulations surrounding the dispensing of medications.

Those pharmacists who own or manage drug stores may supervise personnel and are adept at business, customer relations, and office management. Pharmacy technicians may assist the pharmacist with many of the more routine, basic aspects of the job, freeing the pharmacist to concentrate on more complicated tasks.

Duties and Responsibilities

- Weighing, measuring, and mixing drugs and other medicinal compounds
- Dispensing prepared medications
- Determining the identity, purity, and strength of medications
- Insuring that patients understand the instructions of their prescriptions
- Keeping comprehensive records of all medications dispensed to satisfy requirements of the law
- Advising other health-care professionals and customers about the use of drugs and home health-care supplies

OCCUPATION SPECIALTIES

Hospital Pharmacists

Hospital Pharmacists, or Clinical Pharmacists, work in hospitals, clinics, or nursing homes. They may advise the medical staff on the selection and effects of drugs, perform administrative duties, and work in patient care areas as members of a medical team. They may also engage in the monitoring of drug levels and filling medical orders.

Radiopharmacists

Radiopharmacists prepare and dispense radioactive pharmaceuticals used for patient diagnosis and therapy, applying principles and practices of pharmacy and radiochemistry. They verify that the specified radioactive substance prescribed by a physician will give the desired results in examination and treatment procedures.

Pharmacy Services Directors

Pharmacy Services Directors direct and coordinate the activities and functions of a hospital pharmacy, and plan and implement procedures in the pharmacy according to hospital policy and legal requirements. They also direct pharmacy personnel programs, such as hiring, training, and intern programs.

WORK ENVIRONMENT

Physical Environment

Pharmacists usually wear white lab coats that identify them to customers, work in clean, well-lighted, and well-ventilated areas, and spend most of their workday hours standing. They work forty hours a week or more; sometimes hours may be extended to include nights and holidays. Some pharmacists travel to health-care locations to monitor patients' drug therapies.

Relevant Skills and Abilities

Analytical Skills
- Analyzing data
- Using logical reasoning

Communication Skills
- Expressing thoughts and ideas
- Speaking clearly

Interpersonal/Social Skills
- Being sensitive to others
- Cooperating with others

Organization & Management Skills
- Following instructions
- Paying attention to and handling details

Planning & Research Skills
- Researching information
- Developing solutions

Technical Skills
- Performing scientific, mathematical, and technical work
- Using technology to process information
- Working with machines, tools, or other objects

Human Environment

Pharmacists work with other pharmacists, physicians, and patients, and need to be good listeners and communicators in order to help people.

Technological Environment

Pharmacists work in clean environments where potentially dangerous pharmaceutical products are kept and dispensed, and must wear gloves when manipulating some types of drugs, treatments, and medicines. They also use computers and the Internet for electronic transmission of prescriptions and for other tasks.

EDUCATION, TRAINING, AND ADVANCEMENT

High School/Secondary

In order to be admitted to a four-year pharmacy degree program at a college or university, high school students must have completed at least two years of study in math, chemistry, biology, physics, humanities, and social sciences. High school students must have interest in the sciences and maintain good grades to prepare for postsecondary education.

Suggested High School Subjects
- Algebra
- Applied Math
- Biology
- Bookkeeping
- Chemistry
- College Preparatory
- English
- Geometry
- Humanities
- Merchandising
- Physics
- Science
- Trigonometry

Famous First

The first pharmacists to be regulated by a state were the pharmacists of New York, beginning in 1904. New state regulations enacted then called for pharmacists to receive two years of training and four years of practical experience. Other states soon followed suit. Prior to that time pharmacists—once called apothecaries— were essentially unlicensed; anyone who wanted to could hang out a shingle and dispense lawful drugs. It helped, of course, to have training, an apprenticeship, and a good reputation earned by having satisfied one's customers.

Library of Congress

College/Postsecondary

Pharmacists must earn a doctor of pharmacy degree (PharmD). Admission to a pharmacy program requires at least two years of prior undergraduate coursework. Doctor of pharmacy degree programs usually last four years and must be accredited by the Accreditation Council Pharmacy of Education (ACPE). Doctor of pharmacy coursework usually includes pharmaceutical chemistry, toxicology, pharmacology, ethics, pharmacy administration, and best practices for communicating with patients about health issues and medications. This may be followed by one or more years of postgraduate residency, similar to what medical students undertake.

Related College Majors
- Biochemistry
- Chemistry
- Pharmacy (B. Pharm., Pharm.D.)
- Pre-Pharmacy Studies

Adult Job Seekers

Adult job seekers in the field of pharmacy have generally earned a doctor of pharmacy, but if postsecondary education is not immediately an option, it may be worth joining professional pharmacist associations to develop a better understanding of what the career entails. It may be possible to work closely with a licensed pharmacist as a pharmacy technician, so that supervisors and mentors can help plan a future career through the right educational choices. Doing so is helpful in terms of gaining practical experience, but to advance to a pharmacist position, a doctor of pharmacy degree and a license will be required.

Professional Certification and Licensure

All states require a license to practice pharmacy. After earning a doctor of pharmacy degree, individuals must pass a series of examinations. All states require the North American Pharmacist Licensure Exam (NAPLEX) which tests skills and knowledge. Most states require the Multistate Pharmacy Jurisprudence Exam (MPJE), which tests knowledge of pharmacy law. States that do not require these exams require their own pharmacy law tests. In many places, candidates for licensure must work a certain number of hours in a practice before becoming licensed.

Additional Requirements

Pharmacists need to have a strong background in chemistry, biology, biochemistry, mathematics, and statistics in order to understand medicines, safely monitor and calculate dosages, and study patient profiles. They should demonstrate responsibility, the desire to help others, and attention to detail. Pharmacists must adhere to strict ethical and professional standards, as they have access to powerful narcotics as well as confidential and highly sensitive patient information.

Fun Fact

Nearly 70 percent of Americans are on at least one prescription drug, and more than half take two or more prescriptions. The most common prescribed medications are antibiotics, antidepressants, and painkiller opioids.
Source: Mayo Clinic

EARNINGS AND ADVANCEMENT

Earnings of pharmacists depend on the employee's experience and training and the type of employer. Median annual earnings for pharmacists were $118,264 in 2012. The lowest ten percent earned less than $87,015, and the highest ten percent earned more than $146,937.

Pharmacists usually receive paid vacations, holidays, and sick days; life and health insurance; and retirement benefits. These are usually paid by the employer. Self-employed pharmacists must pay the full cost of any fringe benefit they may have.

Metropolitan Areas with the Highest Employment Level in this Occupation

Metropolitan area	Employment (1)	Employment per thousand jobs	Hourly mean wage
New York-White Plains-Wayne, NY-NJ	11,290	2.19	$55.08
Los Angeles-Long Beach-Glendale, CA	6,250	1.61	$58.61
Chicago-Joliet-Naperville, IL	6,230	1.71	$51.83
Houston-Sugar Land-Baytown, TX	4,740	1.80	$53.18
Philadelphia, PA	4,520	2.48	$52.29
Atlanta-Sandy Springs-Marietta, GA	4,410	1.95	$54.39
Dallas-Plano-Irving, TX	3,860	1.84	$55.06
Phoenix-Mesa-Glendale, AZ	3,570	2.06	$58.99

(1)Does not include specialists such as pediatric cardiologists or surgeons. Source: Bureau of Labor Statistics, 2012

EMPLOYMENT AND OUTLOOK

There were approximately 282,000 pharmacists employed nationally in 2012. About two-thirds worked in retail and community pharmacies, and around another one-fourth worked in hospitals. About one-fourth worked part-time. Employment of pharmacists is expected to grow faster than the average for all occupations through the year 2020, which means employment is projected to increase about 25 percent. This is due to the increased pharmaceutical needs of a larger and older population and greater use of medications. Other factors causing job growth are scientific advances that will make more drug products available, new developments in genome research and medication distribution systems, more sophisticated consumers seeking more information about drugs and coverage of prescription drugs by a greater number of health insurance plans.

Employment Trend, Projected 2010–20

Health Diagnosing and Treating Practitioners: 26%

Pharmacists: 25%

Total, All Occupations: 14%

Note: "All Occupations" includes all occupations in the U.S. Economy. Source: U.S. Bureau of Labor Statistics, Employment Projections Program

Related Occupations
- Chemist
- Medical Scientist

Related Military Occupations
- Pharmacist
- Pharmacy Technician

Conversation With . . .
NANCY E. MONAHAN, RPh
Pharmacist, 29 years

1. What was your individual career path in terms of education, entry-level job, or other significant opportunity?

I graduated from Massachusetts College of Pharmacy and Health Sciences in 1984. While I was a student, I learned of a job at Monahan Pharmacy—which was a small chain of independent drug stores in central Massachusetts—on a bulletin board at school. I took the bus home from Boston every other weekend to work at the store. In late 1986, I started work for CVS, where I worked for 26 years. I started at the Prescription Center Pharmacy (which is a hospital-based retail pharmacy open to anyone) at UMass Memorial in February of 2011.

2. Are there many job opportunities in your profession? In what specific areas?

Many! Don't think of just the pharmacist at the drug store. Hospitals and other health care facilities have staff pharmacists. There are also managerial positions and opportunities with drug companies, the armed services, in pharmacy law, and pharmacy robotic technology. You can specialize in fields like veterinary pharmacy, oncology, nuclear pharmacy, geriatric pharmacy, and diabetes education. Pharmacy can be a launching pad to other careers in health care. One of my classmates from pharmacy school is now a dentist; another went on to become a podiatrist.

3. What do you wish you had known going into this profession?

It is a more physical job than it looks, with long periods of standing. When I started, there were no mandated meal breaks. You ate "on the bench." There are constant work interruptions. You must learn to multitask and have great deal of patience. Also, I was not as aware of the liability issues with pharmacy back then as I am now. That has changed over the years. Pharmacists can be sued for malpractice.

4. How do you see your profession changing in the next five years?

One of the recent changes involves pharmacists becoming certified immunizers, administering flu shots, pneumonia shots and other vaccines. I wouldn't be surprised to see pharmacists eventually get prescribing privileges.

With the advent of accelerated pharmacy schools (editor's note: which can range from three to five years), I believe we have turned out some less empathetic pharmacists as compared to those who are the products of six-year programs. The graduates of the longer programs are immersed more fully in the field.

5. What role will technology play in those changes, and what skills will be required?

Already, most pharmacies are electronically connected to doctors' offices and insurance companies. There are computer systems to warn against drug interactions and potential medical errors. We already have robotics helping us, and some say that robots may eventually replace pharmacists. Robots can dispense pills, but they can't talk to patients about things like side effects.

6. Do you have any general advice or additional professional insights to share with someone interested in your profession?

Pharmacists today are considered more a part of the health care team than they were in previous years. We get more respect from the younger doctors we deal with today and are recognized as an integral part of health care.

Be a pharmacist because you want to help people—not for the money. Salaries have skyrocketed over the past 10 years or so, but if you don't like what you do every day, then it's not worth it.

Patients seem to rely on pharmacists to be more of a liaison with their doctors than they are. In that way, patients have become less responsible for their own health.

SELECTED SCHOOLS

A number of colleges, universities, and professional schools offer programs in pharmacy. Below are listed some of the more prominent institutions in this field.

Ohio State University
College of Pharmacy
500 W. 12th Avenue
Columbus, OH 43210
614.292.2266
www.pharmacy.ohio-state.edu

Purdue University
College of Pharmacy
575 Stadium Mall Drive
West Lafayette, IN 47907
765.494.1361
www.pharmacy.purdue.edu

University of Arizona
College of Pharmacy
1295 N. Martin
PO Box 201202
Tucson, AZ 85721
520.626.1427
www.pharmacy.arizona.edu

University of California, San Francisco
School of Pharmacy
513 Parnassus Avenue
San Francisco, CA 94143
415.476.2732
www.pharmacy.ucsf.edu

University of Kentucky
College of Pharmacy
789 S. Limestone
Lexington, KY 40536
859.323.2755
www.pharmacy.mc.uky.edu

University of Michigan, Ann Arbor
College of Pharmacy
428 Church Street
Ann Arbor, MI 48109
734.764.7312
www.pharmacy.umich.edu

University of Minnesota
College of Pharmacy
308 Harvard Street SE
Minneapolis, MN 55455
612.624.1900
www.pharmacy.umn.edu

University of North Carolina, Chapel Hill
Eshelman School of Pharmacy
301 Pharmacy Lane
CB#7355
Chapel Hill, NC 27599
919.966.9429
www.pharmacy.unc.edu

University of Texas, Austin
College of Pharmacy
2409 University Avenue
Austin, TX 78712
512.471.1737
www.utexas.edu/pharmacy

University of Wisconsin, Madison
School of Pharmacy
777 Highland Avenue
Madison, WI 53705
608.262.6234
www.pharmacy.wisc.edu

MORE INFORMATION

Academy of Managed Care Pharmacy
100 N. Pitt Street, Suite 400
Alexandria, VA 22314
800.827.2627
www.amcp.org

American Association of Colleges of Pharmacy
1727 King Street
Alexandria, VA 22314
703.739.2330
www.aacp.org

American Pharmacists Association
Career Information
2215 Constitution Avenue, NW
Washington, DC 20037-2985
202.628.4410
www.aphanet.org

American Society of Health-System Pharmacists
7272 Wisconsin Avenue
Bethesda, MD 20814
866.279.0681
www.ashp.org

National Association of Boards of Pharmacy
1600 Freemanville Drive
Mount Prospect, IL 60056
847.391.4406
www.napb.net

National Association of Chain Drug Stores
413 N. Lee Street
Alexandria, VA 22313
703.549.3001
www.nacds.org

National Community Pharmacists Association
100 Daingerfield Road
Alexandria, VA 22314
703.683.8200
www.ncpanet.org

Susan Williams/Editor

Physical Therapist

Snapshot

Career Cluster: Health Care, Health and Wellness

Interests: Anatomy and Physiology, Sports Medicine, Physical Education

Earnings (Yearly Average): $80,889

Employment & Outlook: Faster Than Average Growth Expected

OVERVIEW

Sphere of Work

Physical therapists (PTs) provide therapeutic services to patients who have temporary or chronic physical conditions or illnesses that limit physical movement and mobility, thereby negatively affecting patients' life and work. When working with patients, a physical therapist may use techniques such as therapeutic exercise, manual therapy techniques, assistive devices, adaptive devices, hydrotherapy, and electrotherapy. Physical therapists develop patient treatment plans designed to help maintain or recover a patient's physical mobility, lessen pain, increase productivity and independence, and improve quality of life.

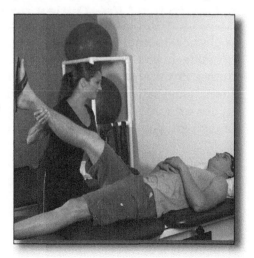

Work Environment

Physical therapists work in rehabilitation facilities, hospitals, nursing homes, physical therapy clinics, and schools. In medical environments, physical therapists work with a team of medical and social service professionals to increase a patient's physical abilities and overall independence. In school settings, physical therapists partner with educational professionals, such as teachers and special education coordinators, to address a student's physical issues. Physical therapists generally work a standard forty-hour workweek, and scheduled appointments are the norm.

Profile

Working Conditions: Work Indoors
Physical Strength: Light Work
Education Needs: Doctoral Degree
Licensure/Certification: Required
Physical Abilities Not Required: No Heavy Labor
Opportunities For Experience: Military Service
Holland Interest Score*: IES

* See Appendix A

Occupation Interest

Individuals attracted to the field of physical therapy tend to be physically strong people who enjoy hands-on work and close interaction with people from diverse backgrounds. Those who excel as physical therapists exhibit traits such as physical stamina, problem solving, empathy, patience, and caring. Physical therapists should enjoy learning, stay knowledgeable about changes in therapeutic techniques, and expect to work as part of a team to effectively address patient needs.

A Day in the Life—Duties and Responsibilities

A physical therapist's daily duties and responsibilities include full days of hands-on patient interaction and treatment, as well as administrative duties. Physical therapists' patients include those experiencing physical limitations and effects from neck and spinal cord injuries, traumatic brain injury, arthritis, burns, cerebral palsy, muscular dystrophy, strokes, limb or digit amputation, or work- or sports-related injuries.

As medical or therapeutic professionals, physical therapists interact with patients or clients on a daily basis and strive to understand the particular challenges faced by each individual. Treatment typically includes a blend of physical techniques and emotional encouragement, since the patient may be in the process of adjusting to a major life change. Some of a physical therapist's daily responsibilities include conducting patient assessments, developing patient treatment plans, and providing physical treatment to patients with severe physical limitations. Physical therapists frequently advise patients on the use of adaptive equipment, such as wheelchairs and orthopedic aids. Some provide early intervention services to young children experiencing physical delays and limitations. Others may offer consultation on or participate in building customized adaptive equipment for patients with special needs not met by existing options. Physical therapists also instruct individuals and groups on physical exercises to prevent injury, lead fitness and health classes and workshops, and counsel patients on physical adaptations that can help the patient to continue to work at his or her chosen occupation. They may also supervise the activities of physical therapy assistants and aides.

During the course of treatment, a physical therapist will consult with a team of physicians, educators, social workers, mental health professionals, occupational therapists, speech therapists, and other medical professionals to help ensure that each patient receives comprehensive care.

A physical therapist's administrative responsibilities include documenting treatment sessions and ongoing patient evaluation. Physical therapists must draft treatment plans, record notes following patient treatment sessions, provide written updates to the other members of a patient's treatment team, and provide insurance companies with patient records and progress notes as required. Independent physical therapists who do not work as part of a school or medical clinic may also be responsible for scheduling appointments and for submitting bills to insurance companies or patients.

Duties and Responsibilities

- Evaluating the physician's referral and the patient's medical records to determine the treatment required
- Performing tests, measurements, and evaluations such as range-of-motion and manual-muscle tests, gait and functional analyses, and body-parts measurements
- Administering manual therapeutic exercises to improve or maintain muscle function
- Administering treatments involving the application of such agents as light, heat, water, and ice massage techniques
- Recording patients' treatments, responses, and progress

OCCUPATION SPECIALTIES

Physical Therapist Assistants

Physical Therapist Assistants help physical therapists provide care to patients. Under the direction and supervision of physical therapists, they give therapy through exercise; therapeutic methods, such as electrical stimulation, mechanical traction, and ultrasound; massage; and gait and balance training. Physical therapist assistants record patients' responses to treatment and report the results of each treatment to the physical therapist.

Physical Therapist Aides

Physical Therapist Aides help make therapy sessions productive, under the direct supervision of a physical therapist or physical therapist assistant. They usually are responsible for keeping the treatment area clean and organized and for preparing for each patient's therapy. They also help patients who need assistance moving to or from a treatment area.

Directors of Physical Therapy

Directors of Physical Therapy plan, direct, and coordinate physical therapy programs and make sure the program complies with state requirements.

WORK ENVIRONMENT

Physical Environment

Physical therapists work in rehabilitation facilities, hospitals, nursing homes, therapy clinics, and schools. Therapeutic office settings used by physical therapists may be shared with other therapeutic professionals, such as occupational, recreational, or speech and language therapists.

Human Environment

Physical therapists work with patients who use physical therapy to improve their strength and mobility, as well as their independence and quality of life. This may include people experiencing balance and strength issues caused by cerebral palsy, spinal cord injuries, or muscular dystrophy; stroke victims experiencing coordination problems or paralysis; and children or adults suffering the physical effects of injuries, abuse, or accidents. Physical therapists usually work as part of a patient treatment team that includes patient families, social workers, teachers, doctors, and additional therapists.

Relevant Skills and Abilities

Communication Skills
- Expressing thoughts and ideas
- Speaking and writing effectively

Interpersonal/Social Skills
- Being patient
- Being sensitive to others
- Cooperating with others
- Working as a member of a team

Organization & Management Skills
- Coordinating tasks
- Managing people/groups
- Paying attention to and handling details
- Performing duties that may change frequently

Planning & Research Skills
- Developing evaluation strategies

Technical Skills
- Performing technical work
- Working with your hands

Technological Environment

Physical therapists use a wide variety of technology in their work. Computers and Internet communication tools are widely used in physical therapy work and practice. Specialized therapies, such as electrotherapy, hydrotherapy, and ultrasound therapy, require technical equipment and training. In addition, physical therapists must learn how to use and teach the use of adaptive devices, such as wheelchairs and orthopedic aids.

EDUCATION, TRAINING, AND ADVANCEMENT

High School/Secondary

High school students interested in pursuing the profession of physical therapy in the future should develop good study habits. High school courses in biology, psychology, anatomy, sociology, and mathematics will prepare students for college- and graduate-level studies. Students interested in the physical therapy field will benefit from seeking internships or part-time work with physical therapists or with people who have physical issues that affect their range of movement or daily life.

Suggested High School Subjects

- Algebra
- Applied Communication
- Applied Math
- Applied Physics
- Biology
- Chemistry
- College Preparatory
- English
- Geometry
- Health Science Technology
- Humanities
- Physical Education
- Physics
- Physiology
- Psychology
- Science
- Trigonometry

Famous First

The first physical therapy school was formed at Walter Reed Army Hospital in Washington, D.C., following the United States' entry into World War I. In 1921 the first research journal in physical therapy, *The PT Review*, was published, and in that same year the first professional organization for physical therapists, the American Physical Therapy Association, was established.

Library of Congress

College/Postsecondary

Postsecondary students interested in becoming physical therapists should complete coursework in physical therapy, if possible, as well as courses on occupational therapy, special education, biology, psychology, anatomy and physiology, sociology, and mathematics. Prior to graduation, college students interested in joining the physical therapy profession should apply to graduate-level physical therapy programs or secure physical therapy-related employment. Those who choose to pursue a master's degree tend to have better prospects for employment and advancement in the field. Membership in the American Physical Therapy Association may help provide postsecondary students with networking opportunities and connections.

Related College Majors
- Adapted Physical Education/Therapeutic Recreation
- Anatomy and Physiology
- Exercise Science/Physiology/Movement Studies
- Health & Physical Education, General
- Physical Therapy
- Sports Medicine & Athletic Training

Adult Job Seekers

Adult job seekers in the physical therapy field should have a master's degree in physical therapy from a college or university accredited by the Commission on Accreditation in Physical Therapy Education. They must also earn the necessary professional licensure. Physical therapists seeking employment may benefit from the networking opportunities, job workshops, and job lists offered by professional physical therapy associations, such as the American Physical Therapy Association and American Board of Physical Therapy Specialties. Advancement in the physical therapy field often depends on the individual's education and specialty certification.

Professional Certification and Licensure

Physical therapists are required to have earned a professional physical therapy (PT) license prior to beginning their professional practice. Upon completion of an accredited master's or doctoral program in physical therapy, candidates take the National Physical Therapy Examination (NPTE) administered by the Federation of State Boards of Physical Therapy. In addition to passing the NPTE, physical therapists are required to register with their state health board, pass a state exam, and engage in continuing education as a condition of their PT license.

Physical therapists may choose to pursue additional, specialized physical therapy certification from the American Board of Physical Therapy Specialties. Certification is available for the following specialties: cardiovascular and pulmonary, clinical electrophysiology, geriatrics, neurology, pediatrics, sports, and women's health.

Additional Requirements

Individuals who find satisfaction, success, and job security as physical therapists will be knowledgeable about the profession's requirements, responsibilities, and opportunities. Successful physical therapists engage in ongoing professional development related to changes in therapeutic techniques, ethical standards, and new technology. Because physical therapists work with vulnerable people and share confidential patient information with other medical professionals, adherence to strict professional and ethical standards is required.

Both entry-level and senior-level physical therapists may find it beneficial to join professional associations as a means of building professional community and networking.

Fun Fact

Brief bouts of dizziness with changes in position or movement of the head – positional vertigo – the most common cause of dizziness, is caused by dysfunction of the inner ear, and can successfully be treated in as little as one session with a physical therapist.

Source: http://www.athletico.com/2011/09/27/the-top-10-things-you-did-not-know-about-physical-therapy

EARNINGS AND ADVANCEMENT

Earnings of physical therapists depend on the type and size of the employer and the physical therapist's length of employment and level of responsibility. Physical therapists in private practice tend to earn more than salaried workers. Salaries are usually higher in rural areas as employers try to attract physical therapists to where there are severe shortages.

Median annual earnings of physical therapists were $80,889 in 2012. The lowest ten percent earned less than $56,837, and the highest ten percent earned more than $114,395.

Physical therapists may receive paid vacations, holidays, and sick days; life and health insurance; and retirement benefits. These are usually paid by the employer. Some employers also provide for paid educational leave.

Metropolitan Areas with the Highest
Employment Level in this Occupation

Metropolitan area	Employment (1)	Employment per thousand jobs	Hourly mean wage
New York-White Plains-Wayne, NY-NJ	7,610	1.48	$40.46
Chicago-Joliet-Naperville, IL	6,740	1.85	$37.33
Los Angeles-Long Beach-Glendale, CA	4,880	1.26	$42.51
Boston-Cambridge-Quincy, MA	3,430	2.00	$37.08
Philadelphia, PA	3,000	1.64	$36.78
Phoenix-Mesa-Glendale, AZ	2,960	1.71	$39.40
Dallas-Plano-Irving, TX	2,830	1.35	$45.41
Nassau-Suffolk, NY	2,570	2.10	$41.68

(1)Does not include self-employed. Source: Bureau of Labor Statistics, 2012

EMPLOYMENT AND OUTLOOK

There were approximately 192,000 physical therapists employed nationally in 2012. Another 120,000 worked as physical therapist assistants or aides. Employment of physical therapists is expected to grow much faster than the average for all occupations through the year 2020, which means employment is projected to increase 35 percent or more. As new medical technologies allow more people to survive accidents and illnesses, but who then require physical therapy, employment opportunities will increase. The rapidly growing elderly population will also contribute to this demand. A growing number of employers are using physical therapists to evaluate work sites, develop exercise programs and teach safe work habits to employees in the hope of reducing injuries.

Employment Trend, Projected 2010–20

Physical Therapists: 39%

Health Diagnosing and Treating Practitioners: 26%

Total, All Occupations: 14%

Note: "All Occupations" includes all occupations in the U.S. Economy. Source: U.S. Bureau of Labor Statistics, Employment Projections Program

Related Occupations
- Activities Therapist
- Athletic Trainer
- Chiropractor
- Occupational Therapist
- Recreational Therapist
- Respiratory Therapist

Related Military Occupations
- Physical & Occupational Therapist

Conversation With . . .
ASHLEY BURNS
Physical Therapist/Certified Orthopedic
Manual Therapist, 5 years

1. **What was your individual career path in terms of education, entry-level job, or other significant opportunity?**

   I completed an entry-level 5½-year Master's in Science physical therapy program at Springfield College. The first two years were spent completing prerequisites; the last three years were the graduate school portion of the program. After graduating with a Master's in Physical Therapy (PT) in 2008, I passed my boards, and began working at Brigham & Women's Hospital. After working for two years, I entered the transitional Doctorate in Physical Therapy program at Massachusetts General's Institute of Health Professions, while still working full-time. Before and after my Doctor in Physical Therapy (DPT), I completed continuing education classes through Maitland Australian Physiotherapy Seminars (MAPS) and passed a two-day exam with three parts: practical, short-answer, and multiple-choice. With this completion, I earned the degree of Certified Orthopedic Manual Therapist. While working at the Brigham, I have had many educational opportunities, including teaching courses, lecturing at outside athletic programs, attending rounds/clinical education series, and publishing articles.

2. **Are there many job opportunities in your profession? In what specific areas?**

   There are many job opportunities in the physical therapy profession, which can be broken down into four different areas: outpatient, inpatient, rehabilitation, and home-care. Within these areas, there are different categories, such as orthopedics, geriatric, neurological, oncology, and cardiopulmonary. There are job openings in all of these areas, but the biggest area in terms of available jobs currently is home care. This is due to the growing geriatric population, which is a result of people living longer, people living healthier lifestyles, and the effects of ever-changing and improving health care.

3. **What do you wish you had known going into this profession?**

   I can honestly say that my education prepared me well for the job, and there weren't a lot of big surprises.

4. How do you see your profession changing in the next five years?

I think in the next five years, patients will be able to come directly to physical therapy without being required to have a referral from their primary care physician to satisfy health insurance requirements. Physical therapists will be more respected for having a doctorate in their field, and will have the ability to screen patients for red flags and determine whether they are appropriate for PT or require further diagnostic screening by a different specialist. (By 2015, all degree programs for physical therapists will be doctorate programs.) In addition, I think physical therapists will eventually be allowed to directly order imaging and to refer patients to other specialists as appropriate.

5. What role will technology play in those changes, and what skills will be required?

Technology is already changing the manner in which health care professionals interact with their patients, charge for billing, and record visits. We have to walk a fine line when seeing patients–typing in all the required information while also listening to a patient, making eye contact, and thinking critically: what is this patient's diagnosis? Physical therapists will need to be computer savvy to ensure all information is recorded accurately.

6. Do you have any general advice or additional professional insights to share with someone interested in your profession?

Physical therapy school is not easy. It is very hard work. You will go to class for eight hours some days, like a job. But it is worth all your time and effort. You will change people's lives by teaching them how to walk again, how to work without pain, return to their sport, or live more comfortably. The rewards of this profession are difficult to put into words. You will have patients who change your own perspective on life, who give you a greater insight into life and give your life meaning. You may think that you are changing their lives, but they effect change in yours. Each day is different from the next, full of variety and challenges. I am constantly learning. As more research is being produced, my evidence-based practice changes. You are keeping your mind active at all times. I honestly wouldn't want to be in any other profession.

7. Can you suggest a valuable "try this" for students considering a career in your profession?

I would suggest observing a physical therapist in a clinic for a few weeks. This will give you a better idea of what physical therapy is all about.

SELECTED SCHOOLS

Many colleges, universities, and professional schools offer programs in physical therapy. Below are listed some of the more prominent institutions in this field.

Emory University
Division of Physical Therapy
1462 Clifton Road NE, Suite 312
Atlanta, GA 30322
404.727.4002
www.rehabmed.emory.edu/pt

MGH Institute of Health Professions
Graduate Program in Physical Therapy
36 First Avenue
Boston, MA 02129
617.726.8009
www.mghihp.edu/academics/physical-therapy

Northwestern University
Department of Physical Therapy and Human Movement Science
645 N. Michigan Avenue, Suite 1100
Chicago, IL 60611
312.908.8160
www.medschool.northwestern.edu/nupthms

University of Delaware
Department of Physical Therapy
301 McKinly Laboratory
Newark, DE 19716
302.831.8910
www.udel.edu/PT

University of Iowa
Graduate Program in Physical Therapy
1-252 Medical Education Building
Iowa City, IA 52242
319.335.9791
www.medicine.uiowa.edu/physicaltherapy

University of Miami
Department of Physical Therapy
5915 Ponce de Leon Boulevard
Coral Gables, FL 33146
305.284.4535
pt.med.miami.edu

University of Pittsburgh
School of Health and Rehabilitation Sciences
4020 Forbes Tower
Pittsburgh, PA 15260
412.383.6558
www.shrs.pitt.edu

University of Southern California
Biokinesiology and Physical Therapy
1540 Alcatraz Street, CHP 155
Los Angeles, CA 90089
323.442.2900
pt/usc.edu

U.S. Army-Baylor University
Physical Therapy Department
3151 Scott Road
Fort Sam Houston, TX 78234
210.221.8410
www.baylor.edu/graduate/pt

Washington University in St. Louis
Program in Physical Therapy
4444 Forest Park Boulevard
St. Louis, MO 63108
314.286.1400
physicaltherapy.wustl.edu

MORE INFORMATION

American Physical Therapy Association
1111 N. Fairfax Street
Alexandria, VA 22314-1488
800.999.2782
www.apta.org

Commission on Accreditation of Allied Health Education Programs
1361 Park Street
Clearwater, FL 33756
727.210.2350
www.caahep.org

Federation of State Boards of Physical Therapy
124 West Street S, 3rd Floor
Alexandria, VA 22314
703.299.3100
www.fsbpt.org

Simone Isadora Flynn/Editor

Physician

Snapshot

Career Cluster: Health Science, Medicine
Interests: Biology, Physiology, Medicine, Patient Care
Earnings (Yearly Average): $296,417
Employment & Outlook: Faster Than Average Growth Expected

OVERVIEW

Sphere of Work

Physicians are doctors who care for sick and injured people. In addition to diagnosing illnesses through interpretation of medical tests, physicians treat injuries that occur accidentally or as a result of disease or illness. Physicians in the United States are divided into two specialties: medical doctors (MDs), who use pharmaceutical and surgical methods to treat patients, and doctors of osteopathic medicine (DOs), who use similar procedures and also incorporate preventative techniques and holistic medical care.

Work Environment

Physicians work in medical office settings and in hospitals. Depending on experience and area of specialization, physicians may divide their time between treating patients, conducting medical research, and offering educational instruction to medical students in both classroom and laboratory settings. The location in which a physician works varies based on whether he or she has a private medical practice, is a researcher for a hospital or a university, or is employed by a pharmaceutical or health organization.

Profile

Working Conditions: Work Indoors
Physical Strength: Light Work
Education Needs: Medical Degree
Licensure/Certification: Required
Physical Abilities Not Required: No Heavy Work
Opportunities For Experience: Military Service, Volunteer Work
Holland Interest Score*: ISR

* See Appendix A

Occupation Interest

Medicine attracts students with demonstrated academic success in biology, physiology, and chemistry. Many professionals who are drawn to the field are those who have excelled academically and want to put their knowledge to use for the benefit of others. Becoming a physician necessitates more than a decade of academic study.

A Day in the Life—Duties and Responsibilities

The day-to-day duties of physicians vary depending on their employers and medical specialties. Physicians who operate their own private medical practices spend their days visiting with patients to diagnose and treat illness and injuries. Private physicians instruct patients on strategies to prevent disease by leading healthier lives. They also prescribe medicines both to treat illness and disease and to prevent future disease.

Physicians employed in the field of medical research spend their days evaluating new treatments, primarily in a laboratory setting. Medical research involves both clinical investigation of the effects of medical treatment on humans over time and investigation of trends in sickness and disease through extensive evaluation of public-health records.

Hospital- and university-employed physicians divide their time between treating patients and instructing medical students while also making occasional forays into medical research. Unlike private practices, in which physicians are also charged with overseeing the administrative and financial aspects of their operations, hospitals and universities offer physicians the assistance of large administrative bodies comprising both medical health professionals and medical students.

Duties and Responsibilities

- Examining patients
- Ordering or performing various tests, analyses, and diagnostics
- Prescribing and administering drugs and treatments
- Providing medical advice to patients and family members
- Following up with patients regarding treatments and conditions
- Staying abreast of medical literature and/or doing research

OCCUPATION SPECIALTIES

General Practitioners

General Practitioners diagnose and treat a variety of diseases and injuries in general practice. They order or execute various tests to obtain information on the patient's condition. They analyze the findings and prescribe drugs and other treatments. They may occasionally make house or emergency calls, and frequently refer patients to specialized physicians and perform minor surgery.

Osteopathic Physicians

Osteopathic Physicians diagnose and treat diseases and injuries of the human body, and examine patients to determine symptoms attributable to impairments of the musculoskeletal system. They treat disorders of bones, muscles, nerves, and other body systems through surgical procedures or manipulative therapy.

Surgeons

Surgeons perform operations to correct deformities, repair injuries, prevent diseases, and improve body functions in patients.

Pediatricians

Pediatricians specialize in the diagnosis and treatment of children's diseases and in preventive medicine for children from birth through adolescence.

Obstetricians

Obstetricians and Gynecologists specialize in the care and treatment of women during and immediately following pregnancy and in diseases of the female reproductive organs.

Cardiologists

Cardiologists diagnose and treat diseases of the heart.

Psychiatrists

Psychiatrists study, diagnose, and treat mental, emotional, and behavioral disorders.

Podiatrists

Podiatrists diagnose and treat disorders and diseases of the foot and lower leg.

Radiologists

Radiologists use x-ray and radioactive substances to diagnose and treat diseases of the human body.

Anesthesiologists

Anesthesiologists administer anesthetics to render patients insensible to pain during surgical, obstetrical, and other medical procedures.

Ophthalmologists

Ophthalmologists diagnose and treat diseases and injuries of the eye.

Dermatologists

Dermatologists diagnose and treat diseases of the skin.

Neurologists

Neurologists diagnose and treat organic (i.e., physiological) diseases and disorders of the human nervous system.

Internists

Internists diagnose and treat diseases and injuries of human internal organ systems.

Family Practitioners

Family Practitioners provide comprehensive medical services for all members of a family, regardless of age or sex, on a continuing basis.

WORK ENVIRONMENT

Physical Environment

Physicians work in a wide variety of academic and medical settings, including laboratories, hospitals, and university classrooms.

Relevant Skills and Abilities

Analytical Skills
- Analyzing information
- Using logical reasoning

Communication Skills
- Listening to others
- Speaking and writing effectively

Interpersonal/Social Skills
- Being able to remain calm
- Being able to work independently
- Cooperating with others
- Providing support to others
- Working as a member of a team

Organization & Management Skills
- Handling challenging situations
- Making decisions
- Managing people/groups
- Paying attention to and handling details
- Performing duties which change frequently

Planning & Research Skills
- Developing evaluation strategies
- Researching information

Technical Skills
- Performing scientific, mathematical, and technical work

Human Environment

Physicians must be excellent interpersonal communicators possessing the capability to explain intricate medical concepts in an understandable manner. As physicians must often discuss sensitive topics with patients, they must be capable of exhibiting tremendous compassion.

Technological Environment

Physicians use a vast array of traditional and contemporary medical devices and diagnostic technology, ranging from complex computer software to highly specialized instruments.

EDUCATION, TRAINING, AND ADVANCEMENT

High School/Secondary

High school students can best prepare to enter the medical field by taking high-level courses in algebra, calculus, geometry, biology, chemistry, and physics. Students who become medical doctors usually demonstrate high levels of achievement in each of these courses as well as extensive extracurricular involvement in high school events such as science fairs and national scholastic science competitions. Volunteerism and charitable work also help high school students attain and hone the interpersonal communication skills relevant to the position.

Suggested High School Subjects
- Algebra
- Biology
- Chemistry
- College Preparatory
- English
- Geometry
- Health Science Technology
- Humanities
- Mathematics
- Physical Education
- Physics
- Physiology
- Psychology
- Science
- Sociology
- Statistics
- Trigonometry

Famous First

The first physician to practice in space was Navy Commander Dr. Joseph P. Kerwin. In 1973, after taking off from Cape Canaveral, Florida, Dr. Kerwin landed aboard Skylab, the first American orbital space station. He and two other fellow astronauts stayed aboard the space station for 28 days, during which Dr. Kerwin performed daily routine medical tests on the crew.

College/Postsecondary

Few professions require as much postsecondary education as that of physician. Aspiring physicians first complete four years of pre-medicine collegiate courses. Premed students must successfully complete collegiate-level courses in organic chemistry, physics, and biology. Such coursework involves investigations into complex topics such as cell biology, genetics, and biochemistry.

Upon the completion of premed studies, aspiring physicians are required to apply and be accepted to a four-year program at one of numerous accredited medical schools. In medical school, students dedicate themselves to a particular realm of medicine while completing coursework in anatomy, internal medicine, and general surgery.

Aspiring physicians must then successfully complete a three- to four-year doctoral program in which they investigate the historical development of and contemporary issues related to their particular realm of medical expertise. Specific medical fields pursued by medical students may include pathology, radiology, clinical medicine, and neurophysiology. Such programs are usually supplemented with hospital residency programs and thesis presentations outlining specific field or laboratory research.

Related College Majors
- Anatomy and Physiology
- Medicine (M.D.)
- Osteopathic Medicine
- Pre-Medicine Studies

Adult Job Seekers

The enormous educational commitment required to become a physician makes adult job seekers who have dedicated a significant portion of their careers to other disciplines a rarity in medicine. Medical students often rely on the contacts and professional networks they construct during their lengthy period of education to lay the groundwork for future professional opportunities. There remain several medicine-centric avenues for adult job seekers to begin new careers in the medical field, particular in the realms of nursing, research analytics, and record keeping.

Professional Certification and Licensure

All physicians must hold and subsequently renew a state medical license, which grants them the right to practice medicine in that state. Medical license applications are reviewed annually by state medical boards.

Additional Requirements

Intense dedication to academics and perseverance in the face of challenging coursework are necessary for completion of the numerous years of study required to become a physician. In addition to the desire to help others, aspiring physicians must also be patient communicators who possess the ability to motivate themselves and those around them in the face of adversity.

Physicians have among the highest earnings of any occupation. Earnings depend on the geographic location, whether the physician is salaried or in private practice, and the physician's specialty, number of years in practice, skill, personality and professional reputation.

EARNINGS AND ADVANCEMENT

Median annual earnings of primary care physicians were $214,536, while those physicians practicing a medical specialty earned $378,298 in 2012. Median annual earnings for select medical specialties in 2012 were: Anesthesiologist, $431,730; Obstetrician/Gynecologist, $298,061; Internist, $217,702; Psychiatrist, $212,736; Pediatrician, $203,677 and Family Practitioner, $200,766.

Physicians may receive paid vacations, holidays, and sick days; life and health insurance; and retirement benefits. These are usually paid by the employer. Most physicians, however, are self-employed and must arrange for their own health insurance and retirement programs. Some employers also provide for paid educational leave.

Metropolitan Areas with the Highest Employment Level in this Occupation

Metropolitan area	Employment (1)	Employment per thousand jobs	Hourly mean wage
New York-White Plains-Wayne, NY-NJ	26,080	5.06	$73.84
Chicago-Joliet-Naperville, IL	12,140	3.33	$72.56
Los Angeles-Long Beach-Glendale, CA	7,740	2.00	$94.73
Atlanta-Sandy Springs-Marietta, GA	6,210	2.75	$97.02
Nassau-Suffolk, NY	6,110	5.00	$97.38
Bethesda-Rockville-Frederick, MD	5,910	10.56	$78.24
Boston-Cambridge-Quincy, MA	5,750	3.36	$62.33
Washington-Arlington-Alexandria, DC-VA-MD-WV	5,170	2.21	$81.05

(1)Does not include specialists including pediatricians, psychiatrists, ophthalmologists, and obstetricians as well as family physicians. Source: Bureau of Labor Statistics, 2012

EMPLOYMENT AND OUTLOOK

There were over 650,000 physicians and surgeons employed nationally in 2012. About one-half worked in an office-based practice, and another one-fourth were employed in hospitals. Employment is expected to grow faster than the average for all occupations through the year 2020, which means employment is projected to increase nearly 25 percent. This is due to continuing growth of the health-care industry. An aging population will create demand for physicians, as will new medical technologies that allow physicians to perform more procedures and treat conditions previously thought to be untreatable.

Newly trained physicians are likely to experience competition as they seek to launch a practice. Those who are willing to locate in inner cities, rural areas and other places where doctors are not in oversupply should have little difficulty.

Employment Trend, Projected 2010–20

Health Diagnosing and Treating Practitioners: 26%

Physicians and Surgeons: 24%

Total, All Occupations: 14%

Note: "All Occupations" includes all occupations in the U.S. Economy. Source: U.S. Bureau of Labor Statistics, Employment Projections Program

Related Occupations
- Cardiologist
- Chiropractor
- Dentist
- Neurologist
- Nurse Practitioner
  Pediatrician
- Radiologist
- Surgeon

Related Military Occupations
- Physician & Surgeon

Conversation With . . .
JOHN TRUDEL
Primary Care Physician, 25 years

1. What was your individual career path in terms of education, entry-level job, or other significant opportunity?

I was premed for four years, then did four years at Albany Medical College, and a three-year residency at Charleston Naval Hospital before becoming an attending physician. I joined the Navy to pay for medical school. I got a scholarship for three years, then gave the Navy six years when I graduated from medical school. Primary care was always what I wanted to do because that was the most interesting and offered the most variety. You never know what you're going to get. Eventually, I switched over to informatics and computers.

2. Are there many job opportunities in your profession? In what specific areas?

There is a shortage of primary care physicians, so there are many opportunities. There are some people in private practice, but many new doctors want to work for someone else. Most of the residents today spend a lot of time thinking about 'work/ life balance.' Nowadays there are restrictions on the number of hours a resident can work, so they have a built-in feeling of 'You can't make me do that.' So now, they want to work 9 to 5, have weekends off, and have someone to take care of their patients at the hospital if you want them to join your practice.

3. What do you wish you had known going into this profession?

I wish I had known how much of this job involves understanding people, human behavior, and feelings and perceptions rather than just science, so that I could have developed those skills. I didn't get any of that kind of training. When my partner was in residency, they would videotape his interactions with patients in the exam room and talk to him about how to sit, how to act. There are consultants you can hire to help people perceive you better, to teach you to let your empathy come through. There are simple things you can do, like sit in a chair and lean forward, as opposed to standing. Or ask patients what they need, and let them talk for two to three minutes, so that they feel heard, even though at one minute and 30 seconds, I know what they need. It's all about perception.

4. How do you see your profession changing in the next five years?

There will be more emphasis on population management, team care, use of nurse practitioners/physician assistants and technology, especially the Electronic Medical Record (EMR). Population management looks at large groups of patients over a long period of time. Traditionally as a physician, you've got to go into a room and see a patient, one patient at a time. Now, using the EMR, if you have a cohort of 40 patients who are diabetic, you can look at what's your blood sugar control. Or how's the average blood pressure of your patients? Are they being told to take an aspirin every day? Over time, you have better outcomes.

5. What role will technology play in those changes, and what skills will be required?

An EMR is just about required to run a practice. Use of data mining, reports, quality measures, and meaningful use of technology are all becoming integrated into medicine now. Becoming facile with the computer and being able to leverage that data will be the difference between being an average provider/organization and an exemplary provider/organization. We are increasingly being measured and compared with our peers by patients and outside groups (government, consumers, insurance companies) and gaining or losing patients based on this information. Also, if used well, this information helps us take better care of patients by prompting us to do things we should and stopping us from doing things we shouldn't.

6. Do you have any general advice or additional professional insights to share with someone interested in your profession?

It remains a noble profession full of people who truly care about what they do: make people better. When I'm sitting in meetings with physicians, they're not talking about what you can do to make their lives better; they're asking what they can do to make their patients' lives better. And that's how it should be. It is a difficult yet rewarding job.

7. Can you suggest a valuable "try this" for students considering a career in your profession?

There are volunteer opportunities in hospitals for individuals interested in the health care field. Many physicians will allow college students to shadow them for a few days. Speak with your primary care physician or contact your group practice to ask for the opportunity.

SELECTED SCHOOLS

There are a variety of good medical schools in the United States. Below are listed some of the more prominent institutions that focus on primary care (as opposed to medical research or specializations).

Oregon Health and Science University
3181 S.W. Sam Jackson Park Road
Portland, OR 97239
503.494.8311
www.ohsu.edu

University of Alabama, Birmingham
School of Medicine
1702 2nd Avenue
Birmingham, AL 35294
205.975.8884
www.uab.edu/medicine

University of California, San Francisco
School of Medicine
513 Parnassus Avenue
San Francisco, CA 94143
415.476.2342
medschool.ucsf.edu

University of Colorado, Denver School of Medicine
1301 E. 17th Place
Aurora, CO 80045
303.724.8025
www.ucdenver.edu/academics/
colleges/medicalschool

University of Massachusetts, Worcester
School of Medicine
55 N. Lake Avenue
Worcester, MA 01655
508.856.8989
www.umassmed.edu

University of Michigan, Ann Arbor
Medical School
1301 S. Catherine Avenue
Ann Arbor, MI 48109
734.763.9600
medicine.umich.edu

University of Minnesota
Medical School
420 Delaware Street SE
Minneapolis, MN 55455
612.625.7977
www.med.umn.edu

University of Nebraska Medical Center
Emile Street
Omaha, NE 68198
765.494.1361
www.unmc.edu

University of North Carolina, Chapel Hill
School of Medicine
321 S. Columbia Street
Chapel Hill, NC 27514
919.966.4708
www.med.unc.edu

University of Washington
School of Medicine
1959 N.E. Pacific Street
Seattle, WA 98195
206.543.2100
www.uwmedicine.org

MORE INFORMATION

American Academy of Family Physicians
11400 Tomahawk Creek Parkway
Leawood, KS 66211
913.906.6000
www.aafp.org

American Association of Colleges of Osteopathic Medicine
5550 Friendship Boulevard, Suite 310
Chevy Chase, MD 20815
301.968.4100
www.aacom.org

American Board of Medical Specialties
222 N. LaSalle Street, Suite 1500
Chicago, IL 60601
312.436.2600
www.abms.org

American College of Surgeons
633 N. St. Claire Street
Chicago, IL 60611
312.202.5000
www.facs.org

American Congress of Obstetricians and Gynecologists
409 12th Street SW
PO Box 70620
Washington, D.C. 20024
202.638.5577
www.acog.org

American Medical Association
515 N State Street
Chicago, IL 60654
800.621.8335
www.ama-assn.org

American Medical Women's Association
Attn: Career Information
100 North 20th Street, 4th Floor
Philadelphia, PA 19103
215.320.3716
www.amwa-doc.org

American Osteopathic Association
Public Relations Department
142 East Ontario Street
Chicago, IL 60611
800.621.1773
www.aoa-net.org

American Podiatric Medical Association
9312 Old Georgetown Road
Bethesda, MD 20814
301.581.9200
www.apma.org

Association of American Medical Colleges
2450 N Street, NW
Washington, DC 20037-1126
202.828.0400
www.aamc.org

National Medical Association
8403 Colesville Road, Suite 920
Silver Spring, MD 20910
202.347.1895
www.nmanet.org

John Pritchard/Editor

Radiation Therapist

Snapshot

Career Cluster: Health Science

Interests: Anatomy, Physiology, Patient Care, Radiography

Earnings (Yearly Average): $79,479

Employment & Outlook: Faster Than Average Growth Expected

OVERVIEW

Sphere of Work

Radiation therapists are radiologic technologists who specialize in administering radiation therapy as a treatment for cancer, under the guidance and supervision of radiation oncologists (cancer specialists). They are trained to read radiation prescriptions, maintain and operate radiation equipment, assist physicians in identifying and locating tumors or masses, and care for patients during and after radiation treatment. They are also responsible for keeping accurate records of the times and amounts of radiation exposure.

Work Environment

Radiation therapists spend their workdays in hospitals, oncology centers, and radiologists' offices. These medical settings are usually clean, bright, and temperature controlled. Radiation therapists generally work forty-hour weeks, which may include days, evenings, weekends, and on-call hours. They may be at risk for backaches, injuries from machine accidents, or exposure to radiation.

Profile

Working Conditions: Work Indoors
Physical Strength: Light Work
Education Needs: Medical Degree
Licensure/Certification: Required
Physical Abilities Not Required: No
Heavy Work
Opportunities For Experience:
Military Service, Volunteer Work
Holland Interest Score*: ISR

* See Appendix A

Occupation Interest

Individuals drawn to the profession of radiation therapist tend to be compassionate, analytical, and detail oriented. Radiation therapists need physical strength, stamina, and good hand-eye coordination to maneuver patients and operate medical equipment. They should find satisfaction in working in a medical environment and solving complex problems. Mental and emotional strength is also essential, as the work requires constant interaction with people who are very ill and may be distraught.

A Day in the Life—Duties and Responsibilities

Radiation therapists may be generalists or may specialize in such areas as treatment planning, computed tomography simulation (imaging and modeling), dosimetry (radiation measurement/calculation), tumor localization, radiation protection (preventative measures), linear accelerator modification (a technique involved in radiation therapy), or high-risk procedures. In general, they help provide radiation treatments to cancer patients.

To determine a treatment plan, radiation therapists assist radiation oncologists with tumor or mass identification and localization. They also sometimes assist a radiation oncologist or   in making radiation dosage decisions. Prior to treatment, therapists must prepare and sterilize specialized radiation equipment called linear accelerators and review the radiologist's or oncologist's prescription to determine the type and extent of treatment required. While administering targeted and localized radiation therapy treatments, a radiation therapist is responsible for ensuring patient comfort and safety. He or she instructs patients on how and where to position themselves in order to improve treatment efficacy and minimize the patient and staff exposure to radiation. The radiation therapist must also monitor patients for adverse reactions during treatment and educate them about the side effects, such as hair loss and vomiting. After treatment sessions, the radiation therapist must report all sessions and side effects to patient oncology teams, notify biomedical equipment technicians or hospital engineers of any radiation equipment failures, and dispose of radioactive medical waste in accordance with U.S. Nuclear Regulatory Commission safety guidelines and regulations.

Radiation therapists are often charged with administrative duties in addition to their clinical responsibilities. They may work with office staff to plan and schedule radiation therapy appointments, greet patients and explain the role of radiation therapy treatments, and document the date, time, amount, and type of radiation therapy treatment administered in each session.

Duties and Responsibilities

- Operating radiation equipment
- Administering radiation to patients
- Recording data regarding radiation dosage, number of treatments, and effects of treatments on patients
- Monitoring safety of those present during radiation treatments

WORK ENVIRONMENT

Physical Environment

Radiation therapists prepare and administer radiation therapy to patients in hospitals, oncology centers, and radiologists' offices. They work with high-end medical equipment in sterile environments and must take every precaution to prevent any radiation exposure.

Relevant Skills and Abilities

Analytical Skills
- Analyzing data

Communication Skills
- Speaking effectively
- Preparing reports

Interpersonal/Social Skills
- Being sensitive to others
- Cooperating with others
- Providing support to others
- Working as a member of a team

Organization & Management Skills
- Making decisions
- Paying attention to and handling details

Technical Skills
- Performing scientific, mathematical, and technical work
- Working with machines, tools, or other objects

Human Environment

Radiation therapists should be comfortable interacting with patients, physicians, laboratory technicians, nurses, scientists, and office staff. Due to the sensitive nature of radiation therapy and cancer treatment, therapists should be empathetic, tactful, and committed to patient confidentiality. Cooperation and communication between radiation therapists and other members of a patient's oncology care team is essential.

Technological Environment

To administer treatments, radiation therapists use linear accelerators, computers, lathes, radiation dosimetry or dosage charts, patient positioning straps, radiation shields, protective aprons and clothing, radiation detectors, closed-circuit cameras, and intercoms. They may also use photo imaging software to evaluate results, radiation dose calculation programs to determine dosing, and electronic medical records to document treatment.

EDUCATION, TRAINING, AND ADVANCEMENT

High School/Secondary

High school students interested in pursuing a career as a radiation therapist should study anatomy and physiology, biology, physics, communications, computer science, psychology, and mathematics, which will provide a strong foundation for college-level work in the field. Students should also consider seeking internships or part-time work in medical settings.

Suggested High School Subjects
- Algebra
- Applied Biology/Chemistry
- Applied Math
- Biology
- Chemistry
- English
- Health Science Technology
- Physics
- Physiology

Famous First

The first person to use radium in the treatment of cancer was Dr. Robert Abbe (1851–1928) of St. Luke's Hospital in New York. In 1904, after visiting Marie Curie in Paris, Abbe wrote a paper that laid out the advantages of using radiation therapy over traditional surgery or x-ray therapy (the latter of which produced very mixed results). His research and experiments led to the founding of the science of radiation oncology. Abbe was also a strong opponent of the use of tobacco, which he considered to be a cancer-causing agent. In that respect, too, he was far ahead of his time.

College/Postsecondary

Postsecondary students interested in becoming radiation therapists should work toward an associate's or bachelor's degree in radiography or radiation therapy from a program accredited by the Joint Review Committee on Education in Radiologic Technology (JRCERT). These programs typically include coursework in anatomy and physiology, research, pathology, patient care, treatment planning, dosimetry, radiation equipment and procedures, and ethics. Postsecondary students can gain hands-on work experience through clinical internships or co-op experiences.

Related College Majors
- Medical Radiologic Technology
- Nuclear Medicine Technology

Adult Job Seekers

Adults seeking employment as radiation therapists should have, at a minimum, an associate's degree in radiography or radiation therapy from a JRCERT-accredited school. Some employers may be willing to hire candidates who have only a certificate in the field, but most prefer to employ radiation therapists who hold a degree. Professional radiology and oncology associations, such as the American Registry of Radiologic Technologists and the American Cancer Society, may offer job-finding workshops and generally maintain lists of available jobs.

Professional Certification and Licensure

Certification is often required of radiation therapists as a condition of employment or promotion. The main option for voluntary radiation therapy certification is the Radiation Therapy Technologist (RTT) designation offered by the American Registry of Radiologic Technologists. Applicants earn the voluntary RTT certification by completing an approved radiation therapy training program, meeting clinical experience requirements, adhering to ethical standards, and passing a national examination. RTT certification is valid for two years. State licensure is usually required for radiation therapists; prospective therapists should consult with the department of health in their home state for specific licensing requirements.

Additional Requirements

High levels of integrity and professional ethics are required of radiation therapists, as professionals in this role have access to confidential medical information. Radiation therapists must be committed to lifelong learning and follow all relevant trends and developments in the field of medicine.

Fun Fact

Employment of radiation therapists is expected to grow by 20 percent between 2010 and 2020, faster than the average for all occupations.

Source: US Bureau of Labor Statistics

EARNINGS AND ADVANCEMENT

With experience, radiation therapists can be promoted to supervisors. Opportunities as instructors for radiation technology programs also exist. Median annual earnings of radiation therapists were $79,479 in 2012. The lowest ten percent earned less than $54,007, and the highest ten percent earned more than $117,183.

Radiation therapists may receive paid vacations, holidays, and sick days; life and health insurance; and retirement benefits. These are usually paid by the employer. Some employers also reimburse their employees for the cost of continuing education.

Metropolitan Areas with the Highest
Employment Level in this Occupation

Metropolitan area	Employment	Employment per thousand jobs	Hourly mean wage
Philadelphia, PA	500	0.28	$38.27
Phoenix-Mesa-Glendale, AZ	410	0.24	$37.32
Houston-Sugar Land-Baytown, TX	370	0.14	$36.81
Los Angeles-Long Beach-Glendale, CA	370	0.09	$45.29
Boston-Cambridge-Quincy, MA	320	0.19	$41.49
Atlanta-Sandy Springs-Marietta, GA	280	0.12	$37.49
Detroit-Livonia-Dearborn, MI	250	0.36	$34.04
Minneapolis-St. Paul-Bloomington, MN-WI	240	0.14	$33.71

Source: Bureau of Labor Statistics, 2012

EMPLOYMENT AND OUTLOOK

Radiation therapists held about 18,000 jobs nationally in 2012. Most worked in hospitals and cancer treatment centers. Although this occupation is very specialized, the need for radiation therapists continues to grow. Employment is expected to grow faster than the average for all occupations through the year 2020, which means employment is projected to increase 20 percent. This increase is due to an aging population, the advanced ability to detect cancer, and the number of cases being treated by radiation.

Employment Trend, Projected 2010–20

Health Diagnosing and Treating Practitioners: 26%

Radiation Therapists: 20%

Total, All Occupations: 14%

Note: "All Occupations" includes all occupations in the U.S. Economy.

Related Occupations
- Radiologic Technologist
- Ultrasound Technician

Conversation With . . .
MEGHAN C. KEARNEY, M.S, RTT
Radiation Therapist, 8 years

1. **What was your individual career path in terms of education, entry-level job, or other significant opportunity?**

   I knew I wanted to stay local (Boston) and focus on the healthcare field which helped narrow my search. I also wanted to choose a university major that would provide me with a stable career had I not gone to immediately to graduate school. After attending a few open houses, I was immediately impressed when I found Suffolk University's clinical program in radiation biology. I was able to do clinical rotations throughout the best hospitals in the city and create a professional network early on, which set me up for a full-time position, immediately following graduation and board examination, at Massachusetts General Hospital.

2. **Are there many job opportunities in your profession? In what specific areas?**

   Currently, there is a fair amount of opportunity in the profession, especially if one is willing to travel. Although there is not a high rate of turnover, many of our students from our affiliated schools are employed after graduating whether it is full time or per diem work. Dosimetry – the behind-the-scenes work that goes into creating treatment plans – is also a great option for students who are more interested in the physics aspect of healthcare versus direct patient care.

3. **What do you wish you had known going into this profession?**

   That is a hard question… I was able to get so much exposure to the field before and during my schooling that I think I was well informed and knew what to expect.

4. **How do you see your profession changing in the next five years?**

   There will be a greater focus on quality imaging modalities and applications within the field of radiation therapy. I think radiation therapists will be expected to have a sophisticated knowledge of cross sectional anatomy and how to apply it in the clinic.

5. **What role will technology play in those changes, and what skills will be required?**

Technology will play the largest and most important role in the future of radiation therapy and adaptability will be crucial. Upgrades and innovative imaging technologies will require therapists to be life-long learners with a strong commitment to patient safety and patient care. The evolving role of radiation therapists requires people who are flexible, versatile and can function and thrive as part of a cohesive team.

6. **Do you have any general advice or additional professional insights to share with someone interested in your profession?**

It is definitely emotionally draining at times but I think anyone who goes into the healthcare field knows that going in. Contrary to what many assume, most of the people that we treat come in smiling and going about their normal daily activity just trying to fight their courageous battle with cancer one day at a time and we get to help them through that.

Any student who participates in clinical rotations as part of their schooling is at an advantage because they are able to get valuable hands-on experience with the culture, work flow and procedures of the clinic. Students who have the opportunity to do clinical rotations should always treat the experience as a working interview. A manager will not underestimate the opportunity to hire someone who earns positive feedback from current employees and functions as a worthy member of the team.

Also, it is important to do some self analysis and figure out what you envision the ideal working environment to include. If you find that you thrive in a team environment and enjoy being social and having face to face interaction with coworkers and patients throughout your day, then you may be a good fit. If not, then it may be best to research other opportunities that would better suit your personality.

7. **Can you suggest a valuable "try this" for students considering a career in your profession?**

I would strongly encourage prospective students to take advantage of any job shadow opportunities. Some schools will arrange for a one-day clinic visit for students interested in applying for the clinical program prior to any commitment.

SELECTED SCHOOLS

Many technical and community colleges offer programs in radiologic technology. Interested students are advised to consult with a school guidance counselor or research area postsecondary schools. The website of the Joint Review Committee on Education in Radiologic Technology (see below), provides a search tool that allows you to locate schools/programs in your state.

MORE INFORMATION

American Healthcare Radiology Administrators
490B Boston Post Road, Suite 200
Sudbury, MA 01776
800.334.2472
www.ahraonline.org

American Medical Technologists
10700 West Higgins, Suite 150
Rosemont, IL 60018
800.275.1268
www.amt1.com

American Registry of Radiologic Technologists
1255 Northland Drive
St. Paul, MN 55120-1155
651.687.0048
www.arrt.org

American Society of Clinical Oncology
2318 Mill Road, Suite 800
Alexandria, VA 22314
571.483.1300
www.asco.org

American Society of Radiologic Technologists
15000 Central Avenue, SE
Albuquerque, NM 87123-3917
800.444.2778
www.asrt.org

Joint Review Committee on Education in Radiologic Technology
20 N. Wacker Drive, Suite 2850
Chicago, IL 60606-2901
312.704.5300
www.jrcert.org

Simone Isadora Flynn/Editor

Radiologic Technologist

Snapshot

Career Cluster: Health Science

Interests: Medical Imaging, Anatomy & Physiology, Health Science Technology

Earnings (Yearly Average): $57,600

Employment & Outlook: Faster Than Average Growth Expected

OVERVIEW

Sphere of Work

Radiologic technologists use x-ray and other imaging technology as a diagnostic tool or as part of a patient treatment plan. They create images of specific areas and parts of the human body, including bones, tissue, blood vessels, and organs. Radiologic technologists may perform such imaging procedures as mammography, x-rays, computed tomography (CT) scans, and magnetic resonance imaging (MRI). Radiologic technologists work under the supervision of radiologists trained to read and interpret medical images. Depending on the type

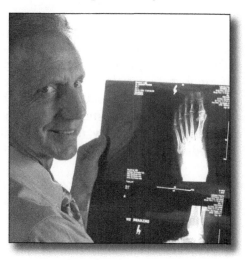

of equipment used, they may also be called x-ray technicians, CT technicians, and so on.

Work Environment

Radiologic technologists/technicians spend their workdays in hospitals, clinics, radiologists' offices, medical imaging and testing centers, and mobile imaging units. Radiologic technologists generally work forty-hour weeks, which may include days, evenings, weekends, and on-call hours to accommodate the needs of patients. They are at risk for injury from machine accidents and exposure to radiation.

Profile

Working Conditions: Work Indoors
Physical Strength: Light Work
Education Needs: Technical/ Community College
Licensure/Certification: Required
Physical Abilities Not Required: No Heavy Labor
Opportunities For Experience: Internship, Military Service, Volunteer Work, Part-Time Work
Holland Interest Score*: SRI

* See Appendix A

Occupation Interest

Individuals drawn to the profession of radiologic technologist tend to be intelligent, focused, analytical, and detail oriented. Radiologic technologists need moderate physical strength, stamina, and good hand-eye coordination to maneuver patients and operate technical equipment. Technologists should enjoy working in a medical environment and solving complex problems. Teamwork and strong communication skills are also important, as radiologic technologists work closely with radiologists to diagnose and treat patients.

A Day in the Life—Duties and Responsibilities

The daily occupational duties and responsibilities of radiologic technologists vary by the individual's area of job specialization and work environment. Radiologic technologists may specialize in use of a particular imaging technology, such as radiation therapy, nuclear medicine, or computed tomography, or in work with a specific patient population, such as pediatric radiology or trauma radiology.

Radiologic technologists spend their days assisting radiologists with preparing and performing imaging tests and treatments. Prior to an imaging session, the radiologic technologist prepares, maintains, and sterilizes the imaging equipment, such as x-ray machines and computerized axial tomography (CAT) scanners. He or she greets patients when they arrive, explains the role of radiologic and magnetic imaging in their diagnosis or treatment, and records patient medical histories. After reviewing the radiologist's test request or prescription to determine the type and extent of imaging, testing, or treatment required, the technologist enters the appropriate scan sequence into the radiologic and magnetic imaging equipment. If soft tissues are to be scanned (a procedure known as fluoroscopy), the radiologic technologist prepares a radiopaque solution for the patient to drink prior to imaging.

During the imaging session, the radiologic technologist directs and positions the imaging equipment close to the patient's body and creates the requested x-ray, video, or computerized images. The technologist must ensure patient comfort and safety throughout the session, instructing the patient how and where to position the body and following all safety guidelines to limit radiation exposure for patients as well as physicians and lab workers.

After the imaging session, the radiologic technologist processes the x-ray film or other image results, disposes of radioactive medical waste in accordance with U.S. Nuclear Regulatory Commission (NRC) safety guidelines and regulations, and reports all imaging findings to the supervising radiologist.

Radiologic technologists often have administrative duties in addition to their technical responsibilities. They may work with office staff to plan and schedule imaging appointments and otherwise participate in the daily operations of the imaging center or office as required. Radiologic technologists are also responsible for recording the date, time, exposure, and type of imaging administered to patients in each session. They must report any equipment failures to biomedical equipment technicians or hospital engineers when necessary. All radiologic technologists are additionally responsible for educating themselves about the administrative, physical, and technical patient privacy safeguards included in the federal Health Insurance Portability and Accountability Act (HIPAA).

Duties and Responsibilities

- Arranging devices to lessen discomfort and prevent a patient from moving
- Positioning the patient for imaging of the desired area
- Adjusting equipment to give a clear and undistorted view of the patient's body
- Determining proper voltage, current, and exposure time for each procedure
- Preparing and administering drugs or chemical mixtures
- Operating x-ray therapy machines to treat patients
- Keeping records and files and preparing reports of procedures

OCCUPATION SPECIALTIES

Chief Radiologic Technologists

Chief Radiologic Technologists coordinate activities of and supervise radiologic technologists engaged in taking radiographs and assisting in X-ray therapy.

Nuclear Medicine Technologists

Nuclear Medicine Technologists prepare, administer, and measure radioactive isotopes in therapeutic, diagnostic, and tracer studies, utilizing a variety of radioisotope equipment.

WORK ENVIRONMENT

Physical Environment

Radiologic technologists perform radiologic and magnetic imaging for diagnostic and therapeutic purposes in hospitals, radiologists' offices, medical imaging and testing centers, and mobile imaging units. These medical settings tend to be clean and comfortable.

Relevant Skills and Abilities

Analytical Skills
- Analyzing information

Communication Skills
- Speaking effectively
- Preparing reports

Interpersonal/Social Skills
- Cooperating with others
- Working as a member of a team

Organization & Management Skills
- Paying attention to and handling details

Planning & Research Skills
- Developing evaluation strategies

Technical Skills
- Performing scientific, mathematical, and technical work
- Working with machines, tools, or other objects

Human Environment

Radiologic technologists should be comfortable interacting with patients, physicians, laboratory technicians, nurses, scientists, and office staff. Owing to the sensitive nature of medical diagnosis, radiologic technologists should be empathetic and tactful when interacting with patients and maintain patient confidentiality at all times.

Technological Environment

To complete their imaging work, radiologic technologists may use x-ray equipment, ultrasound machines, computerized axial tomography scanners, magnetic resonance imaging equipment, film processors, patient positioning equipment, bone densitometers, lead shields, protective aprons and clothing, measuring and dosing equipment, and intravenous pumps. They may also work with databases, electronic medical records, and medical device software.

EDUCATION, TRAINING, AND ADVANCEMENT

High School/Secondary

High school students interested in pursuing a career in radiologic technology should study anatomy and physiology, biology, chemistry, physics, and mathematics, which will provide a strong foundation for work in the field. Students interested in this career path will benefit from seeking internships or part-time work in medical settings.

Suggested High School Subjects
- Algebra
- Applied Biology/Chemistry
- Applied Math
- Biology
- Chemistry
- English
- Geometry
- Keyboarding
- Physics
- Physiology

Famous First

The first use of radioactive tracers in a diagnostic procedure took place in 1925 under the direction of Hermann Blumgart of Harvard University. After first testing the procedure on himself, Blumgart injected a radium preparation into the veins of fifteen patients and observed the rate of blood circulation with an electroscope. From this he was able to identify those who suffered from cardiac disease.

Library of Congress

College/Postsecondary

Postsecondary students interested in becoming radiologic technologists should work toward a certificate, an associate's degree, or a bachelor's degree in radiologic technology from an accredited school. The Joint Review Committee on Education in Radiologic Technology (JRCERT) provides accreditation to over 600 radiography training programs, which are available through universities, community colleges, technical schools, and hospitals. Coursework in anatomy, patient care, medical imaging, computer science, physics, and medical ethics may also prove useful. Postsecondary students can gain hands-on work experience through a program-sponsored clinical internship or co-op experience.

Related College Majors
- Diagnostic Medical Sonography Technology
- Medical Radiologic Technology
- Nuclear Medical Technology

Adult Job Seekers

Adults seeking employment as radiation therapists should have, at a minimum, an associate's degree in radiography or radiation therapy from a JRCERT-accredited school. Some employers may be willing to hire candidates who have only a certificate in the field, but most prefer to employ radiation therapists who hold a degree. Professional radiology and oncology associations, such as the American Registry of Radiologic Technologists and the American Cancer Society, may offer job-finding workshops and generally maintain lists of available jobs.

Professional Certification and Licensure

Certification and licensure is generally required for radiologic technologists as a condition of employment and promotion. The main option for radiologic technologist certification is the Registered Technologist (RT) designation offered by ARRT. Applicants earn this certification by completing an approved radiologic technology training program, meeting clinical experience requirements, abiding by ethical guidelines, and passing an examination. Continuing education coursework is required to maintain certification. Licensing requirements for radiologic technologists vary by state, so technologists should consult with the department of health in their home state for specific licensing requirements.

Additional Requirements

A high level of integrity and professional ethics is required of radiologic technologists as professionals in this role have access to confidential medical information.

Fun Fact

Wilhelm Conrad Rontgen discovered X-rays in 1895, when he was studying the passage of an electric current through low pressure gas. The first X-ray was of his wife's hand, and he received the Nobel Prize in Physics in 1901.

Source: www.nobelprize.org

EARNINGS AND ADVANCEMENT

Earnings of radiologic technologists depend on the size and geographic location of the employer and the training and experience of the employee. Radiologic technologists had median annual earnings of $57,600 in 2012. The lowest ten percent earned less than $38,701, and the highest ten percent earned more than $81,461.

Radiologic technologists may receive paid vacations, holidays, and sick days; life and health insurance; and retirement benefits. These are usually paid by the employer.

Metropolitan Areas with the Highest
Employment Level in this Occupation

Metropolitan area	Employment	Employment per thousand jobs	Hourly mean wage
New York-White Plains-Wayne, NY-NJ	6,650	1.31	$32.86
Chicago-Joliet-Naperville, IL	5,260	1.47	$29.14
Los Angeles-Long Beach-Glendale, CA	4,460	1.17	$29.55
Boston-Cambridge-Quincy, MA	3,830	2.29	$44.15
Philadelphia, PA	3,780	2.08	$28.76
Houston-Sugar Land-Baytown, TX	3,660	1.43	$26.68
Phoenix-Mesa-Glendale, AZ	3,270	1.92	$29.55
Atlanta-Sandy Springs-Marietta, GA	3,190	1.43	$25.42

Source: Bureau of Labor Statistics, 2012

EMPLOYMENT AND OUTLOOK

There were approximately 220,000 radiologic technologists and technicians employed nationally in 2012. Most were employed in hospitals. Most other jobs were in physicians' offices, diagnostic laboratories and imaging centers and outpatient care centers. Employment is expected to grow faster than the average for all occupations through the year 2020, which means employment is projected to increase up to 28 percent. This is a result of new uses being found for imaging technologies in the diagnosis and treatment of diseases, and as an aging population requires more diagnostic testing.

Employment Trend, Projected 2010–20

Radiologic Technologists and Technicians: 28%

Health Technologists and Technicians: 26%

Total, All Occupations: 14%

Note: "All Occupations" includes all occupations in the U.S. Economy. Source: U.S. Bureau of Labor Statistics, Employment Projections program

Related Occupations
- Medical Laboratory Technician
- Radiation Therapist
- Ultrasound Technician
-

Related Military Occupations
- Radiologic (X-Ray) Technician

Conversation With . . .
BETSY S. ELLIS
Radiologic Technologist, 25 years

1. What was your individual career path in terms of education, entry-level job, or other significant opportunity?

I studied journalism/communications in college and was a DJ for two years. Then I moved to North Carolina and got a job in a hospital as a file clerk. I just happened to get a job in the radiology department. I had to take films to get read and I'd listen to the radiologist. Everything was so interesting. I always liked science and medicine. People in the department encouraged me and I applied to a program at Pitt Community College in Greenville, NC. I had heard if you could survive their Associate's Degree program you could work anywhere in the country. The Radiologic Technologist profession is a good choice for those wanting to work with patients and work in the medical field in many different specialties.

2. Are there many job opportunities in your profession? In what specific areas?

X-ray techs are almost always in demand. However, cities with multiple X-ray academic/training programs have fewer jobs available. The areas where X-ray techs are in high demand are: diagnostic X-ray, which covers chest X-ray, plain films, bone X-rays, and operating room for many different procedures; CT scans; special procedures such as angiograms, cardiac catheter; urology; orthopedics; fluoroscopy procedures (upper GI, barium enema); trauma; MRI; and ultrasound.

Within each modality are specialties and, when in a hospital setting, an X-ray tech may experience all the specialties. However, with the increasing growth of large practices—and practices maintaining outpatient surgery centers—office jobs are in demand as well. In an office setting, X-ray techs specialize in one area, such as urology.

As you get into a specialty, doctors will rely on you. They like a second set of eyes. I've had a lot of doctors say, "Do you see anything?" They know we are used to looking at films.

3. What do you wish you had known going into this profession?

When you do your rotations in school, you don't rotate through all the modalities. I wish I'd known how broad X-ray could be. Rotating gives you more knowledge and makes you realize: Wow, there are a lot of things that go on in radiology.

4. How do you see your profession changing in the next five years?

Radiology is constantly changing. We have gone from film to digital. Our modalities have become multi. We now can do 3-D X-ray. I think in the next five years we will see MRI become a more specific modality for prostate biopsies. I also think our images for all procedures will be faster, since digital is getting better and faster each year.

5. What role will technology play in those changes, and what skills will be required?

The X-ray department will be more efficient, producing more films with the speed of the equipment. X-ray techs will need to keep up with all the changes. We have always needed to be multi-taskers and that will increase. X-ray Techs have to continuously cross-train, especially if you're in a specialty field, and keep up with continuing education credits.

6. Do you have any general advice or additional professional insights to share with someone interested in your profession?

You will be busy. You will need to be a multi-tasker. You will need to be able to draw the line between your emotions and your work. This profession sees many, many sad things.

Even if you think you know what you want to do once you graduate, work at a hospital (level one trauma would be best) so that you gain the knowledge and experience of being a versatile X-ray tech. Working a few years in an intense, busy hospital will give you the experience to learn and to work wherever you want. Look into being a travel tech; it's a good way to see places and save some money!

7. Can you suggest a valuable "try this" for students considering a career in your profession?

Call a local X-ray department and ask if you could follow a tech around or come and find out more about what they do. Most places will allow students who are considering the profession of radiologic technologist to come for a visit. Talk to other techs about their job: what they like best, what they like least!

SELECTED SCHOOLS

Many technical and community colleges offer programs in radiologic technology. Interested students are advised to consult with a school guidance counselor or research area postsecondary schools. The website of the Joint Review Committee on Education in Radiologic Technology (see below), provides a search tool that allows you to locate schools/programs in your state.

MORE INFORMATION

American Healthcare Radiology Administrators
490B Boston Post Road, Suite 200
Sudbury, MA 01776
800.334.2472
www.ahraonline.org

American Medical Technologists
10700 West Higgins, Suite 150
Rosemont, IL 60018
800.275.1268
www.amt1.com

American Registry of Radiologic Technologists
1255 Northland Drive
St. Paul, MN 55120-1155
651.687.0048
www.arrt.org

American Society of Radiologic Technologists
15000 Central Avenue, SE
Albuquerque, NM 87123-3917
800.444.2778
www.asrt.org

Joint Review Committee on Education in Radiologic Technology
20 N. Wacker Drive, Suite 2850
Chicago, IL 60606-2901
312.704.5300
mail@jrcert.org
www.jrcert.org

Simone Isadora Flynn/Editor

Radiologist

Snapshot

Career Cluster: Health Science, Medicine
Interests: Anatomy & Physiology, Medicine, Patient Care, Medical Technology
Earnings (Yearly Average): $410,035
Employment & Outlook: Faster Than Average Growth Expected

OVERVIEW

Sphere of Work

Radiologists are medical doctors who assess, diagnose, and treat diseases and other physical problems by means of radiologic technology. They use X-rays, computed tomography (CT) scans, positron emission tomography (PET) scans, magnetic resonance imaging (MRI) technologies, and other radiologic procedures to scan patients for tumors, broken bones, and other internal issues. Based on the images revealed, radiologists determine the causes of symptoms and consult with other physicians on the best course of treatment.

Work Environment

Radiologists work primarily in busy medical environments. Most work in hospitals, while others work in private medical offices or clinics. Because scanning images can be read from virtually any location at any time, radiologists can maintain flexible schedules, and some are able to work off-site, conferring with other physicians through e-mail and hospital communications systems. Prospective radiologists should be aware that although medical facilities have strict protocols regarding patient and staff safety, there is still a risk of exposure to blood and other bodily fluids, and some patients may be panicked or difficult while undergoing radiologic scans.

Profile

Working Conditions: Work Indoors
Physical Strength: Light Work
Education Needs: Medical Degree
Licensure/Certification: Required
Physical Abilities Not Required: No Heavy Labor
Opportunities For Experience: Military Service
Holland Interest Score*: ISR

* See Appendix A

Occupation Interest

Radiologists must be inquisitive and extraordinarily attentive to detail, with exceptional vision and analytical skills and a thorough knowledge of anatomy and physiology. Prospective radiologists should have an aptitude for computers and machinery. They should also excel at communication and teamwork, as they must often collaborate with other physicians regarding a patient's condition.

A Day in the Life—Duties and Responsibilities

Radiologists may meet with patients before an X-ray, mammogram, ultrasound, CT scan, PET scan, or MRI in order to explain the procedure. They may also ask about the patients' medical histories and symptoms so they can better understand any unusual images in the scans. In the case of fluoroscopic and other X-ray procedures, radiologists administer radiopaque substances (such as barium) by mouth, injection, or enema in order to better view soft tissues, internal organs, and physiological systems. Protective lead sheets or vests are used to protect patients from harmful radiation to body areas that are not being scanned. Radiologists and radiologic technologists may work together to properly position the device being used and complete the scan. In many institutions, a radiologic technologist gathers the patient information and performs the scans, leaving the radiologist free to concentrate on diagnosis and treatment plans.

Interventional radiologists, on the other hand, use radiological techniques to treat patients' conditions (by means of nonsurgical or minimally invasive procedures), and so they interact with the patients directly and operate the scanning equipment themselves.

Once the images are taken, radiologists develop and analyze them to locate signs of disease, broken bones, hemorrhages, or any other physiological issues. Radiologists frequently consult with other physicians, including the patient's primary care physician, to determine the patient's condition and the best way to initiate treatment. They are also responsible for keeping records of the procedures performed and their outcomes. They may oversee a technologist's activities and monitor procedures if they do not perform these tasks themselves.

Many radiologists specialize in certain types of scans, patient populations, or conditions. For example, some radiologists specialize in nuclear radiology, using PET scans and gamma imaging for diagnosis and treatment. Others work primarily with children or women. Some radiologists focus on radiation oncology (using radioactive materials to detect and treat cancer), while others specialize in emergency radiology, in which they work with trauma patients.

Duties and Responsibilities

- **Employing x-rays, CT scans, and MRIs to diagnose medical conditions**
- **Reading/analyzing a variety of medical images**
- **Consulting with patients and patient's physicians and providing medical advice**
- **Performing nonsurgical and/or minimally invasive procedures on patients**

WORK ENVIRONMENT

Physical Environment

Radiologists work in hospitals and medical offices. These environments are extremely clean, well lit, well ventilated, and highly organized. Radiologists must be on their feet while scanning is taking place, and the work involved can cause psychological stress, as any mistakes in reading patient images may be disastrous.

Relevant Skills and Abilities

Analytical Skills
- Analyzing data
- Identifying patterns and anomalies

Communication Skills
- Speaking and writing effectively
- Listening attentively
- Expressing thoughts and ideas

Interpersonal/Social Skills
- Being able to remain calm
- Being able to work both independently and as part of a team
- Cooperating with others
- Being sensitive to others
- Having good judgment
- Being objective
- Being persistent

Organization & Management Skills
- Handling challenging situations
- Making decisions
- Managing people/groups
- Paying attention to and handling details
- Performing duties that may change frequently
- Demonstrating leadership

Planning & Research Skills
- Developing evaluation strategies
- Identifying and solving problems
- Identifying resources
- Gathering information

Technical Skills
- Performing scientific, mathematical, and technical work

Human Environment

In addition to patients and their families, radiologists interact and work with many different personnel. Among these professionals are other physicians, radiologic technologists, students, medical assistants, nurses, hospital administrators, emergency medical technicians, and medical equipment manufacturers.

Technological Environment

Depending on their area of specialty, radiologists use a number of different types of patient scanning technologies, which may include MRIs, CT scans, X-ray machines, PET scans and other forms of nuclear radiology, ultrasound and mammography, and angiograms. Radiologists must also use computer programs such as patient information and medical reference databases, high-resolution photo imaging software, and basic office suites.

EDUCATION, TRAINING, AND ADVANCEMENT

High School/Secondary

High school students should study biology, chemistry, anatomy, physics, physiology, and other natural sciences. Math courses such as calculus, algebra, and geometry are also essential. English courses will help students hone their communication skills, and classes in psychology, child development, and health can aid them in developing a positive bedside manner. Volunteer work in local medical centers or hospitals will provide familiarity with the health-care field.

Suggested High School Subjects
- Algebra
- Biology
- Chemistry
- College Preparatory
- English
- Geometry
- Health Science Technology
- Humanities
- Mathematics
- Physics
- Physiology
- Science
- Sociology
- Statistics
- Trigonometry

Famous First

The first full-body scan of a person employing MRI technology was done in 1977 by inventor and physician Raymond Damadian of New York. Damadian went on to found the FONAR Corporation which released the first commercially available MRI scanner in 1980. MRI scanners produce detailed images of soft tissues and fluids that x-ray machines cannot capture well.

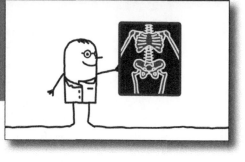

College/Postsecondary

Radiologists must first obtain a bachelor's degree in biology, chemistry, or some related field with a premedical focus, then pass the Medical College Admission Test (MCAT) and attend an accredited four-year medical school program. Medical schools offer hands-on clinical experience as well as classroom and laboratory instruction. Thereafter, aspiring radiologists must complete a minimum of four years of radiology residency training. Those who wish to specialize in a radiology subfield should pursue a one- or two-year fellowship after their residency.

Related College Majors
- Anatomy & Physiology
- Biophysics Medicine (M.D.)
- Osteopathic Medicine
- Pre-Medicine Studies

Adult Job Seekers

Radiologists may find full-time employment as the result of an internship or residency program. They can apply directly to hospitals and medical offices that post openings. Radiologists may also find it helpful to join and network through medical societies and associations, such as the Radiological Society of North America and the American College of Radiology.

Professional Certification and Licensure

All physicians, radiologists included, must pass the U.S. Medical Licensing Examination (USMLE) in order to receive a license from their state's medical board. Radiologists must also complete a board certification exam that focuses primarily on radiology. Further credentials may be necessary to practice in a radiological subspecialty.

Additional Requirements

Aspiring radiologists must be strongly committed to their career goal, as it takes many years of formal schooling to become a practicing radiologist. Additional education is a requirement for ongoing licensure and certification.

Fun Fact

For radiologists, aerobic activities are by far the most popular exercises (over 70%). About 35% of radiologists chose weight training as their second most favored exercise, followed by competitive sports, winter sports, yoga, and tai chi.

Source: Medscape Radiologist Lifestyle Report 2012

EARNINGS AND ADVANCEMENT

Radiologists have among the highest earnings of any occupation. Earnings depend on geographic location, number of years in practice, skill, and professional reputation. According to Allied Physicians, Inc., median annual earnings of radiologists were $410,035 in 2012.

Radiologists may receive paid vacations, holidays, and sick days; life and health insurance; and retirement benefits. Some employers provide for paid educational leave.

Metropolitan Areas with the Highest Employment Level in this Occupation (Physicians and Surgeons)

Metropolitan area	Employment	Employment per thousand jobs	Hourly mean wage
New York-White Plains-Wayne, NY-NJ	26,080	5.06	$73.84
Chicago-Joliet-Naperville, IL	12,140	3.33	$72.56
Los Angeles-Long Beach-Glendale, CA	7,740	2.00	$94.73
Atlanta-Sandy Springs-Marietta, GA	6,210	2.75	$97.02
Nassau-Suffolk, NY	6,110	5.00	$97.38
Bethesda-Rockville-Frederick, MD	5,910	10.56	$78.24
Boston-Cambridge-Quincy, MA	5,750	3.36	$62.33
Washington-Arlington-Alexandria, DC-VA-MD-WV	5,170	2.21	$81.05

Source: Bureau of Labor Statistics

EMPLOYMENT AND OUTLOOK

Radiologists held about 36,000 jobs nationally in 2012. Employment of radiologists is expected to grow faster than the average for all occupations through the year 2020, which means employment is projected to increase about 24 percent. This is due to the continued growth of the health-care industry. Demand for all physicians will continue to increase as consumers are looking for high levels of care using the latest technologies, tests and therapies.

Employment Trend, Projected 2010–20

Health Diagnosing and Treating Practitioners: 26%

Physicians and Surgeons: 24%

Total, All Occupations: 14%

Note: "All Occupations" includes all occupations in the U.S. Economy. Source: U.S. Bureau of Labor Statistics, Employment Projections Program

Related Occupations
- Cardiologist
- Neurologist
- Pediatrician
- Physician
- Surgeon

Related Military Occupations
- Physician & Surgeon

Conversation With . . .
MATTHEW J. BASSIGNANI, MD
Radiologist, 18 years

1. What was your individual career path in terms of education, entry-level job, or other significant opportunity?

I got my undergraduate degree in occupational therapy cum laude from Boston University, and always wanted to go on to medical school. The Allied Health Professions school at BU (Sargent College) allowed me to work with patients sooner than if I had followed a conventional pre-med track. I graduated from BU School of Medicine, completed a residency in Diagnostic Radiology at Tufts-New England Medical Center and a fellowship in Body Imaging at University of Virginia in Charlottesville, VA . I worked as faculty radiologist at the Medical College of Virginia in Richmond, then accepted a position at the University of Virginia where I moved up to associate professor before moving to private practice at Virginia Urology, where I have been medical director for radiology since 2009.

2. Are there many job opportunities in your profession? In what specific areas?

There is a constant need for radiologists because radiology is an all-encompassing specialty. Any patient with a complex issue almost certainly gets one or more diagnostic imaging studies, which is especially true for patients who visit an ED, or emergency department. Imaging subspecialties include pediatrics, musculoskeletal radiology, breast, neuroradiology, chest, cardiac, nuclear medicine, CT, MRI, ultrasound, gastrointestinal and genitourinary imaging and interventional specialties such as angiography.

3. What do you wish you had known going into this profession?

It's hard to say anything would have swayed me one way or the other. Most people who REALLY want to be doctors typically have a laser beam focus on achieving that goal. I love being a doctor. Still, it would have been nice to know that the government would spend so much time regulating the medical industry. For example, the government unilaterally decides how much to pay us for studies for Medicare and Medicaid patients, (about 50 percent of our patient population) regardless of what those services cost our practice. Then insurance companies, which we've already negotiated a fair price with, turn around and pile on. All of a sudden, what used to be a service that made money to support our clinical practice is now a money-loser. It makes it really hard to run a practice. The government represents a huge, overreaching bureaucracy that makes it hard for people to do what they want to do, which is to be a doctor.

4. How do you see your profession changing in the next five years?

It's already happening. Government continues to regulate, which places huge time requirements on physicians to meet those regulations (e.g., quality assurance, quality improvement, accreditation, excessive documentation). Everything has to go through a particular agency that is accredited by the government. Many small practices cannot cope with these bureaucratic hurdles and ultimately sell to large corporations that can manage these myriad requirements. This is leading to the industrialization of the medical field, meaning doctors work for corporations. The patient is a widget and the doctor is processing a widget. How many widgets do you see in an hour? The person who wants to be a general practitioner in his hometown and take care of the people there can't possibly do that anymore.

On a positive note, changes in technology have brought a bounty of new enhancements that allow radiologists to play a central role in patient diagnosis and treatment. These technological advances make radiology a very interesting specialty where one is never bored and there is always something new and useful being developed to help the radiologist do his job better. It is this diverseness of my specialty that keeps me interested and happy in my chosen career.

5. What role will technology play in those changes, and what skills will be required?

Radiologists are typically technophiles and very visually oriented. These two skills make a good radiologist. The ability to communicate complex radiographic findings and their implications also makes a radiologist a valuable resource to referring clinicians. The successful radiologist is someone who works well with patients (not all can) so that the patient understands and respects the role of the radiologist as a consultant to their primary care physician.

6. Do you have any general advice or additional professional insights to share with someone interested in your profession?

You must know early on in your educational career if you want to be a physician because there are so many prerequisites to get into medical school that you really must have "all your ducks in a row." If being a physician is really what you want to do, get practical experience early on. Visit the Association of American Medical Colleges (AAMC) website (www.aamc.org) for information about what is required, including the MCAT (Medical College Admissions Test).

7. Can you suggest a valuable "try this" for students considering a career in your profession?

You need to be certain that you want to be a doctor. The educational path is so long that it would be a shame to get half or all the way through and find out it wasn't exactly what you thought it was. Volunteer in a hospital during high school, working in several different departments or clinics. Make sure you like working with patients, hospital staff, and physicians. But, do not expend all of your energy just getting into medical school. Medical schools really want to make sure that their applicants are well-rounded individuals, so take some electives. Pursue hobbies. Volunteer in your community. Travel outside of the United States, perhaps as part of a relief effort. Be sure that these activities represent a true effort to make yourself a well-rounded applicant. Don't just pad your application.

SELECTED SCHOOLS

There are a number of good medical schools with radiology programs in the United States. Below are listed some of the more prominent institutions in this field.

Duke University
School of Medicine
201 Trent Drive
Durham, NC 27710
919.684.2985
medschool.duke.edu

Johns Hopkins University
School of Medicine
733 N. Broadway
Baltimore, MD 21205
410.955.3182
www.hopkinsmedicine.org

Stanford University
School of Medicine
291 Campus Drive
Stanford, CA 94305
650.725.3900
med.stanford.edu

University of California, San Francisco
School of Medicine
513 Parnassus Avenue
San Francisco, CA 94143
415.476.2342
medschool.ucsf.edu

University of Michigan, Ann Arbor
Medical School
1301 S. Catherine Avenue
Ann Arbor, MI 48109
734.763.9600
medicine.umich.edu

University of Minnesota
Medical School
420 Delaware Street SE
Minneapolis, MN 55455
612.625.7977
www.med.umn.edu

University of Pennsylvania
Perelman School of Medicine
421 Curie Boulevard
Philadelphia, PA 19104
215.662.4000
www.med.upenn.edu

University of Washington
School of Medicine
1959 N.E. Pacific Street
Seattle, WA 98195
206.543.2100
www.uwmedicine.org

Washington University, St. Louis
School of Medicine
1 Brookings Drive
St. Louis, MO 63130
314.935.5000
medschool.wustl.edu

Yale University
School of Medicine
333 Cedar Street
New Haven, CT 06510
203.432.4771
medicine.yale.edu

MORE INFORMATION

American Association for Women Radiologists
4550 Post Oak Place, Suite 342
Houston, TX 77027
713.956.0566
www.aawr.org

American College of Radiology
1891 Preston White Drive
Reston, VA 20191
800.227.5463
www.acr.org

American Medical Association
515 N. State Street
Chicago, IL 60654
800.621.8335
www.ama-assn.org

American Society for Radiation Oncology
8280 Willow Oaks Corporate Drive, Suite 500
Fairfax, VA 22031
703.502.1550
www.astro.org

Radiological Society of North America
820 Jorie Boulevard
Oak Brook, IL 60523
630.571.2670
www.rsna.org

Society for Nuclear Medicine
1850 Samuel Morse Drive
Reston, VA 20190
703.708.9000
www.snm.org

Society for Pediatric Radiology
1891 Preston White Drive
Reston, VA 20191
703.648.0680
www.pedrad.org

Michael Auerbach/Editor

Registered Nurse (RN)

Snapshot

Career Cluster: Health Care

Interests: Medicine, Anatomy & Physiology, Patient Care

Earnings (Yearly Average): $68,571

Employment & Outlook: Faster Than Average Growth Expected

OVERVIEW

Sphere of Work

Registered nurses (RNs) assist physicians in the diagnosis and treatment of various medical conditions and diseases. Their job largely consists of catering to the physical, mental, and emotional needs of patients, educating patients and their families on proper post-treatment care and pain management, and encouraging wellness and preventive health-care measures. Registered nurses can specialize in a type of treatment, medical condition, organ or body system, patient population, or work setting.

Work Environment

Most registered nurses work in health-care facilities, which are clean, organized, and brightly lit. Home health and private duty nurses work in a variety of settings, often traveling to the homes of individual patients. Some nurses provide public health services to schools, nursing homes, or other community centers. Registered nurses are generally subject to irregular schedules, often working shifts of eight to twelve hours at night, on the weekends, and during holidays; some nurses are even on call to assist patients who need round-the-clock care. Their work is usually directed by a head nurse or supervisor.

Profile

Working Conditions: Work Indoors
Physical Strength: Light Work
Education Needs: Doctoral Degree
Licensure/Certification: Required
Physical Abilities Not Required: No Heavy Labor
Opportunities For Experience: Military Service
Holland Interest Score*: IES

* See Appendix A

Occupation Interest

Those interested in becoming a registered nurse should be curious about the human body, its functions, and its susceptibility to diseases. They should enjoy continually researching and learning about new medical conditions, treatments, and trends in the field, as medicine is always changing and developing. Prospective nurses should also be empathetic, kind, reassuring, and committed to helping those in physical, mental, and emotional need. Effective communication, physical and emotional endurance, and a sense of discretion are also helpful.

A Day in the Life—Duties and Responsibilities

Registered nurses juggle many responsibilities during each shift. They may be responsible for a single patient or several patients at a time. Nurses evaluate and record patients' symptoms and vital signs and keep track of changes in their condition. When necessary, they order diagnostic tests, prepare patients for procedures, conduct laboratory tests, and assess test results. Registered nurses prescribe and administer treatments according to the patient's plan of care, which may involve tasks as simple as giving a patient antibiotic medication or as complex as providing life support to trauma patients. They also educate patients and family members on post-hospital care, disease prevention, plans of care, and health improvement methods. In many cases, registered nurses take on managerial roles and must perform various administrative tasks, such as budget planning, inventory maintenance, and staff scheduling.

Often, registered nurses must supervise a specific unit or department, which involves overseeing and instructing other nurses and health-care professionals. They consult with physicians on treatments and plans of care for patients. They regularly assist physicians with patient examinations, treatments, and surgeries, for which they may be required to prepare examination rooms and organize medical equipment. Nurses often follow up with patients, providing continued support and altering plans of care when necessary.

Many registered nurses also perform medical research, studying changes in the field of nursing. Public health nurses focus heavily on the educational aspect of the work and design prevention and wellness programs.

Duties and Responsibilities

- Greeting and familiarizing new patients with hospital routines
- Determining nursing and health needs of patients
- Tending to wounds and injuries
- Preparing patients for surgery
- Aiding the physician during examination and treatment
- Assisting with operations and deliveries by preparing rooms, equipment, and supplies and assisting the physician
- Administering prescribed drugs, injections, and treatments
- Observing and recording the condition of patients, including their vital signs
- Directing and supervising less skilled nursing personnel
- Teaching and counseling patients and their families
- Helping people to improve or maintain their health

OCCUPATION SPECIALTIES

General Duty Nurses

General Duty Nurses provide overall nursing care to patients in hospitals, long-term care facilities, or similar institutions. They also may work in specialized units such as cardiovascular departments, neonatal departments (attending to newborns), intensive care units, surgery units, or addiction/rehabilitation centers.

School and Occupational Health Nurses

School Nurses are responsible for the nursing needs of elementary, middle school, high school, and college students. Occupational Health Nurses provide nursing service and first aid to employees or persons who become ill or injured on the premises of industrial plants or other commercial establishments. Both types of nurse also develop information programs such as health education and accident prevention.

Private Practice and Private Duty Nurses

Private Practice Nurses care for and treat patients in medical offices as directed by physicians. Private Duty Nurses provide constant bedside care to one patient either in a hospital or at the patient's home.

Community Health Nurses

Community Health Nurses instruct individuals and families in health education and disease prevention in community health agencies.

Advance Practice Nurses

Advance Practice Nurses may provide primary and specialty care, and, in most states, they may prescribe medicines. All states specifically define requirements for registered nurses in these four advanced practice roles:

–*Clinical Nurse Specialists* provide direct patient care and expert consultations in one of many nursing specialties, such as psychiatric-mental health.

– *Nurse Anesthetists* *provide* anesthesia and related care before and after surgical, therapeutic, diagnostic, and obstetrical procedures. They also provide pain management and emergency services.

– *Nurse-midwives* provide care to women, including gynecological exams, family planning advice, prenatal care, assistance in labor and delivery, and care of newborns.

– *Nurse Practitioners* serve as primary and specialty care providers, providing a blend of nursing and primary care services to patients and families.

WORK ENVIRONMENT

Physical Environment

The majority of nursing is performed at hospitals, clinics, private homes, and community centers. All nursing work environments must be orderly and sanitary; however, private duty, home health, and public health nurses may have less control over the condition of the physical environments in which they work. Nurses constantly bend, walk, and stand. They must follow strict safety protocols to avoid contracting infectious diseases, being exposed to toxins or radiation, and incurring work-related injuries.

Relevant Skills and Abilities

Analytical Skills
- Expressing thoughts and ideas
- Speaking and writing effectively

Communication Skills
- Listening to others
- Speaking and writing effectively

Interpersonal/Social Skills
- Cooperating with others
- Working as a member of a team
- Being sensitive to others

Organization & Management Skills
- Coordinating tasks
- Following instructions
- Making decisions
- Managing people/groups
- Paying attention to and handling details

Technical Skills
- Performing technical work

Human Environment

Registered nurses regularly work with doctors, other nurses, physician assistants, administrative personnel, and other hospital or clinic staff. Nurses also frequently interact with patients as well as patients' friends and family members. Registered nurses usually report to a head nurse, supervisor, or physician.

Technological Environment

Registered nurses use a wide array of technical equipment to aid them in their daily tasks. They commonly use sterile medical instruments, surgical equipment, stethoscopes, electronic blood pressure monitors, and oxygen masks. As for digital resources, they may use medical reference databases, medical software, and the Internet.

EDUCATION, TRAINING, AND ADVANCEMENT

High School/Secondary

High school students who wish to pursue a career in nursing should start by taking courses in the sciences, sociology, psychology, social work, health and nutrition, English, and technology. Preparatory courses in mathematics, physical education, and communications are also beneficial for the prospective nursing student. During the summer months or during school vacations, students can volunteer at or tour local hospitals, clinics, nursing homes, or community centers where they can provide assistance to patients in need. Through these experiences, students can also become familiar with the various responsibilities of a registered nurse.

Suggested High School Subjects
- Algebra
- Applied Biology/Chemistry
- Applied Communication
- Applied Math
- Biology
- Chemistry
- Child Growth & Development
- College Preparatory
- English
- First Aid Training
- Foods & Nutrition
- Health Science Technology
- Medical Assisting
- Nurse Assisting
- Physical Science
- Physics
- Physiology
- Psychology
- Science
- Social Studies

Famous First

The first nursing school to be developed as part of a university was the School of Nursing at the University of Minnesota, in Minneapolis, in 1909, under the direction of Bertha Erdmann. Six students were admitted to the first class. Superintendent Erdmann soon went on to pioneer a second collegiate nursing school, at the University of North Dakota, in Grand Forks.

Library of Congress

College/Postsecondary

After high school, students can enroll in one of three programs to obtain a postsecondary degree in registered nursing. They can earn a bachelor's degree in nursing (BSN), an associate's degree in nursing (ADN), or a three-year diploma from a hospital. Educational programs in nursing offer courses in biology, chemistry, anatomy, nutrition, physiology, psychology and psychiatry, human development, pharmacology, and patient care for various populations. They also provide practical clinical experience at health-care facilities in many areas of medicine, including pediatrics, mental health, surgery, and maternity. Those who wish to specialize in advanced areas of practice or find employment in administration or education must pursue a master's degree in nursing (MSN). An MSN may take two to four years to complete, depending on whether the applicant already holds a BSN degree.

Related College Majors
- Anatomy & Physiology
- Health Sciences
- Nursing (L.P.N.)
- Nursing (R.N.)
- Nursing Anesthetist
- Nursing Midwifery

Adult Job Seekers

After obtaining one of three nursing degrees, registered nurses can enter the workforce as staff nurses. They generally find employment through school-to-work opportunities, internships, or apprenticeships. They can also apply directly with hospitals or clinics.

Those who have an ADN or diploma may have fewer opportunities for advancement than those with a BSN. Many working registered nurses with an ADN or diploma can complete an RN-to-BSN program through a hospital or health-care facility. Accelerated one-year BSN or two-year MSN programs are available to individuals who have already earned a bachelor's degree in another field. Some employers offer tuition reimbursement for ongoing education as an employment benefit.

Professional Certification and Licensure

All registered nurses must be licensed by their state. To obtain professional licensure, registered nurses must complete an approved nursing program and successfully pass the National Council Licensure Examination (NCLEX-RN). Licensure requirements vary by state, so applicants should consult the National Council of State Boards of Nursing for specific details.

Voluntary professional certification is available in certain nursing specialties and may be a requirement for employment or promotion. Continuing education may be required for ongoing licensure or certification.

Additional Requirements

Registered nurses must always follow and adapt to changes in the medical field. As new trends and recommendations surface, registered nurses should actively seek to understand and learn more about them. Because the field of medicine is vast and the number of illnesses and disorders is so high, registered nurses must seek to evaluate, diagnose, and treat patients with the greatest degree of accuracy possible. They must also remain calm and clear-headed during emergencies and crises, be able to think on their feet, and make quick executive decisions.

EARNINGS AND ADVANCEMENT

Earnings depend on the type of institution (hospital, medical school, doctor's office or medical center), the geographic location and the employee's education, experience and position. Registered nurses who have completed a Bachelor of Science in Nursing degree will be in greatest demand and will be able to advance more quickly. Also, because demand for registered nurses is high, employers have begun to tie salaries to educational preparation.

Median annual earnings of registered nurses were $68,571 in 2012. The lowest ten percent earned less than $46,841, and the highest ten percent earned more than $100,838.

Registered nurses may receive paid vacations, holidays, and sick days; life and health insurance; and retirement benefits. These are usually paid by the employer. The majority of registered nurses must buy their own uniforms.

Metropolitan Areas with the Highest Employment Level in this Occupation

Metropolitan area	Employment (1)	Employment per thousand jobs	Hourly mean wage
New York-White Plains-Wayne, NY-NJ	92,060	17.85	$39.63
Chicago-Joliet-Naperville, IL	72,590	19.94	$34.18
Los Angeles-Long Beach-Glendale, CA	69,540	17.96	$41.82
Philadelphia, PA	43,700	23.97	$34.23
Houston-Sugar Land-Baytown, TX	43,180	16.35	$35.51
Boston-Cambridge-Quincy, MA	43,020	25.14	$42.74
Dallas-Plano-Irving, TX	39,120	18.66	$33.08
St. Louis, MO-IL	33,580	26.34	$28.14

(1)Does not include self-employed. Source: Bureau of Labor Statistics, 2012

EMPLOYMENT AND OUTLOOK

There were approximately 2.7 million registered nurses employed nationally in 2012. Employment is expected to grow faster than the average for all occupations through 2020, which means employment is projected to increase up to 26 percent. This is due to technological advances in patient care, more emphasis on preventative care and an elderly population that requires nursing care. Job opportunities should be excellent, especially for registered nurses with advanced education and training.

Employment Trend, Projected 2010–20

Health Diagnosing and Treating Practitioners: 26%

Registered Nurses: 26%

Total, All Occupations: 14%

Note: "All Occupations" includes all occupations in the U.S. Economy. Source: U.S. Bureau of Labor Statistics, Employment Projections Program

Related Occupations
- Emergency Medical Technician
- Licensed Practical Nurse (L.P.N.)
- Nurse Practitioner

Related Military Occupations
- Registered Nurse

Conversation With . . .
TAMMY GOUDREAU
Registered Nurse, 28 years

1. What was your individual career path in terms of education, entry-level job, or other significant opportunity?

I knew I wanted to be a nurse from when I was little. I went to a three-year nursing school. I wanted to do that because it got me in the hospital right away. I started school in the month of August and by October I was already on the floor doing nursing. They taught us how to make a hospital bed, take blood pressure, pulses. As nursing students, we would work with the nurse and also take care of patients. After I graduated, I was hired as a pediatric nurse. Over the years, I've been a cardiac nurse, an intensive care nurse, and an emergency room nurse. In my current role in the transfer and access center, I work with doctors, nursing homes, and clinics, arranging care for patients

2. Are there many job opportunities in your profession? In what specific areas?

When I became a nurse, there was a shortage of nurses. But job opportunities have decreased over the years. With so many businesses downsizing and letting people go, we've seen an increase in the number of people going into nursing as a second career. However, there are always openings in emergency nursing and critical care areas.

3. What do you wish you had known going into this profession?

I wish I knew how tough it was going to be. Being an emergency room nurse, in particular, is hard. You see a lot and you don't have a chance to process it all. You move from one patient to the next. You have to be very, very flexible, not only with the diagnoses of patients, but also you get pulled in so many directions. You get abused by the patients. Some are alcoholics, some are psychiatric patients. You get called every name in the book. You have to let a lot of things roll off. People are always coming at you. You have people waiting five, six, seven hours to be treated and they yell at you. You have to develop a thick skin.

Through those experiences, I learned to go beyond the surface with patients and dig a little bit deeper to see what was really going on with them.

4. How do you see your profession changing in the next five years?

Unfortunately, with everything being computerized, sometimes it feels like the nurses talk more to the computer than they do to the patient. I don't feel that it's as hands on as it used to be.

I also expect that health care will become more decentralized, with medical technicians delivering the medicine and nurses being more behind the scenes doing the paperwork and writing patient care plans. That's because a med tech and a certified nursing assistant are less costly than a nurse.

5. What role will technology play in those changes, and what skills will be required?

Technology is going to make a big impact on nursing. Certain new technologies, such as the IV pump, for example, means that you don't have to calculate anything anymore. You just plug your numbers into your IV pump and it calculates the dosage for you. We now have bedside ultrasounds that we can use to find a vein. So, computer skills will be increasingly required. Online learning is also changing the way we keep up with our certifications. For example, we take CPR classes online. The only time we show up in person is to demonstrate CPR on a dummy to the instructor

6. Do you have any general advice or additional professional insights to share with someone interested in your profession?

I think it's a wonderful profession as long as you're a caring individual and love speaking to people and taking care of them. You need to have that inside of you. The pay is great, but the hours aren't. You can expect to work holidays and weekends.

7. Can you suggest a valuable "try this" for students considering a career in your profession?

You can volunteer in a hospital. Sometimes the volunteer office will place you where you have a specific interest, like the emergency room or the intensive care unit. Just expose yourself to different areas. If you're interested in medicine, volunteering may persuade you to make it a career. Just remember, you get used to things as a nurse. I don't like the operating room. I couldn't go through the OR rotation in nursing school without almost passing out. But you do get used to these things just by virtue of being exposed to it. The first time I saw a lumbar puncture I almost passed out. But I never questioned whether I should be a nurse.

SELECTED SCHOOLS

A number of excellent nursing programs and schools are available for those interested in pursuing a career in this field. Below are listed some of the more prominent four-year and graduate-level institutions.

Duke University
School of Nursing
307 Trent Drive
Durham, NC 27710
919.684.4248
nursing.duke.edu

Johns Hopkins University
School of Nursing
525 N. Wolfe Street
Baltimore, MD 21205
410.955.4766
nursing.jhu.edu

Oregon Health and Science University
School of Nursing
3455 S.W. U.S. Veterans Hospital Road
Portland, OR 97239
503.494.7725
www.ohsu.edu/xd/education/schools/school-of-nursing/

University of California, San Francisco
School of Nursing
2 Koret Way
UCSF Box 0602
San Francisco, CA 94143
415.476.1435
nursing.ucsf.edu

University of Michigan, Ann Arbor
School of Nursing
400 N. Ingalls
Ann Arbor, MI 48109
734.763.5985
nursing.umich.edu

University of North Carolina, Chapel Hill
School of Nursing
Carrington Hall, CB#7640
Chapel Hill, NC 27599
919.966.4260
nursing.unc.edu

University of Pennsylvania
School of Nursing
418 Curie Boulevard
Philadelphia, PA 19104
215.898.8281
www.nursing.upenn.edu

University of Pittsburgh
School of Nursing
3500 Victoria Street
Pittsburgh, PA 15261
412.624.4586
www.nursing.pitt.edu

University of Washington
School of Nursing
1959 N.E. Pacific Street
Box 357260
Seattle, WA 98195
206.543.8736
nursing.uw.edu

Yale University
School of Nursing
P.O. Box 27399
West Haven, CT 06516
203.785.2389
nursing.yale.edu

MORE INFORMATION

American Association of Colleges of Nursing
1 Dupont Circle NW, Suite 530
Washington, DC 20036
202.463.6930
www.aacn.nche.edu

American Nurses Association
8515 Georgia Avenue, Suite 400
Silver Spring, MD 20910-3492
800.274.4262
www.nursingworld.org

American Society of Registered Nurses
1001 Bridgeway, Suite 233
Sausalito, CA 94965
415.331.2700
www.asrn.org

National Council of State Boards of Nursing
111 E. Wacker Drive, Suite 2900
Chicago, IL 60601-4277
312.525.3600
www.ncsbn.org

National League for Nursing
61 Broadway
New York, NY 10006
800.669.1656
www.nln.org

National Student Nurses Association
45 Main Street, Suite 606
Brooklyn, NY 11201
718.210.0705
www.nsna.org

Briana Nadeau/Editor

Surgeon

Snapshot

Career Cluster: Health Science, Medicine
Interests: Medicine, Anatomy & Physiology, Patient Care
Earnings (Yearly Average): $364,595
Employment & Outlook: Faster Than Average Growth Expected

OVERVIEW

Sphere of Work

Surgeons treat a variety of ailments, including injuries, cancerous tumors, and diseases, using invasive methods. They operate on patients using an assortment of surgical instruments and methods. Most surgeons specialize in a specific field, such as brain surgery, pediatric surgery, or cosmetic surgery. Like others in the medical profession, surgeons examine patients, perform specific tests, and counsel patients on medical issues. They look at patients' medical histories and test results to determine the best surgical procedures to use.

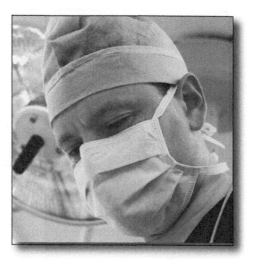

Work Environment

Most surgeons work out of medical facilities, especially hospitals, where they are assisted by nurses and other personnel. The work environment is usually well lit and sterile. While performing an operation, a surgeon typically stands for a long period of time. Many surgeons work irregular hours and often work more than forty hours per week. Travel is a frequent part of a surgeon's career as well, and most spend several hours each week moving between offices and hospitals. Surgeons at times work on call and must be able to travel quickly to a hospital if there is an emergency.

Profile

Working Conditions: Work Indoors
Physical Strength: Light Work
Education Needs: Medical Degree
Licensure/Certification: Required
Physical Abilities Not Required: No Heavy Labor
Opportunities For Experience: Military Service
Holland Interest Score*: IRA

* See Appendix A

Occupation Interest

Like most medical professionals, surgeons must undergo extensive education and training. They are empathetic and believe in making a difference in the lives of others. Surgeons must be very understanding of their patients' needs and strive to educate them as best they can. Since a surgeon's work requires precision and accuracy, the profession calls for great attention to detail.

A Day in the Life—Duties and Responsibilities

The primary duty of a surgeon is to perform operations on patients. In addition to the actual act of surgery, surgeons also examine patients and their medical histories, make diagnoses, and perform specialized tests. Depending on the specialization of the surgeon, the day-to-day activities can vary.

When a surgeon first meets a patient, he or she will analyze the patient's medical history, physical condition, allergies, and other physical aspects. Based on the examination and the patient's symptoms, the surgeon may call for further tests to be administered. Once the surgeon has determined the best surgical method to use, he or she will thoroughly explain what the procedure entails, its risks, and what the recovery will be like. Making the patient feel comfortable is an important aspect of the surgeon's job.

During the operation, nurses, anesthesiologists, residents, and other specialists aid the surgeon, who directs and manages those assisting. Surgical instruments and tools must be checked for sterility. In addition to a variety of small surgical instruments, modern surgeons use miniature cameras and powered tools.

Surgeons also conduct research concerning surgical techniques and instruments that can help improve operating procedures and results. Many surgeons publish their research findings in medical journals and attend related conferences.

Duties and Responsibilities

- Conducting medical interviews
- Evaluating medical test results and x-rays or other images
- Providing medical advice
- Performing surgical procedures on patients
- Overseeing the work of other medical professionals in the operating room
- Following up with patients during their recovery
- Prescribing medication
- Keeping abreast of developments in the field

WORK ENVIRONMENT

Relevant Skills and Abilities

Analytical Skills
- Analyzing information
- Assessing courses of action

Communication Skills
- Listening carefully
- Speaking and writing effectively

Interpersonal/Social Skills
- Being able to remain calm under pressure
- Being patient
- Working as a member of a team

Organization & Management Skills
- Handling challenging situations
- Making decisions
- Managing people/groups
- Organizing information or materials
- Paying attention to and handling details

Planning & Research Skills
- Researching information
- Developing a strategy

Technical Skills
- Performing scientific, mathematical, and technical work
- Working with your hands

Other Skills
- Working in a medical setting

Physical Environment

Surgeons work in various medical facilities, such as hospitals and surgical outpatient centers, as well as their own offices. Travel between hospitals and offices is common as well.

Human Environment

Surgeons work alongside a variety of other individuals in the medical profession, including physicians, nurses, and specialists. They work closely with their patients as well as with patients' families, and the nature of their work requires them to make frequent physical contact with patients.

Technological Environment

Surgeons use a wide range of specially designed instruments and tools, including scalpels, retractors that open tissue, clamps for blood vessels, tubes and needles for injecting fluids, fiber optic endoscopes, and different measuring devices. They may also use tools such as drills (for bone) and dermatomes (for skin grafts).

EDUCATION, TRAINING, AND ADVANCEMENT

High School/Secondary

The education and training requirements for surgeons are highly demanding. A high school diploma is required in order to move on to the postsecondary education and training required of surgeons. High schools offer an assortment of basic and advanced courses that would be beneficial to a student interested in becoming a surgeon. These courses include anatomy, biology, and chemistry.

Suggested High School Subjects
- Biology
- Chemistry
- College Preparatory
- Computer Science
- English
- Health Science Technology
- Physics
- Physiology
- Science

Famous First

The first television broadcast of a surgical procedure occurred in March 1952 in Philadelphia. A local station showed Dr. Isador S. Ravdin of the University of Pennsylvania Hospital operating on a peptic ulcer. In June of that same year the first nationwide surgical broadcast took place when Dr. Samuel Fogelson of Wesley Memorial Hospital in Chicago was shown performing a duodenal ulcer operation.

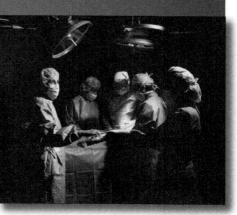

Library of Congress

College/Postsecondary

Eight years of formal education is required for surgeons to complete their schooling. This typically includes four years of undergraduate studies and four years of medical school. Further education may be necessary depending on the surgeon's specialty. An undergraduate studying to be a surgeon should complete courses in biology, physics, chemistry, and mathematics. Learning to communicate well with others both orally and in written form is crucial, so students should also take English and humanities courses. Students can volunteer at hospitals or outpatient clinics in order to gain experience and work alongside professionals.

To continue on to medical school, a student must typically hold a bachelor's or more advanced degree. Applicants must submit transcripts, letters of recommendation, and sometimes essays detailing why they believe they should be selected. An interview with an admissions board is often required. Students must also successfully complete the Medical College Admission Test (MCAT). Medical schools are very competitive, so students should be sure to excel in their undergraduate studies and MCAT. Some medical schools offer combined undergraduate and medical school programs that can last six to seven years.

The first two years of medical school are typically spent in a formal classroom and laboratory where students are instructed in anatomy, biochemistry, pathology, medical ethics, and a variety of related topics. Students acquire practical knowledge and skills, such as how to record a patient's medical history, examine patients, and make diagnoses. The last two years are spent working with patients in hospitals or clinics, where students learn about the procedures and techniques involved in surgery under the guidance of experienced professionals. After medical school, surgeons enter a rotating residency in which they acquire hands-on training in a hospital. Residencies can last anywhere from two to eight years.

Related College Majors
- Anatomy & Physiology
- Medicine (M.D.)
- Osteopathic Medicine
- Pre-Medicine Studies

Adult Job Seekers

An adult job seeker interested in becoming a surgeon should consider the amount of education and training needed. Factors that should also be considered include the irregular hours required of many surgeons and the cost of medical school. Due to the amount of time spent training and the irregular hours, surgeons may spend long periods of time away from their families.

Professional Certification and Licensure

A surgeon must be licensed by his or her state of residence in order to practice. In order to be licensed, a surgeon must graduate from an accredited medical school, pass an examination, and complete one to seven years of graduate medical education. Some states allow license reciprocity.

Additional Requirements

Surgeons must be detail oriented, persistent, and passionate about helping other people. They need to be physically able to work long, irregular hours and should be able to make decisions quickly during emergencies. The nature of the work requires surgeons to follow strict safety procedures.

EARNINGS AND ADVANCEMENT

Surgeons enjoy being at the top of the advancement ladder, but they may continue to take additional training to sharpen or focus their area of expertise. Earnings of surgeons depend on the individual's years in practice, skill, personality, professional reputation, and size of patient load, and the geographic area in which one chooses to practice. They may choose to practice individually or as part of a group. General surgeons had median annual earnings of $364,595 in 2012.

Most surgeons operate as independent contractors with insurance companies and hospitals, and, as such, are self-employed. They are able to have any fringe benefit that they can create for themselves. Surgeons practicing in a group setting can receive benefits, such as paid vacations, holidays, and sick days; life and health insurance; and retirement benefits.

Metropolitan Areas with the Highest Employment Level in this Occupation

Metropolitan area	Employment (1)	Employment per thousand jobs	Hourly mean wage
New York-White Plains-Wayne, NY-NJ	1,550	0.30	$93.18
Los Angeles-Long Beach-Glendale, CA	1,210	0.31	$106.00
Chicago-Joliet-Naperville, IL	870	0.24	$117.06
Minneapolis-St. Paul-Bloomington, MN-WI	710	0.40	n/a
Louisville-Jefferson County, KY-IN	660	1.11	$110.71
Philadelphia, PA	660	0.36	n/a
Washington-Arlington-Alexandria, DC-VA-MD-WV	630	0.27	$116.02
Sacramento–Arden-Arcade–Roseville, CA	590	0.72	n/a

(1)Excludes oral and maxillofacial surgeons. Source: Bureau of Labor Statistics, 2012

EMPLOYMENT AND OUTLOOK

Surgeons held about 43,000 jobs nationally in 2012. Due to the continued growth of the health-care industry, employment of surgeons is expected to grow faster than the average for all occupations through the year 2020, which means employment is projected to increase nearly 25 percent. Job demand will be especially high in rural and low-income areas.

Employment Trend, Projected 2010–20

Health Diagnosing and Treating Practitioners: 26%

Physicians and Surgeons: 24%

Total, All Occupations: 14%

Note: "All Occupations" includes all occupations in the U.S. Economy. Source: U.S. Bureau of Labor Statistics, Employment Projections Program

Related Occupations
- Cardiologist
- Dentist
- Medical Scientist
- Neurologist
- Pediatrician
- Physician
- Radiologist

Related Military Occupations
- Physician & Surgeon

Conversation With . . .
BROOKE BUCKLEY, MD FACS
General Surgeon, 6 years

1. What was your individual career path in terms of education, entry-level job, or other significant opportunity?

I am a so-called "straight arrow." I grew up in a medical family, I always wanted to be a doctor, and I went straight through school without any time off. I went to The Johns Hopkins University undergraduate, as a biology major. One-third of the class there goes into medicine, so the competition is strong. In med school I had friends who went to smaller schools and in some ways they had an easier time applying because they were unique in their schools as opposed to one of many. I went to The Ohio State University College of Medicine. I started off wanting to go into pediatric oncology because I had a friend in college who passed away from cancer. In my third year of med school, when I did my surgery rotation, I fell in love with the people I worked with. I thought I wanted to do pediatrics based on the patient population, but I chose my career based on my colleagues. At the most basic level, surgeons are doers and pediatricians and interns are thinkers. It doesn't mean we don't think, but we can fix stuff. As a surgeon, you get called in when people are at their worst. That certainly means we have much bigger misses when things go wrong, but there's something really satisfying about being able to fly in and fix things. I did my residency at Fairview Hospital, which is part of the Cleveland Clinic system.

2. Are there many job opportunities in your profession? In what specific areas?

The job opportunities are huge. A surgeon shortage of over 20,000 is projected by 2020. Obviously you can't just crank out new surgeons; it takes four years of medical school and a minimum five-year residency. In general surgery, there's huge opportunity because there's so much pressure to become a specialist. General surgeons are badly needed in small communities–as are family doctors and pediatricians.

3. What do you wish you had known going into this profession?

Medical school goes in phases. You're all sorts of excited when you go to med school, because you're going to be a doctor. But residency training is long and there were times that I hated what I was doing, and missing friends' weddings and all the normal things people do. I wish had known there was light at the end of the tunnel. You finish, and all of the reasons you wanted to go to med school are available to you again.

Also, a lot of physicians right now are down on the practice of medicine, which is changing rapidly. But everything in the world is changing and medicine, at the least, is a skill that is portable and undeniable. We will always need doctors who do procedures, like surgeons. Saving someone's life is an amazing honor.

4. How do you see your profession changing in the next five years?

The focus of American health care is changing from treating disease to trying to prevent disease. This means that when patients make it to a surgeon, they will often have more illnesses and have more challenging issues to deal with. This makes being a primary care provider even more challenging and exciting. At the same time, it requires more strategic thinking from the primary care providers to help people stay healthy.

5. What role will technology play in those changes, and what skills will be required?

Medical records increasingly are required to be electronic. Anyone in high school or college now will never know what it's like to have a paper chart. As surgeons, we also need to use a lot of computer-based equipment. Interestingly, video game-type simulation helps doctors acquire skills in fields like robotic and laparoscopic surgery.

6. Do you have any general advice or additional professional insights to share with someone interested in your profession?

I would suggest considering your options in the health field because becoming a doctor is a long and difficult process. If you can be happy as another type of provider –such as a nurse, physical therapist, occupational therapist, physicians' assistant– then seriously consider that role. The road is shorter and less arduous. If you look at those professions and still want to be a physician, go for it with all your heart ... it will be worth it. The long hours will fade away as you become autonomous in helping people live healthier lives.

7. Can you suggest a valuable "try this" for students considering a career in your profession?

I think that for people who have always known they wanted to go into medicine–or even the opposite, people who think they could never be a doctor because they don't like blood–spending time shadowing a doctor is hugely valuable. Getting exposure in high school and college will change your reality in ways you can't anticipate until you try it.

SELECTED SCHOOLS

There are a number of good medical schools with surgery programs in the United States. Below are listed some of the more prominent institutions in this field.

Columbia University
College of Physicians and Surgeons
630 W. 128th Street
New York, NY 10032
212.305.3601
ps.columbia.edu

Duke University
School of Medicine
201 Trent Drive
Durham, NC 27710
919.684.2985
medschool.duke.edu

Harvard Medical School
25 Shattuck Street
Boston, MA 02115
617.432.1000
hms.harvard.edu

Johns Hopkins University
School of Medicine
733 N. Broadway
Baltimore, MD 21205
410.955.3182
www.hopkinsmedicine.org

Stanford University
School of Medicine
291 Campus Drive
Stanford, CA 94305
650.725.3900
med.stanford.edu

University of California, San Francisco
School of Medicine
513 Parnassus Avenue
San Francisco, CA 94143
415.476.2342
medschool.ucsf.edu

University of Michigan, Ann Arbor
Medical School
1301 S. Catherine Avenue
Ann Arbor, MI 48109
734.763.9600
medicine.umich.edu

University of Pennsylvania
Perelman School of Medicine
421 Curie Boulevard
Philadelphia, PA 19104
215.662.4000
www.med.upenn.edu

University of Washington
School of Medicine
1959 N.E. Pacific Street
Seattle, WA 98195
206.543.2100
www.uwmedicine.org

Washington University, St. Louis
School of Medicine
1 Brookings Drive
St. Louis, MO 63130
314.935.5000
medschool.wustl.edu

MORE INFORMATION

American College of Surgeons
633 N Saint Clair Street
Chicago, IL 60611
312.202.5000
www.facs.org

American Medical Association
Attn: Undergraduate Medical
Education
515 N. State Street
Chicago, IL 60610
800.621.8335
www.ama-assn.org

**American Medical Women's
Association**
Attn: Career Information
100 North 20th Street, 4th Floor
Philadelphia, PA 19103
215.320.3716
www.amwa-doc.org

American Surgical Association
500 Cummings Center, Suite 4550
Beverly, MA 01915
978.927.8330
www.americansurgical.info

**Association of American Medical
Colleges**
2450 N Street, NW
Washington, DC 20037-1126
202.828.0400
www.aamc.org

Briana Nadeau/Editor

Ultrasound Technician

Snapshot

Career Cluster: Health Science

Interests: Health Care, Medical Technology

Earnings (Yearly Average): $68,243

Employment & Outlook: Faster Than Average Growth Expected

OVERVIEW

Sphere of Work

Ultrasound technicians, also referred to as diagnostic medical sonographers, use ultrasound machines (which produce and record ultrasonic waves) to produce images of internal organs, fluid buildup, fetuses, and suspicious masses. The field they work in is called medical ultrasonography. Physicians use the digital images, printed images, and recordings created by ultrasound technicians to make diagnoses of illness or to rule out illness. Ultrasound technicians usually specialize in the medical imaging of a specific area of the human body, such as the brain, heart, eyes, blood vessels, uterus and ovaries, or fetus. Some choose to specialize in multiple areas.

Work Environment

Ultrasound technicians spend their workdays in hospitals, doctors' offices, and medical imaging centers, and may perform ultrasounds in medical imaging suites, in operating rooms, on emergency room patients, or at a patient's hospital bedside. Generally, they work forty-hour weeks, but longer hours may be required during busy times. Ultrasound technicians' shifts may include days, evenings, weekends, and on-call hours to meet the medical community's increasing need for diagnostic medical imaging.

Profile

Working Conditions: Work Indoors
Physical Strength: Light Work
Education Needs: Technical/
  Community College, Bachelor's Degree
Licensure/Certification:
  Recommended
Physical Abilities Not Required: No
  Heavy Labor
Opportunities For Experience:
  Volunteer Work
Holland Interest Score*: RSI

* See Appendix A

Occupation Interest

Individuals drawn to the profession of medical ultrasonography tend to be intelligent, analytical, and detail oriented. Those most successful as ultrasound technicians display traits such as good eyesight, hand-eye coordination, focus, problem-solving skills, manual dexterity, calm, and tact. Ultrasound technicians should enjoy working in a medical environment and have solid academic and practical training in ultrasound technology.

A Day in the Life—Duties and Responsibilities

The daily occupational duties and responsibilities of ultrasound technicians are determined by the individual's area of job specialization and work environment. Areas of specialization for medical sonographers include, among others, neurosonography (images of the brain and nervous system), cardiac sonography (images of the heart), abdominal sonography (images of the internal organs), ophthalmic sonography (images of the eye), breast sonography, and obstetrical/gynecological sonography (images of the fetus or female reproductive organs).

During a typical work day, an ultrasound technician will begin by preparing and sterilizing his or her sonographic equipment, reporting any problems to biomedical equipment technicians or hospital staff, working with office or hospital staff to schedule patient appointments, and reviewing physicians' ultrasound orders to determine the type of exam required. When a patient arrives for an exam, the sonographer greets him or her and explains the role of the ultrasound imaging with regard to medical diagnosis and treatment. If the patient cannot be easily moved, the exam may be performed at a patient's bedside with a mobile ultrasound machine. The sonographer instructs the patient on the best way to position his or her body to obtain the most accurate image of the area about which the physician needs diagnostic information, and then uses the machine to take ultrasound pictures or recordings of the internal organ(s), fluid buildup, pregnant uterus, or potentially abnormal tissue masses in the patient's body. Throughout the ultrasound exam, the sonographer works to maintain the safety and comfort of the patient, keeping in mind that the patient may be nervous about the results or worried about a possibly life-threatening health problem. Most hospitals and medical offices do not allow sonographers to make diagnoses, so they must be careful not to express visible reactions to the images they see on the ultrasound screen. Often they may have to communicate this to the patient, and let him or her know that the physician is the person making the actual diagnosis. If a patient's ultrasound is related to a significant or upsetting health issue, he or she may pressure the sonographer to offer an opinion based on the test results, so sonographers should be assertive yet sensitive to the issues involved.

When generating the ultrasound images, the sonographer must analyze and differentiate between pathological and nonpathological findings, in order to focus on the most useful diagnostic images for the physician who will be receiving the images. The sonographer will also provide the physician a written report along with the ultrasound images and recommend further ultrasound imaging tests if the findings are inconclusive or incomplete.

In addition to the range of responsibilities described above, all ultrasound technicians are responsible for educating themselves about the administrative, physical, and technical patient privacy safeguards included in the federal Health Insurance Portability and Accountability Act (HIPA). Some may assist the medical imaging lab with licensure maintenance, and all sonographers must keep complete and detailed records of each examination they perform.

Duties and Responsibilities

- Reviewing the physician's requisition sheet to determine the purpose and type of the examination needed and special considerations involved
- Checking the patient's medical history and prior test results
- Selecting and setting up appropriate equipment for the test
- Planning the procedure and explaining it to the patient
- Assisting the patient in assuming the best physical position to achieve accurate test results
- Completing the final scan while observing the sound wave display screen to make sure the image produced is satisfactory
- Activating equipment that automatically produces a photograph or a printout (called an ultrasonogram) of the ultrasonic pattern

OCCUPATION SPECIALTIES

Neurosonographers

Neurosonographers produce two-dimensional ultrasonic recordings of the nervous system, including the brain.

Cardiac Sonographers

Cardiac Sonographers, also called echocardiographers, produce two-dimensional ultrasonic recordings of the heart.

Ophthalmic Sonographers

Ophthalmic Sonographers produce two-dimensional ultrasonic recordings of the eyes.

Obstetrical/Gynecological Sonographers

Obstetrical/Gynecological Sonographers produce two-dimensional ultrasonic recordings of the pregnant and non-pregnant uterus.

Doppler Technologists

Doppler Technologists produce two-dimensional ultrasonic recordings of blood vessels near the surface of the body.

WORK ENVIRONMENT

Physical Environment

The immediate physical environment of diagnostic medical sonographers varies based on their employer and specialization. Ultrasound technicians perform ultrasounds in hospitals, doctors' offices, and medical imaging centers. Sonographers may perform ultrasounds in stationary medical imaging suites, or they may use a mobile imaging machine to perform ultrasounds on patients in operating rooms, emergency rooms, or patient rooms.

Relevant Skills and Abilities

Communication Skills
- Speaking effectively

Interpersonal/Social Skills
- Cooperating with others
- Working as a member of a team

Organization & Management Skills
- Following instructions
- Making decisions
- Paying attention to and handling details

Planning & Research Skills
- Developing evaluation strategies

Technical Skills
- Performing technical work
- Working with machines, tools, or other objects

Human Environment

Medical sonographers should be comfortable interacting with patients, physicians, laboratory technicians, nurses, scientists, and office staff. Due to the sensitive nature of medical diagnosis, sonographers should exhibit empathy, tact, and confidentiality at all times.

Technological Environment

Ultrasound technicians/ sonographers use a wide variety of tools and equipment to complete their work, including ultrasound scanners, transducers (handheld probes), lubricants, film, positioning pads, computers, and medical imaging software

EDUCATION, TRAINING, AND ADVANCEMENT

High School/Secondary

High school students interested in pursuing a career as a medical sonographer should prepare themselves by developing good study habits. High school–level study of anatomy, physiology, physics, photography, and mathematics will provide a strong foundation for work as a medical sonographer or for college-level work in the field. Due to the diversity of ultrasound technician responsibilities, high school students interested in this career path will benefit from seeking internships or part-time work that expose the students to medical settings.

Suggested High School Subjects

- Algebra
- Applied Biology/Chemistry
- Applied Math
- Applied Physics
- Biology
- English
- Geometry
- Health Science Technology
- Photography
- Physics
- Speech

Famous First

The first medical use of ultrasound was in the late 1940s, the result of work done by Dr. George D. Ludwig of the Naval Medical Research Institute in Bethesda, Maryland. Dr. Ludwig was able to confirm a case of gallstones. His research remained secret under an order by the Department of Defense until 1949, when a paper he wrote was finally released to the public.

College/Postsecondary

Postsecondary students interested in becoming ultrasound technicians should work toward the associate's or bachelor's degree in medical sonography, ultrasound technology, or a related field. The Commission on Accreditation of Allied Health Education Programs has accredited approximately 190 diagnostic medical sonography training programs. Courses in anatomy, physiology, instrumentation, physics, and ethics will prove useful in their future work. Postsecondary students can gain work experience and potential advantage in their future job searches by securing internships or part-time employment in medical settings. .

Related College Majors
- Anatomy & Physiology
- Diagnostic Medical Sonography Technology
- Medical Imaging

Adult Job Seekers

Adults seeking employment as ultrasound technicians should have, at a minimum, an associate's degree in medical sonography from a program accredited by the Commission on Accreditation of Allied Health Education Programs. Adult job seekers should educate themselves about the educational and professional license requirements of their home states and the organizations where they seek employment. Adult job seekers will benefit from joining professional associations to help with networking and job searching. Professional sonography associations, such as the American Registry of Diagnostic Medical Sonographers, the American Registry of Radiologic Technologists, and the Society of Diagnostic Medical

Sonography, generally offer job-finding workshops and maintain lists and forums of available jobs.

Professional Certification and Licensure

Certification and licensure is not legally required for ultrasound technicians, but most employers prefer to hire certified sonographers, so certification may be required as a condition of employment or promotion. Options for voluntary medical sonographer certification include the American Registry for Diagnostic Medical Sonography's Registered Diagnostic Medical Sonographer (RDMS) designation, the Registered Diagnostic Cardiac Sonographer (RDCS) designation, the Registered Vascular Technologist (RVT) designation, and the Physicians' Vascular Interpretation (PVI) designation. These voluntary certifications are earned by completing a sonography training program and passing a national examination. Certification in other areas of specialty is also available.

Additional Requirements

Individuals who find satisfaction, success, and job security as ultrasound technicians will be knowledgeable about the profession's requirements, responsibilities, and opportunities. Since sonographers have access to confidential medical information, they must employ tact and sensitivity when interacting with patients and also adhere to strict ethical and professional standards. Membership in professional sonography associations is encouraged among all medical sonographers as a means of building professional community and networking. Sonographers who obtain registration or certification in multiple areas of specialization will have the best career opportunities.

Fun Fact

An ultrasound exam at 20 weeks of pregnancy is now a standard part of prenatal care, at which time the baby's sex can be determined with 92 percent accuracy. Farmers now use bovine fetal ultrasound for livestock management purposes.

EARNINGS AND ADVANCEMENT

Earnings depend on the type, size and geographic location of the employer and the individual's education, experience and certification. Median annual earnings of ultrasound technicians were $68,243 in 2012. The lowest ten percent earned less than $47,594, and the highest ten percent earned more than $93,799.

Ultrasound technicians may receive paid vacations, holidays, and sick days; life and health insurance; and retirement benefits. These are usually paid by the employer. Those employed by hospitals may also receive dental and optical insurance. Sonographers may be required to purchase their own uniforms.

Metropolitan Areas with the Highest
Employment Level in this Occupation

Metropolitan area	Employment	Employment per thousand jobs	Hourly mean wage
New York-White Plains-Wayne, NY-NJ	2,380	0.46	$31.62
Chicago-Joliet-Naperville, IL	1,240	0.34	$34.01
Los Angeles-Long Beach-Glendale, CA	1,180	0.30	$36.28
Houston-Sugar Land-Baytown, TX	1,130	0.43	$31.66
Dallas-Plano-Irving, TX	1,110	0.53	$31.83
Philadelphia, PA	1,110	0.61	$28.27
Phoenix-Mesa-Glendale, AZ	880	0.51	$35.92
Tampa-St. Petersburg-Clearwater, FL	860	0.76	$25.74

Source: Bureau of Labor Statistics, 2012

EMPLOYMENT AND OUTLOOK

Nationally, there were about 58,000 ultrasound technicians employed in 2012. About one-half of all jobs were in hospitals, while the rest were in medical and diagnostic laboratories, physicians' offices and outpatient care centers. Employment is expected to grow much faster than the average for all occupations through the year 2020, which means employment is projected to increase 40 percent or more. Sonography is becoming more popular with patients than procedures which use radiation, which can cause side effects. A growing and aging population which requires more diagnostic procedures will also create demand for these workers.

Employment Trend, Projected 2010–20

Ultrasound Technicians: 44%

Health Diagnosing and Treating Practitioners: 26%

Total, All Occupations: 14%

Note: "All Occupations" includes all occupations in the U.S. Economy. Source: U.S. Bureau of Labor Statistics, Employment Projections Program

Related Occupations
- Cardiovascular Technician
- Clinical Laboratory Technologist
- Radiologic Technologist

Conversation With . . .
MARGARET KENNEDY
Ultrasound Technologist, 26 years

1. What was your individual career path in terms of education, entry-level job, or other significant opportunity?

Back when I learned ultrasound, there wasn't any formal schooling. Instead, I had a year of on-the-job training in the Women and Children's Department at Rhode Island Hospital. I was working as an X-ray Technician when I did the training. For the boards (licensing exams), I taught myself what I needed to learn in order to pass. Today, most programs are two-year programs. My first ultrasound job was at Beth Israel Hospital in Boston. From there, I was able to explore different aspects of ultrasound technology, from management to teaching to sales. Today, I work two part-time jobs, one in a mobile unit.

2. Are there many job opportunities in your profession? In what specific areas?

Ultrasound is expected to grow more than any other radiological modality in coming years. In general, the more areas you are registered in (i.e., abdominal, obstetrics, gynecology, vascular), the more desirable you will be. To be registered or certified, you have to pass the exams. You could specialize in just obstetrics/gynecology, but the rule of thumb is the more you can do, the more desirable you are to employers. There are jobs in different settings, from hospitals to mobile units. For a new sonographer—which is another word for an ultrasound tech—you really have to be in a hospital environment because you have support there. If you're not sure what you're looking at, you can ask another sonographer or a radiologist for help. In a mobile unit, there's not that interaction with colleagues. The plus side is that you don't get involved in office politics, but there is a sense of isolation.

3. What do you wish you had known going into this profession?

The field has changed so much. It's more about the numbers now in the medical field—get them in and get them out. I feel like the stress has gotten higher. Ultrasound or sonography is not like taking a picture, like an X-ray, where the picture is straightforward. I'm the one who is telling the doctor what I see. That's a lot of pressure. Also, after many years, it can get monotonous. You have to watch for signs of burn out.

4. How do you see your profession changing in the next five years?

I think ultrasound will continue to grow and that the technologists who perform ultrasound exams will become more and more responsible for interpreting exams. Typically today the ultrasound techs show pictures to the radiologist, who dictates what he or she sees. But some places are using computerized reports generated by the sonographer, and the radiologist looks at that report, as opposed to the actual images.

Patients today expect instant results and it is the sonographer's job to assure the patient without disclosing the results of the exam. The general rule is that the ultrasound tech cannot tell the patient what the scan has shown—and this can be a very stressful part of the job.

Also, the population in general is becoming more obese, so repetition injuries like carpal tunnel and shoulder injuries are common in ultrasound techs. If someone is heavier, I have to push harder, and you can't see as well. Last month, I had a patient who was 340 pounds. This week, I had a 290-pound guy.

5. What role will technology play in those changes, and what skills will be required?

As far as performing ultrasounds, I don't anticipate any major changes. The resolution of the machines will continue to improve and 3D ultrasounds will be more prevalent. But the same skills will be required, like good hand/eye coordination and an excellent understanding of cross-sectional anatomy.

6. Do you have any general advice or additional professional insights to share with someone interested in your profession?

Whatever program you enroll in, be sure you have at least a full year of scanning as part of the program, because the more you do it, the better you are at it. You have to be able to understand what you're looking at.

One of the personality traits required for this job is the ability to remain cool under pressure. When you are scanning someone who has something wrong with them, the sonographer must "pretend" everything is OK. This may sound deceitful, but the reality is the patient will want to follow-up with questions that you will not be able to answer.

SELECTED SCHOOLS

Many technical and community colleges offer programs in medical sonography. Interested students are advised to consult with a school guidance counselor or research area postsecondary schools. The website of the Commission on Accreditation of Allied Health Education Programs (see below) provides a search tool that allows you to locate a school/program in your state.

MORE INFORMATION

American Institute of Ultrasound in Medicine
Publications Department
14750 Sweitzer Lane, Suite 100
Laurel, MD 20707-5906
800.638.5352
www.aium.org

American Registry of Diagnostic Medical Sonographers
51 Monroe Street, Plaza East One
Rockville, MD 20850-2400
800.541.9754
www.ardms.org

American Registry of Radiologic Technologists
1255 Northland Drive
St. Paul, MN 55120-1155
651.687.0048
www.arrt.org

American Society of Radiologic Technologists
15000 Central Avenue, SE
Albuquerque, NM 87123-3917
800.444.2778
www.asrt.org

Commission on Accreditation of Allied Health Education Programs
1361 Park Street
Clearwater, FL 33756
727.210.2350
www.caahep.org

Joint Review Committee on Education in Diagnostic Medical Sonography
6021 University Boulevard,
Suite 500
Ellicott City, MD 21043
443.973.3251
www.jrcdms.org

Society of Diagnostic Medical Sonography
2745 Dallas Parkway, Suite 350
Plano, TX 75093-8730
800.229.9506
www.sdms.org

Briana Nadeau/Editor

What Are Your Career Interests?

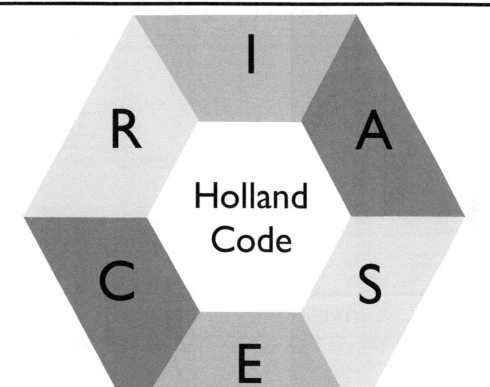

This is based on Dr. John Holland's theory that people and work environments can be loosely classified into six different groups. Each of the letters above corresponds to one of the six groups described in the following pages.

Different people's personalities may find different environments more to their liking. While you may have some interests in and similarities to several of the six groups, you may be attracted primarily to two or three of the areas. These two or three letters are your "Holland Code." For example, with a code of "RES" you would most resemble the Realistic type, somewhat less resemble the Enterprising type, and resemble the Social type even less. The types that are not in your code are the types

you resemble least of all.

Most people, and most jobs, are best represented by some combination of two or three of the Holland interest areas. In addition, most people are most satisfied if there is some degree of fit between their personality and their work environment.

The rest of the pages in this booklet further explain each type and provide some examples of career possibilities, areas of study at MU, and co-curricular activities for each code. To take a more in-depth look at your Holland Code, take a self-assessment such as the SDS, Discover, or a card sort at the MU Career Center with a Career Specialist.

Realistic *(Doers)*

People who have athletic ability, prefer to work with objects, machines, tools, plants or animals, or to be outdoors.

Are you?	independent	Can you?	Like to?
practical	ambitious	fix electrical things	tinker with machines/vehicles
straightforward/frank	systematic	solve electrical problems	work outdoors
mechanically inclined		pitch a tent	be physically active
stable		play a sport	use your hands
concrete		read a blueprint	build things
reserved		plant a garden	tend/train animals
self-controlled		operate tools and machine	work on electronic equipment

Career Possibilities
(Holland Code):

Air Traffic Controller (SER)	Dental Technician (REI)	Laboratory Technician (RIE)	Property Manager (ESR)
Archaeologist (IRE)	Farm Manager (ESR)	Landscape Architect (AIR)	Recreation Manager (SER)
Athletic Trainer (SRE)	Fish and Game Warden (RES)	Mechanical Engineer (RIS)	Service Manager (ERS)
Cartographer (IRE)	Floral Designer (RAE)	Optician (REI)	Software Technician (RCI)
Commercial Airline Pilot (RIE)	Forester (RIS)	Petroleum Geologist (RIE)	Ultrasound Technologist (RSI)
Commercial Drafter (IRE)	Geodetic Surveyor (IRE)	Police Officer (SER)	Vocational Rehabilitation
Corrections Officer (SER)	Industrial Arts Teacher (IER)	Practical Nurse (SER)	Consultant (ESR)

Investigative *(Thinkers)*

People who like to observe, learn, investigate, analyze, evaluate, or solve problems.

Are you?	intellectually self-confident	Can you?	Like to?
inquisitive	Independent	think abstractly	explore a variety of ideas
analytical	logical	solve math problems	work independently
scientific	complex	understand scientific theories	perform lab experiments
observant/precise	Curious	do complex calculations	deal with abstractions
scholarly		use a microscope or computer	do research
cautious		interpret formulas	be challenged

Career Possibilities
(Holland Code):

Actuary (ISE)	Chemical Engineer (IRE)	Geologist (IRE)	Physician, General Practice (ISE)
Agronomist (IRS)	Chemist (IRE)	Horticulturist (IRS)	Psychologist (IES)
Anesthesiologist (IRS)	Computer Systems Analyst (IER)	Mathematician (IER)	Research Analyst (IRC)
Anthropologist (IRE)	Dentist (ISR)	Medical Technologist (ISA)	Statistician (IRE)
Archaeologist (IRE)	Ecologist (IRE)	Meteorologist (IRS)	Surgeon (IRA)
Biochemist (IRS)	Economist (IAS)	Nurse Practitioner (ISA)	Technical Writer (IRS)
Biologist (ISR)	Electrical Engineer (IRE)	Pharmacist (IES)	Veterinarian (IRS)

Artistic *(Creators)*

People who have artistic, innovating, or intuitional abilities and like to work in unstructured situations using their imagination and creativity.

Are you?
creative
imaginative
innovative
unconventional
emotional
independent
Expressive

original
introspective
impulsive
sensitive
courageous
complicated
idealistic
nonconforming

Can you?
sketch, draw, paint
play a musical instrument
write stories, poetry, music
sing, act, dance
design fashions or interiors

Like to?
attend concerts, theatre, art
    exhibits
read fiction, plays, and poetry
work on crafts
take photography
express yourself creatively
deal with ambiguous ideas

Career Possibilities
(Holland Code):

Actor (AES)
Advertising Art Director (AES)
Advertising Manager (ASE)
Architect (AIR)
Art Teacher (ASE)
Artist (ASI)

Copy Writer (ASI)
Dance Instructor (AER)
Drama Coach (ASE)
English Teacher (ASE)
Entertainer/Performer (AES)
Fashion Illustrator (ASR)

Interior Designer (AES)
Intelligence Research Specialist
    (AEI)
Journalist/Reporter (ASE)
Landscape Architect (AIR)
Librarian (SAI)

Medical Illustrator (AIE)
Museum Curator (AES)
Music Teacher (ASI)
Photographer (AES)
Writer (ASI)
Graphic Designer (AES)

Social *(Helpers)*

People who like to work with people to enlighten, inform, help, train, or cure them, or are skilled with words.

Are you?
friendly
helpful
idealistic
insightful
outgoing
understanding

cooperative
generous
responsible
forgiving
patient
kind

Can you?
teach/train others
express yourself clearly
lead a group discussion
mediate disputes
plan and supervise an activity
cooperate well with others

Like to?
work in groups
help people with problems
do volunteer work
work with young people
serve others

Career Possibilities
(Holland Code):

City Manager (SEC)
Clinical Dietitian (SIE)
College/University Faculty (SEI)
Community Org. Director
    (SEA)
Consumer Affairs Director
    (SER)Counselor/Therapist
    (SAE)

Historian (SEI)
Hospital Administrator (SER)
Psychologist (SEI)
Insurance Claims Examiner
    (SIE)
Librarian (SAI)
Medical Assistant (SCR)
Minister/Priest/Rabbi (SAI)
Paralegal (SCE)

Park Naturalist (SEI)
Physical Therapist (SIE)
Police Officer (SER)
Probation and Parole Officer
    (SEC)
Real Estate Appraiser (SCE)
Recreation Director (SER)
Registered Nurse (SIA)

Teacher (SAE)
Social Worker (SEA)
Speech Pathologist (SAI)
Vocational-Rehab. Counselor
    (SEC)
Volunteer Services Director
    (SEC)

Enterprising *(Persuaders)*

People who like to work with people, influencing, persuading, leading or managing for organizational goals or economic gain.

Are you?		Can you?	Like to?
self-confident	ambitious	initiate projects	make decisions
assertive	agreeable	convince people to do things	be elected to office
persuasive	talkative	your way	start your own business
energetic	extroverted	sell things	campaign politically
adventurous	spontaneous	give talks or speeches	meet important people
popular	optimistic	organize activities	have power or status
		lead a group	
		persuade others	

**Career Possibilities
(Holland Code):**

Advertising Executive (ESA)	Credit Analyst (EAS)	Foreign Service Officer (ESA)	Politician (ESA)
Advertising Sales Rep (ESR)	Customer Service Manager	Funeral Director (ESR)	Public Relations Rep (EAS)
Banker/Financial Planner (ESR)	(ESA)	Insurance Manager (ESC)	Retail Store Manager (ESR)
Branch Manager (ESA)	Education & Training Manager	Interpreter (ESA)	Sales Manager (ESA)
Business Manager (ESC)	(EIS)	Lawyer/Attorney (ESA)	Sales Representative (ERS)
Buyer (ESA)	Emergency Medical Technician	Lobbyist (ESA)	Social Service Director (ESA)
Chamber of Commerce Exec	(ESI)	Office Manager (ESR)	Stockbroker (ESI)
(ESA)	Entrepreneur (ESA)	Personnel Recruiter (ESR)	Tax Accountant (ECS)

Conventional *(Organizers)*

People who like to work with data, have clerical or numerical ability, carry out tasks in detail, or follow through on others' instructions.

Are you?		Can you?	Like to?
well-organized	practical	work well within a system	follow clearly defined
accurate	thrifty	do a lot of paper work in a short	procedures
numerically inclined	systematic	time	use data processing equipment
methodical	structured	keep accurate records	work with numbers
conscientious	polite	use a computer terminal	type or take shorthand
efficient	ambitious	write effective business letters	be responsible for details
conforming	obedient		collect or organize things
	persistent		

**Career Possibilities
(Holland Code):**

Abstractor (CSI)	Claims Adjuster (SEC)	Elementary School Teacher	Medical Records Technician
Accountant (CSE)	Computer Operator (CSR)	(SEC)	(CSE)
Administrative Assistant (ESC)	Congressional-District Aide (CES)	Financial Analyst (CSI)	Museum Registrar (CSE)
Budget Analyst (CER)	Cost Accountant (CES)	Insurance Manager (ESC)	Paralegal (SCE)
Business Manager (ESC)	Court Reporter (CSE)	Insurance Underwriter (CSE)	Safety Inspector (RCS)
Business Programmer (CRI)	Credit Manager (ESC)	Internal Auditor (ICR)	Tax Accountant (ECS)
Business Teacher (CSE)	Customs Inspector (CEI)	Kindergarten Teacher (ESC)	Tax Consultant (CES)
Catalog Librarian (CSE)	Editorial Assistant (CSI)		Travel Agent (ECS)

BIBLIOGRAPHY

General

American Medical Association, Health Care Careers Directory. Chicago: American Medical Association, 2013.

DeLaet, Roxann, Introduction to Health Care & Careers. Philadelphia: Lippincott, Williams & Wilkins, 2011.

Gerdin, Judith, Health Careers Today, 5th ed. Maryland Heights, MO: Mosby, 2011.

Makely, Sherry, Shirley Badasch, and Doreen S. Chesebro, Becoming a Health Care Professional. Upper Saddle River, NJ: Prentice Hall, 2013.

Medicine

Agabegi, Steven S., and Elizabeth D. Agabegi. Step-Up to Medicine, 3rd ed. Philadelphia: Lippincott Williams & Wilkins, 2012.

Association of American Medical Colleges, Medical School Admission Requirements (MSAR): Getting Started. Washington, D.C.: Association of American Medical Colleges, 2013.

Gawande, Atul, Complications: A Surgeon's Notes on an Imperfect Science. London: Picador, 2003.

Groopman, Jerome, How Doctor's Think. Boston: Mariner, 2008.

Jauhar, Sandeep, Intern: A Doctor's Initiation. New York: Farrar, Strauss & Giroux, 2009.

Laine, Christine, and Michael A. LaCombe, eds., On Being a Doctor 3: Voices of Physicians and Patients. Philadelphia: American College of Physicians, 2007.

Miller, Robert H., and Daniel M. Bissell, Med School Confidential: A Complete Guide to the Medical School Experience: By Students, for Students. New York: St. Martin's/Griffin, 2006.

Smart, John, Stephen Nelson, and Julie Doherty, Planning a Life in Medicine: Discover If a Medical Career is Right for You and Learn How to Make It Happen. Framingham, MA: Princeton Review, 2011.

Sweet, Victoria, God's Hotel: A Doctor, a Hospital, and a Pilgrimage to the Heart of Medicine. New York: Riverhead Books, 2013.

Transue, Emily R., On Call: A Doctor's Days and Nights in Residency. New York: St. Martin's Press, 2005.

Dentistry & Allied Dental Occupations

American Dental Education Association, ADEA Official Guide to Dental Schools. Washington, D.C., 2013.

Bird, Doni L., Modern Dental Assisting, 10th edition. Philadelphia: Saunders, 2011.

Darby, Michele Leonardi, and Margaret M. Walsh, Dental Hygiene: Theory and Practice, 3rd ed. Philadelphia: Saunders, 2009.

Picard, Alyssa, Making the American Mouth: Dentists and Public Health in the Twentieth Century. New Brunswick, NJ: Rutgers University Press, 2013.

Rule, James T., and Muriel J. Bebeau, Dentists Who Care: Inspiring Stories of Professional Commitment. Hanover Hills, IL: Quintessence Publishing, 2005.

Wynbrandt, James, The Excruciating History of Dentistry: Toothsome Tales & Oral Oddities from Babylon to Braces. New York: St. Martin's/Griffin, 2000.

Nursing & Nursing Assistants

Carter, Pamela J., Lippincott's Essentials for Nursing Assistants: A Humanistic Approach to Caregiving, 3d ed. Philadelphia: Lippincott Williams & Wilkins, 2012.

Chenevert, Melodie, Mosby's Tour Guide to Nursing School, 6th ed. Maryland Heights, MO: Mosby, 2010.

Fitzpatrick, Joyce, and Emerson E. Ea, 201 Careers in Nursing. New York: Springer, 2011.

Gutkind, Lee, ed., I Wasn't Strong Like This When I Started Out: True Stories of Becoming a Nurse. Pittsburgh: In Fact Books, 2013.

Katz, Janet R., A Career in Nursing: Is It Right for Me? Maryland Heights, MO: Mosby, 2007.

Peterson's, Nursing Programs 2014. Lawrenceville, NJ: Peterson's, 2013.

Shalof, Tilda, A Nurse's Story: Life, Death, and In-Between in an Intensive Care Unit. Toronto: Emblem Editions, 2005.

Technicians and Technologists

Davis, Bonnie K., Phlebotomy: From Student to Professional, 3rd ed. Albany: Delmar, 2012.

Dye, Chuck, Diagnostic Medical Sonographers: Stories From People Who've Done It. Santa Monica, CA: 101 Publishing, 2012.

Gurley, La Verne, Introduction to Radiologic Technology, 7th ed. Maryland Heights, MO: Mosby, 2010.

Hillman, Bruce, and Jeff Goldsmith, The Sorcerer's Apprentice: How Medical Imaging Is Changing Health Care. New York: Oxford University Press, 2010.

LeVine, Harry, III, Medical Imaging (Health and Medical Issues Today series). Westport, CT: Greenwood Press, 2010.

Sherry, Clifford, Opportunities in Medical Imaging Careers, rev. ed. New York: McGraw Hill, 2006.

Stern, Jane, Ambulance Girl: How I Saved Myself by Becoming an EMT. New York: Broadway Books, 2004.

Pharmacy, Dietetics & Administration

Bell, Jenna A., Kyle W. Shadix, and Milton Stokes, Launching Your Dietetics Career. Chicago: American Academy of Nutrition and Dietetics, 2012.

Campbell, T. Collin, with Howard Jacobson, Whole: Rethinking the Science of Nutrition. Dallas: BenBella Books, 2013.

Gable, Fred, Opportunities in Pharmacy Careers. New York: McGraw Hill, 2003.

Kelly, William N., Pharmacy: What It Is and How It Works. Boca Raton, FL: CRC Press, 2002.

Levin, Bruce Lubotsky, Peter D. Hurd, and Ardis Hanson, Introduction to Public Health in Pharmacy. Sudbury, MA: Jones & Bartlett, 2008.

Wildman, Robert, The Nutritionist: Food, Nutrition, and Optimal Health. New York: Routledge, 2012.

Williams, Trenor, and Anita Samarth, Electronic Health Records For Dummies. Hoboken, NJ: Wiley, 2010.

Ziesemer, Brandy, Medical Office Management and Technology: An Applied Approach. Philadelphia: Lippincott, Williams & Wilkins 2013.

Physical Therapy & Chiropractic

Cunliffe, Christina, Becoming a Chiropractor: Is Chiropractic Really the Career for You? London: BPP Learning, 2013.

Goodman, Holly, Physical Therapists: Stories from People Who've Done It. Dallas: 101 Publishing, 2012.

Painter, Kirk, So You Want to Be a Therapist? How to Become a Physical or Occupational Therapist. Seattle: Amazon Books, 2013.

INDEX

T

Tampa 22
tartar 54
Teacher's College Columbia University 89
Texas Chiropractic College 39
The Institute for Integrative Nutrition 89
The PT Review 241
Therapeutic Recreation 241
thermography 38
The University of Connecticut 62
tongue depressors 211
tongue forceps 56
toothbrushes 56
tooth pulp 67
tooth-wear 46
topical anesthetics 56
Towson 99
toxic chemicals 121
toxicology 227
traction units 30
transportation 195
trauma dentistry 42
traumatic brain injury 236
treatment 53, 55
treat teeth 55
Trigonometry 31
Troy 35
Tuberculosis 149
Tucson 233
Tufts-New England Medical Center 301
Tufts University 77

U

ultrasonography 334, 335
ultrasound 334, 335, 336, 339, 340, 341, 342,
    343, 345, 346, 347
ultrasound machines 334
ultrasound technician 335, 340
ultrasound therapy 239
UMass Memorial 231
undergraduate 227
United States Medical Licensing Examination
    7
University of Alabama, Birmingham 264
University of California 264
University of California, Los Angeles 179

University of California, San Francisco 179
University of Cincinnati 219
University of Colorado 219
University of Colorado, Denver 219
University of Delaware 248
University of Iowa 248
University of Kentucky 233
University of Maryland, Baltimore 77
University of Maryland Dental School 50
University of Massachusetts, Worcester 264
University of Medicine and Dentistry 217
University of Miami 248
University of Michigan, Ann Arbor 233
University of Minnesota 233
University of Nebraska 77
University of Nebraska Medical Center 264
University of North Carolina, Chapel Hill 265
University of North Dakota 313
University of Pennsylvania 319
University of Pennsylvania Hospital 325
University of Pittsburgh 319
University of Rochester 179
University of Southern California 248
University of Texas, Austin 233
University of the Pacific 77
University of Virginia 301
University of Virginia in Charlottesville 301
University of Washington 304
University of Western States 39
University of Wisconsin, Madison 233
urinalysis 143, 144, 147
U.S. Army-Baylor University 249
U.S. Medical Licensing Examination 298
USMLE 298
U.S. Nuclear Regulatory Commission 281

V

vaccinations 210
vacuuming 197
Vancouver 35
vascular catheters 18
Vascular Technologists 17
veneers 42
Virginia Urology 301
Visiting Nurse's Association of America 110
vitamin 79
Volunteer Work 80

WITHDRAWAL